Bankrupt in America

Markets and Governments in Economic History
A series edited by Price Fishback

Also in the series:

Bankrupt in America

A History of Debtors, Their Creditors, and the Law in the Twentieth Century

MARY ESCHELBACH HANSEN
AND BRADLEY A. HANSEN

THE UNIVERSITY OF CHICAGO PRESS   CHICAGO AND LONDON

The University of Chicago Press, Chicago 60637
The University of Chicago Press, Ltd., London
© 2020 by The University of Chicago
All rights reserved. No part of this book may be used or reproduced in any manner what-
soever without written permission, except in the case of brief quotations in critical articles
and reviews. For more information, contact the University of Chicago Press, 1427 E. 60th
St., Chicago, IL 60637.
Published 2020
Printed in the United States of America

29 28 27 26 25 24 23 22 21 20   1 2 3 4 5

ISBN-13: 978-0-226-67956-3 (cloth)
ISBN-13: 978-0-226-67973-0 (e-book)
DOI: https://doi.org/10.7208/chicago/9780226679730.001.0001

Library of Congress Cataloging-in-Publication Data

Names: Hansen, Mary E., author. | Hansen, Bradley A., 1963– author.
Title: Bankrupt in America : a history of debtors, their creditors, and the law in the
    twentieth century / Mary Eschelbach Hansen, Bradley A. Hansen.
Other titles: Markets and governments in economic history.
Description: Chicago : University of Chicago Press, 2020. | Series: Markets and
    governments in economic history | Includes bibliographical references and index.
Identifiers: LCCN 2019024349 | ISBN 9780226679563 (cloth) | ISBN 9780226679730 (ebook)
Subjects: LCSH: Bankruptcy—United States—History—20th century.
Classification: LCC HG3766 .H35 2020 | DDC 346.7307/8—dc23
LC record available at https://lccn.loc.gov/2019024349

Contents

Figures

Tables

Preface and Acknowledgments

This book has been a long time in the making. We developed its framework in our independent and coauthored work over the last twenty years. We published a substantial amount of the work on bankruptcy before World War II that we summarize here as journal articles. Bradley described the origins of the first permanent bankruptcy law in the US and the development of corporate reorganization.[1] Together we traced how the earliest boom in personal bankruptcy led to the development of the view of the US law as particularly friendly to debtors.[2] We then showed how formal and informal institutions influenced business bankruptcy rates in the 1920s.[3] Finally, we traced the history of collection law in Illinois and demonstrated the importance of state collection law in a consumer's decision to use the federal bankruptcy law during the Great Depression.[4] Recently, Mary showed that new debt instruments quickly appeared on the balance sheets of the bankrupt early in the century.[5] She and Nic Ziebarth documented how the banking and credit crises early in the Great Depression led creditors to put the squeeze on debtors in relatively good condition.[6] These articles form the basis for chapters 2 and 3. Portions of those chapters and their appendices are copyrighted by Cambridge University Press and are reprinted with permission.

We suspected that the framework would be useful to understand the whole of the twentieth century. Our work digitizing the complete set of published bankruptcy statistics and collecting documents from a sample of bankruptcy case files allows us to show it here, in chapters 4 through 6.

We could not have produced this book without substantial help.

Seed funding for the collection of the bankruptcy data came from the Department of Economics, the College of Arts and Sciences, and the

Office of the Provost at American University. Rutgers and Loyola Marymount University contributed through support of Mary's friend and coauthor Michelle McKinnon Miller. Significant funding came from the Institute for New Economic Thinking, the Alfred P. Sloan Foundation (Grant Number 2011–6–16), the Endowment for Education of the National Conference of Bankruptcy Judges, the National Science Foundation Economics Program and Law and Social Sciences Program (SES-1324468 and SES-1355742). The NSF also contributed to computing resources through grant BCS-1039497.

It would not have been possible to collect the case file data without the assistance of the enthusiastic and patient staff at the National Archives. In particular, we thank Rebecca Warlow and Mary Rephlo in NARA administration and the staff at the Atlanta, Kansas City, and Philadelphia regional offices.

A number of collaborators participated in the data collection project. Michelle McKinnon Miller and Tarun Sabarwal were key. Lendol Caldor, Rich Hynes, and Robert Lawless freely shared advice. Dov Cohen, Robert Lawless, Joseph Mason, and John Parman contributed to grant proposals and helped to hone our thinking

Four of Mary's recent PhD students worked on bankruptcy-related topics and contributed to the data and to the ideas in this book. They are Jess Chen, Matt Davis, Megan Fasules, and Dongping Xie. An additional fourteen graduate students from American University, Rutgers, and the University of Kansas worked on the project. They are Tanima Ahmed, Namuna Amgalan, Anne-Christine Barthel, Huancheng Du, Jeremy Duchin, Yue Feng, Amineh Kamranzadeh, Aubrey Land, Moon Oulatta, Chris Penney, Matthew Reardon, Smriti Tiwari, Audrey Wright, Phanwin Yokying, and Amanda Zarka.

Many undergraduates worked on the data. Zach Duey and John Pedersen made key contributions. At American University, additional undergraduate research assistants were Sarah Adler, Gregory Applebach, Drew Badlato, Maxwell Blumenthal, Jason Boim, Quinn Creamer, Kelsey Fritz, Ben Gregson, Gregory Koppell, Andy Lin, Benjamin Miller, Yami Payano, Sean Post, Anthony Primelo, Robert Pryor, Mariya Tsyglakova, Kevin Werner, and Alex Young.

At the University of Kansas, undergraduate research assistants included Alec Bachman, Natalie Craig, Brian Danley, Saran Davaajargal, Lorgens Estabine, Daniel Hilliard, Austin Johnson, Ian Lally, Christopher Lansford, Daria Milakhina, Megan Nelson, Alec Rothman, and

Jonathon Sestak. At Loyola Marymount University (Los Angeles), they included Rahul Daryanani, Derek Dunaway, Niki Flocas, Marissa Hamilton, Yasmin Hellman, Ayanna Leaphart, Courtney Ramsey, Isabelle Rebosura, and Austin Zuckerman. Finally, at the College of William & Mary, undergraduate assistance came from Bryan Burgess, Robert O'Gara, and Xin Sui.

Our colleagues provided formal and informal feedback. Referees and editors improved our journal publications, and several anonymous reviewers contributed to the manuscript at the proposal and final stages. Participants at the annual meetings of the Economic History Association, the Economic and Business History Society, the Eastern Economic Association, and attendees of the NBER Enterprising America conference and of the Washington Area Economic History Seminars and Workshops provided comments. Suggestions from Jeremy Atack, Bill Collins, Noel Johnson, Mark Koyama, Bob Margo, Gabe Mathy, John Murray, Hugh Rockoff, David Skeel, and Mary Tone Rodgers were especially valuable. At American University, Bob Feinberg, Tom Husted, and Kara Reynolds listened patiently as we talked—seemingly endlessly—about our progress and our trials. Richard Hynes and Robert Seamans shared data from related studies.

The influence of our mentors will be obvious to economic historians. Mary learned the science and art of doing economic history from Jeremy Atack; Brad learned from Doug North. Many others, of course, shaped our work. In particular, we would like to acknowledge Lee Alston, Rick Chaney, and Larry Neal. Mary sends special shout-outs to Francine Blau and the late Cynthia Taft Morris, who by their examples, taught her so much about how to navigate academic life.

Of course, there can be no book without its editors. Series editor Price Fishback suggested that the interaction of the government and markets in the evolution of bankruptcy was the sort of story that the University of Chicago Press designed this series to highlight. At the University of Chicago Press, Joe Jackson and Jane MacDonald guided the book through the editorial process, while Susan Karani led the production team. Assistance from Alicia Sparrow and copyediting by Lisa Wehrle were much appreciated. Romina Kazandjan carefully read the first draft and, in addition to finding many typos, helped us to make the book more accessible.

Finally, we thank our parents and grandparents for teaching us how to strive for success without losing sight of what is important in life, and we thank our children for reminding us of those lessons every day.

CHAPTER ONE

Introduction

O n December 11, 2002, Glenda Clutch filed a bankruptcy petition at the US district court in Baltimore.[1] She owed most of her debt to auto finance companies. About three years before her bankruptcy, GMAC had repossessed a van, leaving her with an $8,000 deficiency. Just the month before her bankruptcy, she returned a car that she had recently purchased from a dealership. At the time she filed her petition, she listed personal property valued at $1,725, including $25 in liquid assets, $660 in home furnishings, $250 in clothing, and a 1990 Mazda with estimated value of $850. Under Maryland law, all of her property was exempt from collection. She retained it after receiving her discharge on March 24, 2003, just three months after filing.

Clutch was one of about 1.5 million people who filed for personal bankruptcy in 2002. Three years later, personal bankruptcy in the US hit an all-time high. In 2005, more than 2 million—6 of every 1,000 people—filed. Though personal bankruptcy rates stabilized after 2005, bankruptcy remains an important tool for financially distressed households and a matter of concern for their creditors. A lot of money is at stake. For instance, in 2010, bankrupt households owed more than $459 billion that could be discharged,[2] an amount equal to 3.1 percent of US gross domestic product and nearly as large as the year's Medicare budget.[3]

Today bankruptcy is a fundamental feature of the American economy, but the country did not even have a bankruptcy law for most of its first century. Demand for a permanent bankruptcy law in the late nineteenth century came from trade creditors—mainly wholesalers and manufacturers—who provided credit to other businesses. They wanted a law to deal with business failures. They did not imagine that bankruptcy would eventually come to be dominated by cases like Clutch's, a person with no business interests and few assets, but with significant debt amassed in the course of everyday life. This book explains how bankruptcy in America went from an option that Congress seldom used, to an indispensable tool for businesses, to a central element of the social safety net for households.

To understand how bankruptcy came to occupy its current role in its current form, we trace the changes in bankruptcy law since the 1890s together with the changes in its use. The details of the bankruptcy law, in combination with the details of other state and federal laws governing debtor-creditor relations, local legal culture, and social and economic conditions, determine how the bankruptcy law is used. Changes in how the bankruptcy law is used give rise to changes in interest groups and changes in beliefs about the appropriate function of bankruptcy, which in turn result in changes in the laws. In other words, the bankruptcy rate and the laws that affect it evolve together through their interaction. The interaction explains four principal facts about bankruptcy.

The first fact is that bankruptcy was once rare but is now common. The left-hand side of figure 1.1 shows that the number of bankruptcy cases filed each year increased from just over 10,000 in 1899 to more than 1,000,000 in the late 1990s and early 2000s. The right-hand side of the figure shows that the bankruptcy rate increased from 1 per 10,000 people annually in the first decades of the twentieth century to about 1 per 300 people at the beginning of the twenty-first. During the decades of particularly rapid growth in bankruptcy, the supply of consumer credit increased. Further, supply increased on the extensive margin. Most often, the liberalization of state laws governing usury rates created opportunities for creditors to lend profitably to borrowers who had previously been unable to obtain credit. The usury laws and other state laws mattered; changes in the bankruptcy law by itself did not push bankruptcy rates up.

Second, most early users of the bankruptcy law were business owners, but now most bankrupts are consumers. The share of bankruptcy petitions filed by businesses, which is visible in figure 1.1 as the distance between the total number of bankruptcy petitions (the dotted line) and the number of personal petitions (the solid line), began declining in the 1920s and dropped off dramatically between the 1930s and 1940s. Because the authors of the bankruptcy law expected that its purpose would be to liquidate the inventories and other assets of bankrupt businesses

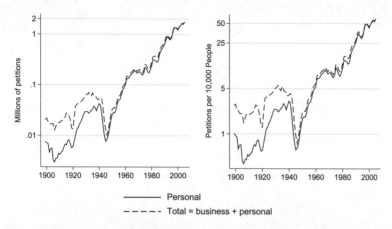

FIG. 1.1. Left panel shows bankruptcy petitions, and right panel shows national bankruptcy rates. Bankruptcy grew, but not at a constant rate. *Source*: See appendix to chapter 1.

for the benefit of their trade creditors, they did not create procedures that would discourage consumers from using the law. After personal bankruptcy took off, views about the purpose of bankruptcy law adapted to the way people used it. Lawmakers, judges, and even creditors came to see relief of the debtor as paramount and liquidation as secondary. At the same time, businesses developed ways to handle insolvency outside of bankruptcy. Personal bankruptcy cases far outnumbered business bankruptcies by World War II.

Third, the bankruptcy rate varies dramatically between places. Figure 1.2 shows that in the state where bankruptcy is used the most in any given year (typically Alabama or Utah), the bankruptcy rate reached 25 per 10,000 people in the 1950s. In the states where it is used the least, the bankruptcy rate did not reach that level until the 1990s. Figure 1.3 shows that state-to-state differences are persistent; many high-rate states in 1920 were still high-rate states in 2000. The persistence in bankruptcy is the result of persistence in the broader legal framework within states. In particular, more people use the bankruptcy law when state laws on garnishment and wage assignment—or state court rulings about the collection laws—make it easier for creditors to collect from debtors in default. While there is much less variation in collection laws today than there was in 1920, collection laws remain an important determinant of the bankruptcy rate. Because of the large and persistent variations in bankruptcy rates between states, trends in the national bankruptcy rate can be understood only in terms of trends in state bankruptcy rates.

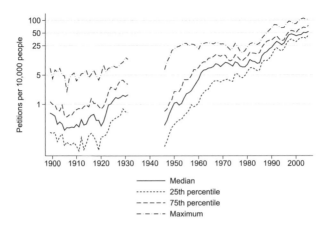

FIG. 1.2. Differences in the bankruptcy rate across states were always large. Immediately after World War II, rates diverged. After a period of convergence in the late 1960s and early 1970s, rates diverged again. State level data not available for 1932–45. *Source*: See appendix to chapter 1.

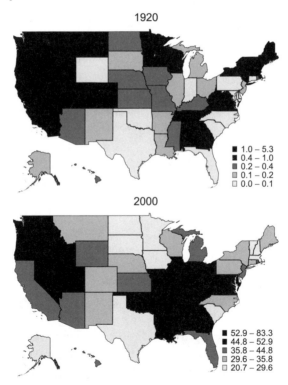

FIG. 1.3. The states with the highest personal bankruptcy rates throughout the century include Alabama, Georgia, Tennessee, and Utah. The Carolinas and Texas have always had low rates. *Source*: See appendix to chapter 1.

The fourth fact is seldom noted, but it is clear in both panels of figure 1.1. Growth in bankruptcy has not been steady. The bankruptcy rate increased at a rapid rate in the 1920s, in the 1950s and early 1960s, and in the 1980s. It increased slowly, and even decreased, in the 1930s and in the late 1960s.

In the 1920s, an interest group emerged to persuade lawmakers to see the rising number of bankrupts as victims of the many small, local creditors who competed, sometimes unscrupulously, for their business. The response of many states was to try to drive "loan sharks" out of businesses by creating a legal market for small consumer loans. This, ironically, fueled bankruptcy. In the 1930s, personal bankruptcy grew modestly while business bankruptcy declined. Yet Congress overhauled bankruptcy law during the Great Depression. It made changes in response to the use of collections and foreclosure to liquidate farms and businesses that were temporarily insolvent yet fundamentally sound. Congress created new ways for farmers and businesspeople to use bankruptcy to pay their debts over time. Later in the decade, Congress also created a way for personal bankrupts to pay their debts over time.

In the 1960s, a new interest group argued to Congress and to the US Supreme Court that the bankrupt were still victims of their creditors. Both Congress and the Supreme Court responded by limiting the ability of creditors to collect through garnishment. Also in the 1960s, a separate interest group argued for reform of the federal bankruptcy law to decrease the bankruptcy rate. However, by the time Congress finished debating the reforms, restrictions on garnishment had already decreased the growth of the bankruptcy rate. The reforms that Congress eventually enacted aimed to encourage more people to use the pay-over-time procedures but did not aim to decrease the number of people using the bankruptcy law. In the 1980s and 1990s, the interest group seeking reform of the federal bankruptcy law reemerged. This time, credit card issuers took the lead. It took a few tries, but in 2005, they convinced Congress to require, rather than merely encourage, people to use pay-over-time to gain access to the protections of bankruptcy.

What Is Bankruptcy? Why Have a Bankruptcy Law?

In everyday speech, *insolvency, default, failure,* and *bankruptcy* are synonyms. However, a person can fail to pay her debts without using the legal procedure known as bankruptcy. We focus on the legal procedure and its use.

Bankruptcy is federal law. The US Constitution explicitly empowers Congress to enact uniform laws on it.[4] When Congress does not exercise its option, state laws and common law govern debtor-creditor relations. But federal bankruptcy law, like the English law on which it is based, provides two important things that state and common law cannot: collective proceedings and the opportunity for the discharge of all debts.

State collection laws usually distribute assets on a first-come, first-served basis. Under a first-come, first-served rule, creditors are paid in the order in which they file claims. The first creditor to file a claim may be fully paid while the last to file a claim receives nothing. In bankruptcy, all of the creditors owed by the debtor participate. Other collection efforts are automatically stayed (stopped) when bankruptcy proceedings begin. In bankruptcy, the proceeds from liquidating the debtor's assets are divided on a pro rata basis among creditors with similar claims. For example, if any creditor with an unsecured claim receives a payout, all receive one. If one creditor's claim is 5 percent of all unsecured claims, then it receives 5 percent of the total payout to unsecured creditors.

Second, state laws did not always include all debts, leaving some creditors with recourse and other creditors with none. To make matters worse, even if state legislatures intended that debtors would receive a discharge of all debts, creditors challenged the constitutionality of state law that tried to discharge debts held by out-of-state creditors or debts contracted before the passage of the law.[5]

Both features of federal bankruptcy law have benefits.[6] A collective proceeding with pro rata distribution eliminates a wasteful duplication of effort, in which every creditor monitors a debtor. It also prevents a race of diligence, in which a creditor acts on the first sign of a debtor's financial weakness. In the worst-case scenario, the race of diligence is like a bank run. It causes the failure of a fundamentally sound but temporarily insolvent debtor.

The discharge of debts has several economic rationales.[7] The best known is that the discharge provides a fresh start. People burdened by debt that they believe they cannot repay have little incentive to earn income beyond whatever local law exempts from collection because any additional income goes to their creditors. Discharge thus provides an incentive for work. Discharge also acts like insurance for entrepreneurs. It encourages risk taking. In places where the law is more forgiving, people are more likely to start new businesses.[8] Indeed, some of America's most famous entrepreneurs, including F. Augustus Heinze, Henry Ford, and Walt Disney, went bankrupt before they became successful. Finally, discharge provides an incentive for debtors to cooperate with bankruptcy proceedings. This final reason appears to have been important for the introduction of discharge into English bankruptcy law in 1705.[9] Each bankruptcy law in the US has provided collective proceedings and the possibility of a discharge.

Histories of US Bankruptcy Law and Its Use

Congress passed bankruptcy laws in 1800, 1841, and 1867. Each law followed an economic downturn.[10] Each law prompted complaints about excessive costs, and Congress repealed each one after a few years.[11] In 1898, Congress passed a law that endured. Congress amended and expanded its 1898 Bankruptcy Act many times but did not replace it until 1978. Congress also amended the 1978 Act many times. This book discusses major amendments through 2005.

Although there were many short-lived bankruptcy laws in the nineteenth century, the first expansive history of bankruptcy law was not written until Congress debated the major amendments of the Great Depression. In 1935, legal historian Charles Warren declared, "Every bankruptcy law has been the product of some financial crisis or depression."[12] The economic crises of the nineteenth century caused many businesspeople to become insolvent through no fault of their own, which created demand for a bankruptcy law. Congress responded to provide relief. Bankruptcy procedures, however, were costly. Debtors and creditors often had to travel far to a federal court, and administrative costs were high because bankruptcy required a complete accounting of the debtor's assets and liabilities. Even then, creditors seldom got much out of bankruptcy. After each crisis passed, demand for repeal developed quickly. Warren's interpretation became a standard part of the legal literature.[13]

The growth in the bankruptcy rate in the 1980s—on the heels of the 1978 replacement of the 1898 act—revived interest in the history of bankruptcy law. The new wave of research emphasized the effect of long-run economic, social, and political forces on the law.[14] The research of two authors is particularly important for our story.

One of the authors of this book, Bradley A. Hansen, reexamined the origins of the 1898 act.[15] He described how commercial associations and the Republican Party had been promoting a bankruptcy law for nearly twenty years before Congress passed the 1898 act.[16] The chief advocates for it were merchants and manufacturers who provided trade credit to retailers throughout the country. The merchants and manufacturers wanted a bankruptcy law to deal with the everyday problems of growing interstate commerce. In this new view, the Panic of 1893 was important mainly because it shifted the political balance. The panic led to Republican control of both houses of Congress and the presidency, which finally allowed the long-sought-after legislation to pass.

Legal historian David Skeel showed how the interaction between pro-debtor populist ideology and interest groups composed of legal professionals and creditor groups shaped the bankruptcy law.[17] After creditors got their bankruptcy law in 1898, the bankruptcy bar prevented efforts to move bankruptcy procedures out of court and into an administrative bureaucracy. New Deal reforms to corporate bankruptcy sidelined elite lawyers and strengthened the lawyers who represented small business and personal bankrupts. This latter group joined with pro-debtor interests in resisting the demands of consumer creditors to force personal bankrupts into repayment.

The growth in the bankruptcy rate in the 1980s also spurred statistical analyses of the determinants of the bankruptcy rate. Although the rapid increase in the national bankruptcy rate was initially blamed on the 1978 changes to the bankruptcy law,[18] accounting for changes in the way bankruptcy petitions were counted and for changes in the economy explained much of the increase in the bankruptcy rate in the 1980s.[19] Two other legal changes that occurred in the late 1970s probably increased the bankruptcy rate.[20] In 1977, the Supreme Court ruled that laws prohibiting lawyers from advertising were unconstitutional, and, in 1978, it ruled that the usury limit on a credit card was determined by the state where the bank that issued the card was, not the state the card holder lived in.[21] The first decision made people more aware of bankruptcy and bankruptcy lawyers. The second increased the supply of consumer credit.

Just as changes in the legal environment over time were associated with rising bankruptcy rates, differences in the legal environment across states were associated with geographical differences in bankruptcy rates.[22] As noted above, in states that protected more of a debtor's assets from collection actions or from liquidation in bankruptcy, more debtors used the bankruptcy law. In states that protected more of a debtor's income from garnishment, fewer debtors sought protection from their creditors in bankruptcy. Studies of default and bankruptcy among credit card holders reinforced the importance of accounting for interactions between state collection law and federal bankruptcy law. In states that protected many assets, both default and bankruptcy were higher.[23]

In addition to the state legal environment, studies identified economic and social determinants of the bankruptcy rate.[24] Greater levels of social capital, proxied by larger shares of people holding traditional values regarding commitment and people belonging to tight-knit communities, decreased the bankruptcy rate by decreasing the likelihood of default. Other things equal, people became more likely to default as the bankruptcy rate rose during the 1980s, and people were more likely to file for bankruptcy in places that had higher bankruptcy rates in the past. These patterns suggested that the social stigma of bankruptcy fell as bankruptcy became more common. Of course, the patterns were also consistent with the argument that the cost of filing declined as more people gained information about the benefits of bankruptcy.

Beyond social capital and stigma, social pressure to borrow had the potential to increase household debt. For example, families pressured to purchase a home in a good neighborhood to obtain access to quality schools and a safe environment may have sought relief in bankruptcy.[25] In general, unemployment and economic instability increased bankruptcy,[26] while generous unemployment and welfare benefits decreased it.[27]

Empirical studies of bankruptcy, which now number in the hundreds, typically emphasize one of the three categories of determinants of bankruptcy. Each one typically emphasizes how either law or economics or society influences bankruptcy. Regardless of which determinant is the focus of the study, each scholar typically takes one of two sides of a policy debate about how to control bankruptcy rates. On one side are scholars who believe deteriorating economic conditions for middle- and lower-income households increase the default rate, which drives increases in the bankruptcy rate. These scholars recommend regulating lenders and improving other aspects of the social safety net as ways to reduce bankruptcy. On the other side are scholars who believe that increases in the bankruptcy rate in the twentieth century were the result of an overly generous federal bankruptcy law. They argue that the federal law alone encouraged households to act strategically in their decisions to borrow, default, and use the bankruptcy law to obtain a discharge of their debt. These scholars recommend restricting access to liquidation in bankruptcy. In 2005, Congress complied. Although bankruptcy rates fell, consumer borrowing and default did not.

Since the early 2000s, we, along with other scholars,[28] have developed a more nuanced understanding of the ways in which society, the economy, and the law interact to determine the bankruptcy rate. Our story of twentieth-century bankruptcy occupies a middle ground in the scholarly debate. We recognize that economic conditions, social changes, and federal bankruptcy law mattered. In particular, we emphasize how the legal environment influences, and is influenced by, social and economic factors. Additionally, although nearly all research on bankruptcy addresses only bankruptcy's recent past, we emphasize how recent events connect to events that unfolded over the twentieth century.

Our Approach

The essence of our approach is to recognize that bankruptcy is the final step on a long path. Figure 1.4 shows the path. A debtor's choice of bankruptcy, on the bottom right of the figure, is preceded by many choices. The choices are made both by debtors and by creditors. The first step is for a would-be debtor to ask for a loan. Then, the creditor denies or approves the loan. Borrowing and lending do not typically lead to bankruptcy, but the path to bankruptcy always begins with borrowing and lending.

Of the people who seek and obtain loans, only those who default continue to be at risk of becoming bankrupt. Default, however, does not necessarily lead to bankruptcy. If no creditors pursue collection of the debt in default, a debtor is unlikely to seek the protection of the bankruptcy law. Even if a creditor does attempt to collect, the debtor may choose to let the collection proceed rather than choose to file for bankruptcy.

To be precise, then, the bankruptcy rate is the product of three components. The first component is the fraction of the population that owes debt, or the rate of indebtedness. The second is the fraction of the indebted who do not pay, or the rate of default. The third is the fraction who are in default and who choose to file for bankruptcy rather than allowing creditors to pursue collection of the debt.

Recognizing the steps along the path to bankruptcy is important because it reminds us of the many factors other than bankruptcy law that

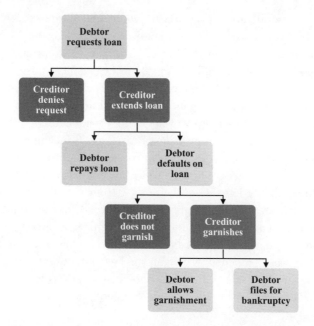

FIG. 1.4. Filing for bankruptcy is the final step on a path that begins with a prospective debtor requesting a loan. Only a fraction of loan requests are granted by creditors; only a fraction of debtors default; creditors seek garnishment in only a fraction of defaults; and only a fraction of debtors who are garnished choose bankruptcy. Anything that influences the choices of debtors and creditors at each step can influence the bankruptcy rate.

influence the bankruptcy rate. Anything that influences the supply of credit, or the demand for it, can influence the bankruptcy rate by influencing the rate of indebtedness, which, again, is the outcome of the first two steps along the path in figure 1.4. Similarly, anything that influences the default rate can also influence bankruptcy, and anything that influences the benefits and costs of using the bankruptcy law can influence the bankruptcy rate.

Moreover, things that influence choices near the end of the path can also influence earlier choices. For instance, a change in the bankruptcy law that increases its benefits may also increase the probability that debtors choose default. An increase in default reduces the expected return on lending for creditors, which decreases the supply of credit and reduces the rate at which people successfully obtain credit. Because the later decisions along the path influence earlier decisions, we cannot use economic theory alone to predict the effect of a change in the bankruptcy law.[29] The effect of legal changes on the bankruptcy rate must be determined empirically. In the section titled "Our Evidence" below, we summarize how we account for economic, social, and legal influences on the bankruptcy rate. A complete accounting appears in the appendices.

Recognizing that the bankruptcy rate is the product of its three components yields a second, and crucial, insight. The three components are not added together, they are multiplied. They interact. Because they interact, growth in debt and growth in default do not cause a one-for-one increase in personal bankruptcy. There are periods during which bankruptcy grew more quickly than consumer credit, and there are periods during which consumer credit grew while bankruptcy did not. For example, as shown in the left side of figure 1.5,[30] from 1920 to 1930 and from 1955 to 1965, the effect of the expansion of credit on the bankruptcy rate was amplified by pro-creditor garnishment. In contrast, from the late 1960s to the mid-1970s, credit continued to expand, but its effect on bankruptcy was dampened by a change in law that limited garnishment. Similarly, the right side of figure 1.5 shows that periods with increased risk of default, such as long recessions,[31] did not always see rapid growth

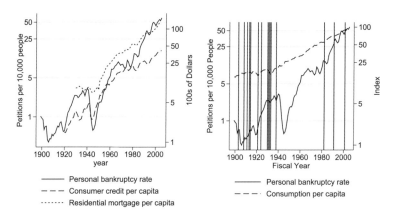

FIG. 1.5. Left panel shows personal bankruptcy rates and two measures of consumer indebtedness: total consumer credit per capita and residential mortgage lending per capita (both in 1982–84 dollars). Though the contours of bankruptcy rates and consumer credit are similar, in some periods credit grew more quickly than bankruptcy; in other periods bankruptcy grew while credit shrank. Right panel shows consumer bankruptcy rates and two measures of business cycles, which are indicative of causes of default. Periods of expansion (i.e., rapid increases in consumption) coincide with rapid increases in the personal bankruptcy rate. Fiscal years with recessions of at least twelve months in duration (vertical lines) are not always accompanied by a spike in bankruptcy. *Sources*: See text and appendix to chapter 1.

in bankruptcy. Our empirical analysis shows that a significant plotline in the story of bankruptcy in the twentieth century revolves around the interaction between consumer credit, state collection laws, and federal bankruptcy law.

We use the fact that the bankruptcy rate is a product of its three component rates to structure our narrative, and we use it to organize documentary and statistical evidence. We use both documentary and statistical evidence because our approach to understanding bankruptcy in the US is influenced by both the cliometric and new institutional approaches to economic history.

The new institutional approach to economic history emphasizes the role of institutions in explaining economic performance, and it attempts to explain the evolution of institutions over time. We present the main chapters of this book in the narrative style frequently used to write the history of institutions. We tell the story of what happened. Of course, a narrative is accessible to an interdisciplinary audience. More important, we present a narrative because it helps us to be clear about the main point: At any one time, the bankruptcy law and how people use it can be understood only in light of their past evolution.

Cliometrics uses economic theory and statistics to understand the past. It tells structured stories using numbers. The appendices explain our statistical methods in detail. Although we do not give these methods pride of place, the reader will find that economic theory and econometric models are central to how we do history.

Complementarity of History and Cliometrics

The conclusions of cliometric research sometimes diverge from the conclusions of historians who use other, less quantitative, methods.[32] However, the two approaches do not conflict; they complement each other. In fact, it would not be possible for us to trace the interaction between bankruptcy law and the bankruptcy rate without using the tools of the cliometrician *and* the tools of the historian.

Consider first the limitations of economic theory and econometrics in explaining the evolution of bankruptcy. Neither can account for the outsized influence of particular individuals. Jay Torrey, the author of the 1898 Bankruptcy Act, chose to give creditors control of liquidation when he wrote the sections of the act that govern procedures. He rejected the example of the procedure followed in England, which gave technocratic administrators control, even though other proponents of bankruptcy legislation had presented proposals with administrative control. As we shall show, Torrey's choice played a central role in the evolution of bankruptcy law. Similarly, economic theory cannot readily explain why Walter Chandler, a congressman during the Great Depression, was willing to keep pressing Congress to add a way for personal bankrupts to repay their debts through bankruptcy. We show that Chandler's determination was central to the outcome of the 1938 reforms. The 1938 reforms, in turn, determined the way a group of consumer creditors would pursue reforms in the 1990s and 2000s.

Now consider the limitations of history in telling the story of the evolution of bankruptcy. Traditionally, historical analysis does not provide the tools for measurement that economics does. Though economics has little to say about the origins of Chandler's views, it has some excellent tools for measuring the impact of his views. In particular, we base conclusions in several chapters on regression analysis. Using regression, we summarize the impact of legal decisions, state laws, and key social and economic variables on the bankruptcy rate. By setting up our regressions carefully and consistently, we can do three things that are particularly useful to understanding the evolution of bankruptcy. First, to some extent, we can determine which changes in laws and credit markets *caused* an increase or decrease in the bankruptcy rate, as opposed to being simply correlated with changing rates. Second, we can estimate about how many bankruptcies were caused, or were avoided, by the changes in the law. Finally, we can show that particular interactions really matter. There were truly important interactions between the decisions people made along the path to bankruptcy, such as to obtain credit, and decisions made by legislators and judges to change law or its interpretation.

New Institutional Analysis

New institutional economic historians frequently write in the narrative style familiar to historians, but they use the economic way of thinking to explain how institutions change over time. The economic way of thinking, also called rational choice, uses a simple but powerful organizing principle for understanding human behavior. Economists expect people to take an action if its benefits exceed its costs. If the benefits of an action increase, economists expect more people to take the action.

Some people reject the economic way of thinking because they believe all economic models lack realism. They worry about assuming that people have perfect information and perfect foresight or that people care only about material wealth. But the economic way of thinking does not require these unrealistic assumptions. An economic approach to bankruptcy does not imply that people typically borrow with the intent to default, declare bankruptcy, and receive a discharge. In fact, there are a number of reasons to expect that such strategic behavior is atypical, and there is little evidence that it is common.[33] Our economic approach simply implies that groups of people respond in predictable ways to changes in expected costs and benefits.

Similarly, people try to change an institution when they expect the net benefits of the change to be positive. The method people use to change an institution is specific to the type of institution and to the particulars of the case under study. As the discussion above makes clear, to tell the story of bankruptcy in twentieth-century America, we explain multiple types of institutional change, including legislation and court decisions at the state and national levels. Each type of change and each incidence of change has its own story.

Nonetheless, the stories have a common thread. Each institutional change in bankruptcy moved in a direction that was influenced by previous moves. In researching this book, we considered the possibility that forces external to bankruptcy created the changes in the costs and benefits that were at the heart of people's desires to change bankruptcy and related laws. Ultimately, though, we could not ignore how earlier law, and how people were using it, influenced the people who sought to change the bankruptcy law.[34] Oftentimes, the people who sought to change other laws also referenced bankruptcy. We were observing a path-dependent process.

Many social scientists believe that studying path dependence is the key to answering fundamental questions about institutions,[35] including questions about how institutions evolve over time and why institutions sometimes persist even when they seem to have negative consequences for economic growth, political participation, or justice. But not all social scientists agree that an emphasis on path dependence enhances our understanding of institutions.[36] Douglass North suggests that theoretical discussion is unlikely to reveal whether the idea is useful. He urges historians to "do the empirical work necessary to identify the precise sources of path dependence."[37] We do the empirical work. We conclude that path dependence explains the development of bankruptcy and related law more completely than existing interpretations do. At each juncture, interest groups, party politics, and other factors changed bankruptcy and related law. At the same time, the interest groups, politics, and other factors at each juncture had themselves been determined, at least in part, by earlier bankruptcy law and its uses.

Our Evidence

We use an assortment of primary and secondary sources, including books, journal articles, newspapers and trade periodicals, records of Congress, and personal papers of key players. In addition, we use data on bankruptcy from the published works of government agencies and from the original court records of bankrupts.

Congress tasked the attorney general to report the statistics of bankruptcy in an annual report. The Administrative Office of the US Courts took over this duty after its creation in 1939. Except for a few years during the Great Depression, administrations published data for each federal district court. We digitized these reports for the whole of the twentieth century. Unfortunately, Congress often changed its mind about what information it wanted, so constructing consistent series for the whole century required some thought. The appendix to chapter 1 describes the construction of the series.

We typically aggregate the statistics from the federal district courts to the state level and take the state bankruptcy rate as the dependent variable in our regression analysis. In addition to the fact that many states are served by a single federal district court, the collection laws that influence the choice to use bankruptcy once in default are state laws.

As noted above, our regression analysis also accounts for the economic and social factors that influence the many choices on the path to bankruptcy. In each regression, we include measures of the state economic and social conditions that influence the rate at which people get credit and the rate at which people default. Many economic and social determinants of the bankruptcy rate have been widely studied in a modern context. To the greatest extent possible, we include historical proxies. For example, one key economic variable is the unemployment rate. A higher unemployment rate increases default. When we study the decades for which modern state-level unemployment data are unavailable, we proxy unemployment with information about business failures or information about the timing of recessions. As an additional example, a widely discussed social variable is stigma. A decline in the stigma of bankruptcy decreases the social cost of filing and increases the likelihood that debtors in default will choose to file. Stigma, of course, is hard to measure, but we proxy it with variables sociologists have used, such as church membership. We conduct a separate regression analysis for each historical period, in part because the measures that are available at the state level vary by historical period, and in part because the literature and the historical record suggest that the importance of particular variables waxed and waned over time.

The regressions used in each chapter are described in detail in the appendix to the chapter. They tell us that we must look beyond changes in social conditions, changes in economic conditions, or changes in the bankruptcy law to understand the surges in the bankruptcy rate that are clear in figure 1.1. Our regressions tell us to focus on how federal legal/institutional change *interacted* with state law and economic conditions to determine the bankruptcy rate in states. The empirical evidence led us to the study of how the use of the bankruptcy law in states then fed back into federal legal/institutional change.

Finally, we digitized key documents from a sample of federal court case files in bankruptcy matters dating from 1899 to 2002. Again, we describe the sample in the appendix to chapter 1. We use the court documents in two ways. First, we begin each chapter with the salient facts about a particular bankruptcy case. We chose the cases because they illustrate clearly and concisely the theme of the chapter. Chapter 2 also ends with an example case because it highlights the dramatic change in who used the bankruptcy law. Second, we compiled data about changes over time in the types of creditors and debts owed by bankrupts. These data show, for example, that new debt instruments, such as credit cards, appeared in the portfolios of the bankrupt quickly after they were invented.

This book is the first to use consistently constructed state-level statistics on bankruptcy rates, together with extensive samples of documents from court cases, to construct a century-long history of bankruptcy. We begin in the last years of the nineteenth century, a time when interstate trade was growing rapidly and the US was without a bankruptcy law.

Chapters in Brief

Chapter 2 examines the origins and consequences of the 1898 Act to Establish a Uniform System of Bankruptcy. As noted in the first section above, the authors of the law were businesses that wanted an efficient procedure to deal with the failure of other businesses. They gave little thought to personal bankruptcy, and the law that they designed for businesses provided little obstacle to the discharge of consumer debts. As access to consumer credit expanded, personal bankruptcy grew both relative to business bankruptcy and in absolute terms. However, personal bankruptcy did not grow evenly across the US. It was mainly in states that made it easy for creditors to collect that households sought the protection offered by federal bankruptcy law. This pattern in personal bankruptcy led to a shift in beliefs about the causes of bankruptcy and, subsequently, beliefs about the purpose of bankruptcy law. Initially, creditors, debtors, legislators, judges, and other legal professionals agreed that the purpose was to satisfy the claims of creditors efficiently. By the end of the 1920s, many interested parties stressed the importance of providing relief to victims of unscrupulous creditors through the discharge. The increasing number of bankruptcy cases, especially personal bankruptcy cases, also led to changes in organized interest groups, as legal professionals came to work alongside creditors to try to shape the law.

In early 1929, a group of New York legal professionals, aided by the Hoover administration, tried to refocus attention on efficient collection. Chapter 3 explains that, as the downturn became the Great Depression, reformers found that neither the country nor Congress was interested in their ideas for improving efficiency. Instead, President Herbert Hoover pushed Congress to use the bankruptcy law to relieve debtors from the intense pressure caused by the collapse of trade credit by adding new ways for business and farm debtors to delay payment. As the Depression wore on, new business formation fell. Business failure and bankruptcy fell with it. From this point, business and corporate bankruptcy evolved separately from personal bankruptcy. This book follows personal bankruptcy.[38]

During the early years of the Depression, personal bankruptcy cases increased but, again, primarily in states with pro-creditor collection law. Representatives from those states convinced Congress that workers really wanted to pay their creditors if they, too, could have a procedure that granted them more time. Congressional debates around the proposals that eventually became Chapter XIII (now known as Chapter 13) pitted those who viewed the procedure as a means to enable people to pay their debts and avoid the stigma of bankruptcy against those who balked at the idea of requiring debtors to pay by making the courts a collection agency for creditors. This theme was reprised several times over the next seventy years.

Chapter 4 examines the increase in bankruptcy between 1945 and 1965. It begins by showing that demand for Chapter XIII probably was not as great as its advocates imagined it to be. People rarely used the procedure for spreading payments over time except in places where bankruptcy court officials pushed it. Growth in consumer credit returned to its pre-Depression levels, as did growth in the personal bankruptcy rate. Bankruptcy grew everywhere, but it rocketed past its previous peak in states with pro-creditor garnishment.

Pro-creditor garnishment law did not survive the consumer rights movement of the 1960s. By 1970, Congress and the Supreme Court limited the ability of states to enforce their pro-creditor collection laws. Chapter 5 shows that the changes in the garnishment law reduced the state-to-state variation in the bankruptcy rate and caused the national bankruptcy rate to level off. An effort to reform bankruptcy began as a response to the growth of bankruptcy in the 1950s and 1960s, but it moved slowly. By the time recommendations were made to Congress, the rising bankruptcy rates were no longer regarded as a problem. Almost all of the changes to personal bankruptcy in the 1978 Bankruptcy Reform Act (BRA) encouraged debtors to use the law.

Of course, filing rates rose after 1978. The debtor friendliness of the 1978 changes set the stage for a new bankruptcy crisis, but increasing importance of banks that issue credit cards was the most important force. The Supreme Court's 1978 decision in *Marquette National Bank of Minneapolis v. First Omaha Services Corp.* led directly to the growth in the market for credit cards. Banks could now profit from offering cards to high-risk consumers, and this put more people on the path to bankruptcy. Card issuers used some of their profits to lobby for changes to bankruptcy law. They argued that debtors should be *required* to repay under Chapter 13 unless they could demonstrate that doing so would not be feasible. In 2005, Congress passed their bill, despite objections from legal professionals, scholars, and even some creditors. Today personal bankrupts who seek liquidation and discharge under Chapter 7 must show that they do not have sufficient income to repay. At the turn of the twenty-first century, credit card issuers won the argument that retailers began in the 1930s.

Appendix to Chapter 1

The appendix to each chapter details the sources and methods underpinning the quantitative conclusions presented in the main text. The appendices also serve as the codebook and guide to the replication code and data set. We archived the replication code and data at the Interuniversity Consortium for Political and Social Research (https://www.icpsr.umich.edu/icpsrweb/).

The appendix to the current chapter describes the data we used to construct the bankruptcy rate, describes the source of the data on individual bankruptcy cases, discusses two counting problems in calculating long series on bankruptcy, and discusses the overall setup of the regression analysis used throughout the book.

Data on the Bankruptcy Rate

The federal government originally published statistics on the number of petitions for bankruptcy filed in each federal district court each year after the passage of the 1898 Bankruptcy Act.[39] Congress tasked the attorney general to report the statistics of bankruptcy in the annual report to Congress on the activities of the Department of Justice. The Administrative Office of the US Courts took over this duty after its creation in 1939. We digitized the data that were previously available only in hard copy and appended data that were published electronically.[40] We merged the bankruptcy data with population count data to compute the annual bankruptcy rate for each federal district court and each state. We merged the resultant data on the bankruptcy rate with data from numerous other sources to perform regression analyses.

CALCULATING BANKRUPTCY FILINGS

Over time, the government changed both the type of information reported and the terminology used to distinguish between business and personal bankruptcy cases. The only consistent series published for every fiscal year is total filings, which is equal to the sum of business and personal filings. Because patterns in business filings and personal filings are different, it was essential to construct consistent series for each. We use the published data to estimate filings by businesses and filings by consumers for each year.

For 1898 to 1932, the occupation information necessary to separate personal bankruptcies from business bankruptcies is available only for cases that each court *closed* during the year, not for cases that debtors filed at each court during the year. Personal bankruptcies are those identified in the published reports as "wage earner" cases. Prior to 1932, we proxy filings in a district i and year t by the one-year lag of the number of wage earner bankruptcy cases that were closed in year $t+1$.

For fiscal years 1933 through 1945, there are no data on personal bankruptcy at the district or state level. There are only national statistics on closings of wage earner cases. We use the national data in figures 1.1 and 1.5 of the text and again assume a one-year lag between filing and closing.

Data on filings by occupation begin in 1946. For fiscal 1946–78, we define personal cases as those filed in each federal district court by "employees" or "other nonbusiness" debtors during each federal fiscal year. There is a gap in the series from 1948 to 1959. To fill it, we estimate the share of all petitions that were personal by linear interpolation of employee plus other nonbusiness filings reported for 1946–47 and 1960–78. We then multiply the estimated share by total number of petitions. After 1978, the government labels personal filings as "nonbusiness" filings.

CALCULATING THE PERSONAL BANKRUPTCY RATE

We define the personal bankruptcy rate in a state as the number of personal petitions (as defined above) filed in the district courts of the state for every 10,000 persons in the population of the state that year. (Some publications define the bankruptcy rate as filings per household. A brief section below shows a comparison.)

For years prior to 1929, we interpolate population estimates from decennial census counts of counties by assuming a constant rate of growth within counties between censuses.[41] We aggregate county populations to the state level. For 1929 through 1969, we use annual estimates of state population reported by the Bureau of Economic Analysis (BEA) for the purpose of computing personal income per capita.[42] For 1969 and later years, we take annual county-level population estimates from the Survey of Epidemiology and End Results (SEER) and again aggregate to states from counties.[43] We use these population estimates in regression analysis in all chapters when we measure variables on a per capita basis.

To compute the bankruptcy rate at the level of the federal court district (rather than the state), we calculate the district population using historically accurate federal court district boundaries as given in the federal statutes.[44]

Data on Individual Bankruptcy Cases

In several chapters, we describe the liabilities of bankrupts by using new samples of bankruptcy cases. (See the preface and acknowledgments for a list of funders.) Descriptive statistics are calculated for a sample of personal bankruptcies in Missouri (1898–1945; from the Federal Court for the Eastern District meeting at St. Louis and the Federal Court for the Western District meeting at Kansas City) and Maryland (1940–2000; from the Maryland District Court at Baltimore). The Missouri sample contains all cases in every tenth box in permanent storage at the National Archives.[45] The Maryland sample contains all cases in every thirty-third box that was in storage at the Federal Records Center (a part of the National Archives) in March 2012. After we collected the Maryland sample, the National Archives moved the sampled boxes to permanent storage. For both the Missouri and Maryland samples, if the sampled box contained fewer than five cases, we also sampled the next box. Table 1A.1 shows the annual average sample size by decade, along with statistics on the total number of cases filed in the district, which we take from the published data described in the previous section. Together the Missouri and Maryland samples contain cases for almost every year of the twentieth century.

The Missouri and Maryland samples are part of an effort to construct a nationally representative sample of case files for the twentieth century. At the time of this writing, we have drawn samples for thirty courts in eighteen states. In several chapters of *Bankrupt in America*, we rely on conclusions reached in papers published by us or in doctoral dissertations written by our students that use the samples.

We take the example cases that begin and/or end chapters from the samples. In addition to examples from Maryland and Missouri, we use examples from Alabama and Maine. Like the Maryland sample, the Maine sample contains all cases in every thirty-third box. Like the Missouri sample, the Alabama sample contains the cases in every tenth box. For each example case used in the text, we provide an archival citation. As required by our Internal Review Board protocol (American Univer-

TABLE IA.I. **Size of Missouri and Maryland samples**

| | Annual average of | | | |
	Petitions: published statistics	Petitions: sample	Percent business: published statistics	Percent business: sample
Missouri				
1898–1909	408	25.6	68.6	35.7
1910–19	584.2	35.5	71.5	44.1
1920–29	1158.4	73.9	63.8	32
1930–39	1797.9	110.4	92.5	23
Maryland				
1950–59	98.3	26.5	38.5	51.2
1960–69	262.9	36	25.1	19.6
1970–79	1088.5	37.1	16	9.3
1980–89	5204.5	36.1	9.7	11.5
1990–99	19519.1	40.4	9	2.3

Source: See appendix to chapter I.

sity Protocol Number 12012), in the text we changed the names of the personal bankrupts to protect their privacy.

By special agreement with the National Archives, to construct the sample, we photographed and subsequently encoded key documents for each case. In *Bankrupt in America*, we use data from two types of the key documents, the petition and the detailed schedules of debts.

PETITION

The date that the court clerk wrote or stamped "filed" on the debtor's petition marks the official beginning of a case. In a small number of photographs taken for the sample, the filing date does not appear or is not legible. We use the date the debtor signed the petition as the approximate filing date. If neither date filed nor date signed was on the photographs, the case is assigned the date of filing of the next case in the sample. (Cases were generally numbered sequentially.) If a case that was missing a date happened to be the last case in a sampled box, then it was assigned the filing date of the previous case.

A second important piece of information on the petition is the name, or names, of the debtor(s). We use the name of the debtor, as well as the occupation listed on the petition (when given), to identify the case as a personal case or a business case. When debts were contracted in the course of doing business, a business name is typically listed as an alias for the debtor(s). (For example, "John Smith, doing business as Smith Furniture Store," or "Brown & Smith" filing as a business partnership between "James Brown" and "John Smith.") Note that the occupation listed by the debtor on the petition is the occupation at the time of filing, which does not always reveal whether debts were amassed for business purposes. We identify some additional business cases because a group of creditors initiated the case. Except in limited circumstances, the bankruptcy law did not allow creditors to initiate an "involuntary" case against debtors who were not in business.

Extant documents do not make it clear how the court clerks determined the occupational breakdowns of closed cases that they sent to Washington for tabulation and publication. They may, for example, have asked the referee or trustee for the information if they could not deduce it from case documents or did not know the filer personally.

Table 1A.1 shows that the Missouri and Maryland samples contain fewer business cases and more personal cases than official statistics report. If the debtor filed voluntarily and did not reveal a business name on the petition, the case may be misclassified. Businesses may also be underrepresented because of sampling by box rather than by case. Many business cases are large, requiring them to be stored in multiple boxes. In contrast, most personal cases are short, so each sampled box contains many cases. Our sample for Mississippi created using a similar strategy also undercounted business bankrupts, but the businesses in the sample come from the same industries as the population of all businesses.[46]

SCHEDULES OF DEBTS

At the time the debtor files a petition, the debtor submits a number of forms, known as "schedules," that contain detailed information on assets owned and debts owed. (In older cases, debtors sometimes filed schedules shortly after the petition.) We use statistics on the types of debt owed by the bankrupts in chapters 2, 4, and 6.

The amounts of assets and debts of the bankrupt generally reflect the balance sheets of the typical bankrupt, though there are few other samples available, and none provides more than cross-sectional snapshots.[47] Because historical household balance sheet data are scarce, we do not know whether the types of debts and creditors of the bankrupt are representative of the debts of households generally. Representativeness likely depends on what happens as households enter financial distress. On one hand, the demand for short-term credit increases as one's financial condition worsens. On the other hand, the supply of short-term credit probably decreases.

We limit our analysis in this book to debts reported on schedules for secured and unsecured debt. We exclude priority debt (such as taxes) and choses in action. The Missouri sample contains 3,614 secured and 49,701 unsecured debts. The Maryland sample contains 3,605 secured and 25,900 unsecured debts.

To examine changes in the supply of credit, we also coded the types of creditors who were listed by the bankrupt. We defined the following primary categories: utility or commercial business, private person, financial institution, medical provider, department store, credit card company, and other. In the Missouri sample, 16 percent of debts have missing or illegible creditor information. In the Maryland sample, only 7 percent of debts have missing information.

Under the 1898 act, spouses filed on separate petitions. To avoid double-counting debts, we excluded the second case filed by a couple. We identified two filers as a couple if they had the same surname and if the cases were filed within a week.

Counting Issues

This section discusses two issues that arise in the calculation of the bankruptcy rate. The first is whether the bankruptcy rate should be calculated as bankruptcies per person or bankruptcies per household. The second is whether the bankruptcies should refer to the number of legal petitions for bankruptcy protection or the number of persons covered by bankruptcy protections.

CHOOSING A DENOMINATOR FOR THE BANKRUPTCY RATE

One basic but seldom discussed technical question is: What is the appropriate denominator for the consumer bankruptcy rate? What is the population at risk? Though researchers typically compare the number of bankruptcy petitions to the size of the population, there are three reasons that the number of households or of families may be the appropriate denominator:[48]

1. Children cannot enter into debt contracts.
2. For the first three-quarters of the twentieth century, women faced considerable discrimination in the consumer credit market,[49] so it was mostly

men, alone or on behalf of their households, who were at risk for becoming bankrupt.

3. After 1978, married couples could file on a single petition.

While population estimates are available at the state level for every year beginning in 1929, the number of households/families is not. We interpolate population for inter-census years by assuming constant growth. The choice of denominator does not affect patterns in the bankruptcy rate,[50] even though household size changed considerably across the period studied.[51] The growth of the personal bankruptcy rate, and both state and national levels, does not depend on whether the number of people or the number of families is used in the denominator of the rate.

PETITIONS OR PETITIONERS?

The 1978 BRA allowed couples with shared debts to file on one petition instead of two. Therefore, the number of petitions filed after the BRA went into effect is not comparable to the number of petitions previously. The number of people in bankruptcy—the number of petition*ers*—is more comparable before and after the BRA.

Because we define the bankruptcy rate as petitions per 10,000 people, the bankruptcy rates reported in *Bankrupt in America* understate the share of people who use the law after the BRA.[52] If the share of joint petitions was constant over time, then we could account for the change in the law by the inclusion of a dummy variable indicating "After BRA" in regression analysis.

Unfortunately, there is limited information on whether the share of joint petitions was constant. The number of joint filings were reported for only three years in the early 1980s. When we recalculate the personal bankruptcy rate as the people in bankruptcy divided by the population, the result is about five percentage points higher in the average state. There is not much variation across the three years of data. In the sample of case files for Maryland, the share of joint cases in the Maryland sample ranged from about 30 percent to about 40 percent over the 1980s, but there was no trend.

Regression Methods

Figure 1.4 shows that bankruptcy is the last step on a long path that begins with a consumer seeking a loan. The debtor continues along the path only if a creditor extends the loan. Of the consumers who go into debt, only those who default are at risk of bankruptcy. Of the debtors who default, only a fraction choose bankruptcy. The bankruptcy rate is therefore the product of three component rates. The first is the fraction of the population that owes debt. The second the fraction of the indebted who do not pay. The third is the fraction of those who do not pay who decide that the benefits of using the bankruptcy law outweigh the costs. More parsimoniously, the definition of the bankruptcy rate is

$$\textbf{(1)} \qquad \frac{Bankruptcy\ Petitions}{Population} = \frac{InDebt}{Population} * \frac{InDefault}{InDebt} * \frac{Files}{InDefault}$$

We organize all regression analyses for *Bankrupt in America* around the definition in equation (1).[53] The next sections discuss strategies for specification and estimation that apply to regressions included in all of the chapters of this book. Sources of data and results for regression analyses are presented in the appendices to chapters 2–5.

FRAMEWORK

All of the regression analyses of the bankruptcy rate in this book measure the extent to which the rate is influenced by variables that influence indebtedness (*InDebt*), variables that influence default (*InDefault*), and variables that influence the choice to use bankruptcy (*Files*). The basic model is:

$$\textbf{(2)} \qquad Rate_{st} = \alpha + \beta Files_{st} + \ InDefault_{st} + \delta InDebt_{s,t-1} + \varepsilon_{st},$$

where the dependent variable is the bankruptcy rate (*Rate*) in a state s and fiscal year t.

The vector *InDebt* contains the variables that influence the demand and supply of credit that are typically included in economic and sociological studies. These include income, race, and laws governing the interest rate. The specific elements of *InDebt* vary across the chapters because of differences in historical context and because of the limitations in the availability of data. In chapters 2 and 6, we focus on changes to state usury laws, which are an element of *InDebt*. Because a person typically does not obtain credit, default, and file for bankruptcy in quick succession, we lag the elements of *InDebt* by one year.

The vector *InDefault* contains variables associated with difficulties

paying bills, as studied by social scientists in many disciplines including economics and sociology. These include unemployment and divorce.
The elements of *InDefault* also vary across the chapters. Details appear
in the appendices to the individual chapters. We do not lag the elements
of *InDefault*.

The vector *Files* captures the legal rules that determine much of the
costs and benefits of choosing bankruptcy. Sociologists have tended to
study nonfinancial costs such as stigma. Economists and lawyers have
tended to study financial costs and benefits. As emphasized in the text,
the regression results presented throughout the book show that the most
consistently important variable in *Files* is the wage exemptions in garnishment. Also included are the homestead and personal property exemptions. Indicators for the passage of changes in the federal bankruptcy
law itself, especially the Bankruptcy Reform Act of 1978, are included
whenever the year of the change is included in the period under study.
We proxy other costs and benefits (such as stigma) when feasible for the
relevant periods as indicated by our reading of results in the literature.
Again, we discuss the specific variables in the appendix to each chapter.

ADDRESSING ENDOGENEITY OF THE LAW

In all studies of the influence of laws on economic outcomes, a common
concern is the possible endogeneity of the law. We considered the possibility that states changed their laws governing creditor-debtor relations
in response to economic conditions; however, historically states rarely
changed exemptions. For example, only seven states changed homestead exemptions in the first half of the twentieth century. While some
states responded to the establishment of minimum federal exemptions
in 1978–79,[54] they did so mainly to restore the state's generosity vis-à-via
other states. The best predictor of the property exemptions in a state in
the 1990s were the exemptions the state had allowed in 1920. We therefore consider laws to be exogenous to bankruptcy rates.

Estimating equation (2) with state fixed effects minimizes omitted
variable bias. However, many of the legal variables in *Files* do not change
over time. Studies employing fixed effects therefore underestimate the
importance of the elements of *Files*.[55] Recent studies of modern bankruptcy use county or zip code level data to get around this problem.[56]
Of course, the historical bankruptcy rate cannot be measured for units
smaller than the federal district court, and many states have only one
district court. The effects of time-invariant variables can be estimated

using random effects,[57] but the results are highly sensitive to our choice of which variables are assumed to be endogenous. Consequently, in most of our regression analyses, we compare results with state fixed effects to simple pooled cross-section, time series ordinary least squares.

ACCOUNTING FOR INTERACTIONS

Because the elements of the bankruptcy rate in equation (1) are multiplied, not added, we typically include interactions in the regressions. Of greatest interest are the interactions between elements of *Files* and other independent variables. A change in the propensity to file for bankruptcy $\left(\frac{Files}{InDefault}\right)$ *amplifies* changes in the default rate or indebtedness rate. For example, equation (3) below allows the elements of *Files* to amplify the effect of the determinants of the default rate on the bankruptcy rate:

$$
(3) \quad Rate_{st} = \alpha + \beta Files_{st} + \mu InDefault_{st} + \delta InDebt_{s,t-1} + \gamma \beta Files_{st} * InDefault_{st} + \varepsilon_{st}.
$$

CHAPTER TWO

The Intended and Unintended Consequences of the 1898 Bankruptcy Act

On August 9, 1898, John Ellman, a dry-goods merchant,[1] filed a bankruptcy petition at the US district court in St. Louis.[2] It was only the third case filed in St. Louis after the 1898 bankruptcy law went into effect the previous month. Ellman's insolvency dated back to 1893, when his partnership with Max Simon failed.[3] By 1898, Ellman owed 163 creditors a total of $144,000. His smallest debt was $3.75; his largest was $6,000. Nearly all of his creditors were other merchants and manufacturers who had sold him stock on account. Some creditors were in Missouri and nearby Illinois, but most were back east. He had sourced products ranging from corsets to pencils from New York, Massachusetts, Maryland, Pennsylvania, Ohio, and Wisconsin.

Ellman's $125 in cash and $110 in personal property were exempt from liquidation. The only proceeds from the bankruptcy procedure came from cashing out two life insurance policies with value of $94.72. Of this amount, $41.62 went to administrative expenses. The largest disbursement was for $17.89, which went to cover the fees and expenses of the officer of the court who managed the case. Dividends to his creditors totaled $53.10.

The court closed Ellman's case in October 1899. By 1904, he had set up a new business as a "merchandise broker."[4] By 1920, Ellman had amassed enough capital to go into business as a clothing manufacturer.[5]

The failure of John Ellman's business was exactly what merchants and manufacturers had in mind when they drafted and lobbied for the

1898 Bankruptcy Act. However, by 1930, business owners like Ellman were no longer the main users of the bankruptcy law. Employees who had used their regular wages to obtain credit for personal consumption filed most of the bankruptcy petitions after the mid-1920s. The transformation of bankruptcy from a procedure for businesses that wanted to manage the liquidation of another business to a procedure for households who had defaulted on personal debt was an unanticipated and unintended outcome of the 1898 Bankruptcy Act. The transformation of the use of bankruptcy changed the interest groups that lobbied for later changes to the bankruptcy law.

The Origins of the 1898 Bankruptcy Act

For centuries, merchants relied on unsecured credit to finance trade, both local and long distance. Suppliers, such as wholesalers and manufacturers, sent inventory to customers, particularly retailers. Customers paid after selling the items, usually within three to six months. Most customers paid without incident. When customers in the US failed to pay, creditors had to turn to the law. For example, when many businesses were unable to pay after the Civil War, Congress passed a bankruptcy law. But creditors complained of high costs and low dividends, and Congress repealed the law in 1878. After 1878, creditors again had to use state collection laws.

State laws increased the cost of credit and diminished the amount of profitable business. As discussed in chapter 1, advocates for a new federal law saw three specific shortcomings. First, the details of the laws differed from state to state. Lucius Eaton, a member of the St. Louis Merchants Exchange, for instance, explained, "It would simplify and abridge credit . . . if creditors were not required by the aid of local counsel to investigate the laws of every state in which they give credit."[6] Second, some states discriminated against creditors who were not citizens of that state. In 1898, the Retail Grocers and Merchants Association complained that California statutes "are practically to the effect that all claims on the part of California creditors must be settled by their assignees before any money whatever is to be paid to other creditors."[7] The practice of discriminating against out-of-state creditors was not isolated to California, and many state courts upheld such laws.[8] The effect of discrimination, according to John Bartlett of the Minneapolis Chamber of Commerce, was that the "manufacturer and the wholesaler who offers his wares in a State where the laws are notoriously inadequate for their protection, must add to their original profit an amount as security, or insurance if you please, against loss in that State."[9] Third, many state laws provided for a first-come, first-served distribution of assets, rather than a distribution proportional to the debt owed. Beyond the advantage to local creditors from proximity, first-come, first-served collection created a wasteful race to be the first to the courthouse. According to Jay Torrey, president of the National Convention of Representatives of Commercial Bodies, "[I]f a creditor suspects his debtor . . . is in financial trouble, he usually commences an attachment suit, and as a result the debtor is thrown into liquidation irrespective of whether he is solvent or insolvent. . . . [If the creditor] does not pursue that course some other creditor will."[10] The laws also prevented creditors from helping debtors who might be in trouble. Torrey explained, "[U]nder the laws as they exist in most of the States, an embarrassed debtor cannot call a meeting of his creditors without inviting his own financial ruin."[11]

The difficulties of operating under state collection laws became increasingly important as the US and its economy grew after the Civil War.[12] Manufacturers and wholesalers used the expanding communication and transportation networks to send commercial travelers throughout the country. The number of merchants doubled during the years from 1870 to 1900, while the number of commercial travelers increased more than tenfold.[13] As long-distance trade expanded, merchants and manufacturers believed that a federal bankruptcy law could provide a more level playing field for creditors, result in fewer commercial failures, incentivize private workouts, and lower the cost of credit.

In particular, commercial creditors wanted a bankruptcy law that would avoid the high expenses and low dividends that had led to the demise of previous bankruptcy laws.[14] To obtain the specific law they wanted, they needed to present a unified voice in Washington. Fortunately for them, the cost of forming a national organization to lobby for bankruptcy legislation was falling, while the benefit of doing so was rising. The cost of organizing was falling because of the growth of commercial associations, such as trade associations, boards of trade, and chambers of commerce. Before these special interest and local organizations formed in the last quarter of the nineteenth century, it would have been virtually impossible to organize a national lobby.[15]

In 1881, three years after the repeal of the 1867 Bankruptcy Act, the New York Board of Trade and Transportation organized a National

Convention of Boards of Trade. The convention asked Judge John Lowell to draft a bankruptcy bill. Senator George Hoar (R-MA) introduced the Lowell bill in the Senate in 1882. The next year, Senator John Ingalls (R-KS) introduced an alternative bill that differed in details but shared a key provision. While the 1867 bankruptcy law relied on court appointees to settle claims, the Lowell and Ingalls bills relied on government officials to oversee the administration of bankruptcy cases and the investigation of the bankrupts. Judge Lowell argued that "officialism" would provide "supervision over the speedy and economical settlement of bankrupt estates which creditors cannot be relied on to furnish."[16]

Neither bill passed. In 1889, merchants and manufacturers tried again. This time, 304 commercial associations met as the National Convention of Representatives of Commercial Bodies.[17] Jay Torrey—lawyer, businessman, and president of the convention—drafted the bill for which the convention lobbied throughout the 1890s. In contrast to Judge Lowell and Senator Ingalls, Torrey believed that creditor control, not officialism, would provide the best remedy for the high fees and expenses that had plagued previous American bankruptcy laws. Under the Torrey bill, the court was required to schedule a meeting of creditors within thirty days of the filing of a petition for bankruptcy. The creditors selected a trustee, and they were to play an active role in the examination of bankrupts, ensuring the highest possible dividends and preventing a dishonest bankrupt from receiving a discharge.

The members of the convention probably knew that it would not be easy to pass the Torrey bill. Bankruptcy fell squarely into the ideological divide that already existed between Democrats and Republicans.[18] Republicans supported bankruptcy as part of a broader program of promoting a national market. Congressman George W. Ray (R-NY) said, "We have tried to so frame the bill as to promote business intercourse and the giving of credit. Under its provisions, when in operation, the manufacturer and merchant in New England will not hesitate to extend credit to the trader in New Orleans. The merchants and traders of the great Northwest will not fear to extend it to those asking it all throughout the South."[19] Democrats opposed the Torrey bill precisely *because* it promoted a national economy. They argued that a national bankruptcy law would take away one of the few advantages that small local businesses had over large national businesses.[20]

In 1889, during the Fifty-first Congress, Republicans controlled both houses of Congress and the White House. The House passed the Torrey bill. The Senate was more concerned with tariffs and monetary issues and did not take it up.[21] In the Fifty-fourth Congress, Republicans held a majority in the House, but in the Senate they held just forty-four seats, while Democrats held forty, Populists held four, and Silver Republicans held two.

In the Fifty-fifth Congress, Republicans again held a majority in both houses and had President William McKinley in the White House. The bankruptcy bill introduced in the House was the Torrey bill.[22] The Senate passed a different bankruptcy bill, but it was also a Republican bill. A conference committee was created to resolve the differences.

David De Armond (D-MO) declared, "No man can read a page of [the conference report] without finding upon that page indisputable evidence that the bill originated with those who have debts to collect." He continued, "[S]carcely can the insolvent get through under this law and with this machinery if those who take the other side—the creditors—choose to bar the exit and deny him a discharge."[23] However, neither the conference report nor the Torrey bill required debtors to pay a certain percentage of the debt or get creditor consent to obtain a discharge, as previous bankruptcy laws had done. Some legal scholars wrote that the relative debtor friendliness of the Torrey bill reflected the fact that Republicans knew that a limited discharge was "a battle they could not win."[24] However, proponents of the bankruptcy legislation had argued for some time that making a discharge contingent on anything other than the honesty of the debtor would thwart two fundamental objectives of the law: preventing a "race of diligence" and avoiding the preferential treatment of any one creditor. Judge Lowell, for instance, noted that requiring creditor consent would lead to situations in which "certain creditors, the most avaricious and the least scrupulous, will take advantage of any power which may be given them over the debtor's discharge by exacting terms from him, either of present payment or of promises for the future."[25] Torrey himself similarly argued that leaving any honest debtor—an employee, but especially his or her boss—with a debt burden was also bad public policy:

> If [the petitioner] is an honest man he ought to be discharged from the obligation to the end that he may be, if he can, a proprietor, instead of a salaried clerk. If he is held down by the burden of debt . . . it is not possible that he can make any considerable payment of obligations and at the same time provide education and maintenance of the average family.[26]

The conference report took its most debtor-friendly elements, the court's protection from creditors and the promise of a fresh start, directly from the Torrey bill.[27] These provisions were not added merely as "concessions to pro-debtor interests" designed "to minimize defections and to pick up a few Democratic votes."[28] Voting, predictably, fell along party lines.[29] More than 80 percent of Democrats voted against the bill. Democrats wanted only another temporary bankruptcy law to deal with insolvencies caused by the depression of the 1890s. Fourteen representatives switched from voting *nay* on the House bill to voting *yea* on the conference report, but the switches were not necessary. The conference report passed in the House by a vote of 134 to 53, with 112 *yea* votes cast by Republicans. In the Senate, the conference report passed 43 to 13. Five senators who had previously voted *yea* on the Senate version voted against the conference report, and three who had voted *nay* in the Senate voted *yea* on the conference report.[30] The US got its first permanent bankruptcy law in 1898 because the Republican Party finally had sufficient control of Congress to get its bankruptcy bill to a Republican president.

Bankruptcy Procedure

The 1898 Bankruptcy Act made the US district courts the courts of bankruptcy. "Any person, except a municipal, railroad, or banking corporation" who owed debts could use the law. The 1898 act allowed a debtor to declare "voluntarily" in a petition to the court that he or she was unable to pay and willing to liquidate assets to satisfy the creditors' claims. With the petition, the debtor provided a detailed list of all assets and liabilities. The act allowed a creditor to file a petition "involuntarily" against a debtor who had defaulted, but only if the debtor did not primarily generate his or her income as a farmer or as a "wage earner." A debtor brought involuntarily to court provided complete financial information in response to the petition.

The act also allowed a debtor to avoid liquidation by negotiating a "composition." In a composition, the debtor promised to pay a stated percentage of all debts over a stated period. The remainder was discharged. A composition required the consent of a majority of creditors, both in total number and in terms of the amount of debt owed. Compositions were rare, but the procedure was a precursor to business reorganization and "wage earner workout plans" that were incorporated into bankruptcy later.

Under the act, the district court judge appointed a referee to oversee administration of the case and act on the judge's behalf. Referees were typically lawyers, though the act did not specify that they must be trained in law. There was to be one referee in each county that was part of the judicial district.[31] By delegating authority to local referees, the act tried to reduce the high travel costs previously associated with bankruptcy. However, referees were always subject to review by judges, who retained authority in all bankruptcy matters.

After a debtor filed a petition, the court notified creditors to stop any efforts to collect outside of bankruptcy. The "automatic stay" of collections was (and is still) an important benefit of using the law. The referee quickly scheduled a meeting of the creditors. At the meeting, the creditors could elect a trustee to represent them, as mentioned above. If the creditors deferred, the referee would appoint one.

The debtor retained any assets that the state declared to be exempt from collection. A secured creditor retained its claim on collateral. Unsecured creditors were divided into those with priority and those without it. Priority creditors included governments that were owed taxes and employees who were owed wages. The trustee liquidated any assets that were neither collateral for a secured claim nor exempted by state law. He then distributed the proceeds. Because bankruptcy was to be self-financing, referees, trustees, and attorneys were compensated from filing fees or fees (commissions) levied on the bankrupt's estate. Any remaining funds were paid to the creditors. Again, creditors received payment on a pro rata basis.

After the bankrupt's estate was settled, the debtor could petition the court for discharge. If the debtor had complied with the law, the court would grant a discharge of nearly all of the remaining debts.

Republicans meant the 1898 act to be permanent, but Democrats tried to repeal it almost immediately. Democrats continued to claim, with perhaps a touch of hyperbole, "[T]he present act is the most oppressive law, so far as the unfortunate debtor is concerned, that has ever been enacted."[32] Involuntary bankrupts were "subject to every inquisitorial method and harsh measure that commercial lawyers and hard-hearted creditors can suggest," read the 1902 report of the Minority of the House Judiciary Committee.[33] That year, 60 out of 80 Democrats voted for a repeal; 117 out of 121 Republicans voted against it.[34]

Meanwhile, Republicans easily passed amendments to close loopholes, respond to legal decisions, and generally make the law more useful for businesses.[35] Alimony, child support, and liabilities from causing intentional harm were added to the list of debts that could not be discharged. One amendment eliminated a loophole that allowed liabilities arising from fraud to be discharged if the creditor did not obtain a judgment before the discharge was granted. Another amendment restored a provision that was struck from the original Torrey bill: A debtor could be denied a discharge for obtaining credit on a false statement or for concealing, destroying, or conveying property with the intent to hide it from a creditor. In 1898, the House sponsor of the bill had argued that this provision was not necessary because the law did not discharge the specific debts arising from those actions, but in 1902 Republicans argued that including them as grounds for denial of a discharge was in keeping with the philosophy that only honest bankrupts should receive a discharge.[36]

In 1910, Democrats were still seeking a repeal, but they were beginning to lose steam. In the House, Democratic support for a repeal had fallen to two-thirds. Republicans, on the other hand, continued to argue that the law "encourages commercial activity, no matter how distant the creditor and the debtor may be."[37] They claimed it had "done more to increase the credit of the poorer sections of this country than any law that was ever put on the books."[38]

The primary difference between the 1898 act and the earlier, short-lived bankruptcy laws was that the act worked well enough that merchants and manufacturers themselves did not change their minds and seek its repeal. The National Association of Credit Men lobbied for amendments and against a repeal on behalf of the trade creditors who had drafted the 1898 act.[39]

The Intended Effects of the 1898 Bankruptcy Act

The bankruptcy bar also opposed repeal,[40] in no small part because bankruptcy quickly became a primary occupation of the federal courts. In 1900, there were more than 20,000 bankruptcy cases but only 10,628 private civil suits.[41] For its first two decades, the law worked much as commercial creditors had predicted. They predicted that it would be used mostly by businesses. In the average district, business petitions outnumbered farmer petitions by about nine to one, and they outnum-

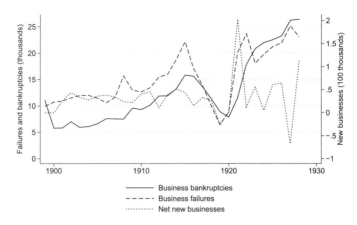

FIG. 2.1. Nationally, business bankruptcies from 1898–1929 tracked business failures (left axis). The relationship between bankruptcy, failure, and new business formation (right axis) was also close until the mid-1920s. *Source*: See appendix to chapter 2.

bered personal petitions by almost two to one. The first wave of debtors to file were business owners who, like John Ellman, had been insolvent for years. After that, a large and constant proportion of all business failures reported by R. G. Dun were handled under the bankruptcy law each year. Figure 2.1 shows that the total number of business bankruptcies tracked business failures.[42] Moreover, for businesses the bankruptcy law worked uniformly across the states. In a typical year, about 85 percent of business failures were handled in federal bankruptcy proceedings, and the share was nearly identical in every state.[43]

Just as the variation in the business failure rate between states explains the variation in the business bankruptcy rate, the increase in business failures over time explains the increase in business bankruptcy from 1900 to 1930. The best predictor of the trend in business failure is the trend in new business formation.[44] Indeed, one of the most striking features of figure 2.1 is the dip in both bankruptcy and new business formation during the US involvement in World War I (1917–18). The postwar spike in new business formation, combined with the recession of 1920–21, then led to a spike in business failures. After 1921, the correlation weakens,[45] but, in general, the increase in business bankruptcy in the early twentieth century was a sign of economic dynamism, not economic stagnation.

Recall that commercial creditors wanted to reduce the incentives for a race of diligence. They claimed that the law did exactly that. The National Association of Manufacturers agreed: "Many thousands of worthy men were saved by it, who, if it had been absent would have been forced into insolvency and ruin."[46] After the Panic of 1907, the National Association of Credit Men reported that "[t]he law undoubtedly stayed the hand of many an anxious creditor who, unable to secure a preference to himself, joined in extending help to his embarrassed debtor, thus tiding over many a deserving business man." The Los Angeles Board of Trade and the journal *Bradstreet's* reached similar conclusions.[47]

One mechanism for extending help to a debtor was "debt adjustment." Adjustment bureaus facilitated the renegotiation of terms ("adjustment") when there were several creditors involved. Local chambers of commerce or boards of trade sponsored the bureaus. Only three bureaus are known to have existed before 1898.[48] Because the bankruptcy law reduced the incentive for individual creditors to initiate liquidation, it made more bureaus possible. By 1929, adjustment bureaus known to the National Association of Credit Men were handling nonbankruptcy adjustment cases involving total liabilities of more than $31 million.[49] Out-of-court cooperation "contrasted with the hasty and intolerant policy of creditors prior to the enactment of the National Bankruptcy Act,"[50] and ultimately led to fewer petitions for bankruptcy by businesses.

The Unintended Effects of the 1898 Bankruptcy Act

The commercial creditors who wrote the 1898 act believed that some employees would benefit from it, but they did not predict that so many households would eventually use the law to obtain a discharge of consumer debt. The personal bankruptcy rate was less than 1 per 10,000 persons in most states and most years from 1899 to 1923. It more than doubled before the start of the Great Depression. Petitions for personal bankruptcy overtook business bankruptcy petitions in the 1920s, as noted in chapter 1 and illustrated in figure 1.1. How did so many personal petitions come to be filed under a law that was drafted by creditors, regarded by its opponents as pro-creditor, and amended to make obtaining a discharge more difficult?

Paradoxically, the law was amenable to personal bankruptcy precisely *because* trade creditors were so focused on business bankruptcy. They designed the administration of the 1898 Bankruptcy Act with the belief that creditors would actively control the proceedings. Creditors, after all, were the ones with the stake in ensuring honesty and the highest possible dividends. The presumption of creditor control made sense for business bankruptcy because most businesses had inventory, capital equipment, and accounts receivable to liquidate. Yet creditors were not interested in controlling personal bankruptcy cases because there were no assets to liquidate after the debtor was granted all exemptions allowed under state law.

As personal cases overtook business cases, the number of "no-asset" cases increased. Before 1918, no-asset cases never accounted for as much as 50 percent of cases in any year. A 1929–30 study found that 85 percent of personal bankrupts in Boston had only exempt assets. An additional 9.4 percent had less than $100 in assets.[51] Not surprisingly, a survey of bankruptcy referees in 1930 found that creditors appeared at 64 percent of the meetings arranged by the court for business cases, but they appeared at only 23 percent of the meetings in personal cases.[52] There was no one to examine the bankrupt or oppose a discharge, so discharges were denied in less than one-half of 1 percent of personal bankruptcy cases.[53] As more households gained access to consumer credit in the 1910s and 1920s,[54] the absolute number of defaults among consumers rose, and more people sought the discharge in bankruptcy.

Growth of Consumer Credit

Innovations in the supply of credit drove the increase in consumer debt.[55] Residential mortgage lending grew, both locally and interregionally. Companies created new methods to finance inventory. New types of financial institutions created new vehicles for making small loans to the growing number of workers earning regular wages. Buying on installment and borrowing for consumption became ubiquitous.[56]

Commercial banks, mutual savings banks, and building and loan associations were all players in nonfarm mortgage lending. Life insurance companies collaborated with mortgage companies to stabilize direct mortgage lending across long distances.[57] Second mortgages were common.[58] Because of these developments, nonfarm residential debt grew from $9 to $30 billion, the ratio of residential debt to wealth rose from about 15 to almost 30 percent, and nonfarm home ownership rose from 41 to 46 percent.[59] Developers created new methods for financing the construction of apartment buildings, hotels, and other real estate developments using long-term bonds. Despite the fact that residential building began to decline in 1926,[60] new issues of mortgage bonds were three times greater in 1926–28 than they had been between the recessions of 1920–21 and 1923–24.[61]

In the 1920s, retail sales made on credit increased from about 20 percent to more than 50 percent.[62] Sales finance companies facilitated an increase in credit extended for the purchase of durable goods. Sales finance companies purchased installment contracts from the retailers who originated them. Most also extended loans to retailers for the purchase of inventory from manufacturers. The sales finance industry grew quickly after 1915.[63] In 1918–19, just under 20 percent of low- to middle-income families were using installment loans to buy furniture and appliances. About 5 percent were using an installment plan to buy an automobile. In contrast, during the 1920s, 60 to 70 percent of car sales were on installment. Sales of other consumer durables increased similarly, and many of these sales were on installment plans.[64] In the year before the start of the Great Depression, 25 percent of households nationwide and 40 percent of upper-middle-income federal employees had installment debt.[65]

Data from our sample of bankruptcy case files confirms that the supply of installment credit grew especially quickly during the 1920s. Figure 2.2 shows the prevalence of installment debt in a sample of 338 personal bankruptcy cases filed in Missouri from 1900 to 1930. The share of bankrupts with installment debt rose from less than 10 percent in the 1910s to 25 percent in 1929. In 1920, a bankrupt household was less likely to owe installment debt than the typical household was. By 1929, the bankrupt household was about as likely as the typical household to owe installment debt secured by furniture, an appliance, or a car. Of course, the pattern in the data does not mean that installment debt caused the bankruptcies of the people in the sample. What the data show is that installment contracts were increasingly available to households that, over the couple of years of the contract, found themselves deciding to seek the protections of bankruptcy rather than continue to struggle to pay. In other words, the pattern in the data suggests that there was growth in the supply of installment credit at the extensive margin, with some proportion of new installment credit going to people who had not been able to get it earlier. The growth in installment credit put more people on the path to bankruptcy.

A large number of lenders, operating on different business models, lent cash to working-class households. Industrial banks (most famously

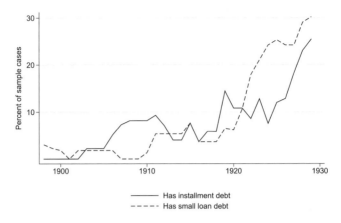

FIG. 2.2. The share of personal cases in the Missouri sample showing installment loans and debts to small loan companies grew substantially in the 1920s, putting more people on the path to bankruptcy. *Source*: See appendix to chapter 2.

the Morris Plan Banks) were lending $360 million per year just twenty years after their creation. Remedial loan societies, credit unions, and banks were each comparatively small, but together loaned a substantial amount. Pawnbrokers and personal finance companies allowed people to borrow against personal items, household goods, or future wages. From 1916 to 1930, loans from personal finance companies grew by a factor of thirty.[66] By 1930, cash loans from all sources totaled $2.86 billion annually.[67]

The supply of small loans seems to have increased even more rapidly than the supply of installment loans during the 1920s. Figure 2.2 shows that, in the sample of Missouri bankrupts, small loans from personal finance companies were more prevalent than installment loans, and grew more rapidly, after about 1920. Like today's payday loan agencies, companies that issued small loans in the 1920s were a source of stop-gap funding for families. People used small loans to pay for unexpected expenses or to make ends meet when wages fell below preexisting obligations such as installment loans. The rapid increase in the propensity of bankrupts to owe at least one small loan lender is therefore a good indicator of how quickly the innovations in consumer credit increased the number of people who were on the path to bankruptcy.

The largest consumer lenders by volume were loan sharks: small loan agencies that violated state usury laws. They may have made up to

25 percent of all cash loans to households in 1930. Earlier in the century, the market share of loan sharks was likely larger. The next section explains how many states tried to reduce it.[68]

Despite the rapid increase in consumer credit per capita (see again figure 1.3), default rates on consumer credit remained low throughout the 1920s. Because missing an installment payment triggered repossession and forfeiture of equity, households preferred to reduce other consumption rather than default.[69] Evans Clark, who at the time was the executive director of the Twentieth Century Fund, declared, "Almost universal experience shows a loss ratio of less than one per cent of the total loans or credit advanced and only in the rarest cases do such organizations show as high a ratio as two per cent."[70] A study of small loan agencies in Massachusetts in 1928 reported that total losses were 0.4 percent, and that 58 percent of the agencies reported no losses.[71]

Even with a constant rate of default, the bankruptcy rate increased as the number of indebted households increased. Bankruptcy law ceased to be predominantly the collection tool for creditors that its authors intended. It became primarily a tool for insolvent consumers to halt collection efforts, especially garnishment, and to receive a discharge of their debts.

State Laws and Bankruptcy Rates

A quick look back at figures 1.1 and 1.2 reveals that, nationally, the personal bankruptcy rate more than doubled in the 1920s, but the difference in bankruptcy between states in any year dwarfed its growth over any decade. None of North Carolina's 2.5 million people filed for personal bankruptcy in 1920; more than 5 of every 10,000 residents of Alabama filed. In 1930, the rate in Alabama was 13 per 10,000, and it was 0.04 per 10,000 in North Carolina. The variation in state laws that governed the relationship between consumers and their creditors caused much of the state-to-state variation in personal bankruptcy. State laws influenced the choices that consumers and creditors made along the path to bankruptcy. Two types of laws were particularly important: laws regulating lending and laws regulating collection procedures. Among laws regulating lending, usury law was of particular importance. Important collection laws included wage assignment, property exemptions, and garnishment.

Lending and Usury Rates

Governments for centuries have regulated the interest rates that lenders can charge. The American colonies had usury laws,[72] and after the establishment of the US, individual states continued to promulgate them. As credit markets became more complex, so did usury laws. By the turn of the twentieth century, most states had multiple usury rates. Each usury rate defined the highest interest rate that a specific type of lender could charge on a given type of transaction. Usury rates, and the severity of the penalty for charging more than the allowed rate on a transaction, varied substantially in 1900. In the nineteenth century, states had actively responded to credit booms and busts by decreasing or increasing the usury rates.[73] In the twentieth century, changes were one way. States raised or removed usury rates on important consumer transactions. About half of states raised the usury rates between 1909 and the start of the Great Depression.

In the first decade of the twentieth century, social reformers believed that usury laws limited the supply of legal loans to poor but honest borrowers. The limited supply of legal loans drove consumers to unscrupulous loan sharks. To solve the problem, the Russell Sage Foundation drafted a Uniform Small Loan Law and began to promote it to state legislatures. The small loan law established regulations for lenders. Lenders who obtained licenses could charge higher interest rates for loans under about $300,[74] or about 20 percent of average annual wages. About half of all states passed a version of the Uniform Small Loan Law between 1909 and 1933.[75] (For a list, see table 2A.1 in the appendix to chapter 2.) Loans from licensed lenders grew from $8.25 million at the end of 1916 to $255 million at the end of 1929.[76]

How much of the increase in lending was caused by the small loan laws? Usually when there is an increase in the consumption of something like lending, it is difficult to tell whether the increase is rooted in an increase in demand, an increase in supply, or an increase on both sides of the market. For example, income was increasing during this period. The increase in income probably increased demand for all types of credit, including small loans.

In the case of the increase in the amount of small loan lending during the 1920s, the problem is simplified. Because usury rates are typically set below the market-clearing interest rate,[77] the observed amount of lending is determined entirely by what lenders are willing to supply. Small loan laws increased the amount of credit that existing lenders were willing to extend and probably also increased the number of lenders in the market. We do not need information about demand to be confident that the passage of small loan laws increased the amount of credit supplied to the working class, allowing them to better smooth consumption.

Because small loan laws aimed to make lending to relatively risky borrowers more profitable, the laws also increased the proportion of people in debt in the states that passed them. The increase in indebtedness caused by small loan laws put more people on the path to bankruptcy. As states passed small loan laws, the personal bankruptcy rate rose. Before states passed small loan laws, their bankruptcy rates were, on average, 0.85 per 10,000 people. After passage of a small loan law, their bankruptcy rates were 1.98 filings per 10,000 people, more than twice as high. For comparison, the average bankruptcy rate in states that never passed a small loan law before the Great Depression was 0.92 per 10,000, or about the same as the rate before the small loan law in states that passed them. Later in this section, we use regression analysis to argue that passage of the small loans laws caused some of the increase in personal bankruptcy, but that the impact depended on the characteristics of the law governing collection procedures in the state.

Collection Procedures

States regulated the collection of debt. The collection remedies available to the creditor depended first on whether the debt was secured. If the debt was secured with property, the creditor could repossess the property if the debtor defaulted, as mentioned above. If the debt was not secured by property, creditors, especially personal finance companies and retailers selling on installment, often asked a debtor to sign a wage assignment at the time the loan was extended.

WAGE ASSIGNMENT

In a wage assignment, at the time the debtor signs a contract he or she also grants the creditor the authority to obtain payment directly from the debtor's employer in the event of default. The creditor avoids court costs and delays.

Many states restricted wage assignments.[78] For instance, in 1905, Illinois enacted legislation that required that an assignment be in writing, be acknowledged before a justice of the peace, entered on the justice's docket, and presented to the employer. If the borrower was married, the spouse had to agree to the assignment. The assignment was void if the transaction was usurious.[79] In 1908, however, the Illinois Supreme Court ruled that the wage assignment law violated the due process clause of the Illinois Constitution. Like other due process cases, this one turned on the balance between individual liberty and the exercise of police powers. Proponents of the law argued that although it restricted liberty, it did not violate the constitution because it was a legitimate use of the state's police powers: Laboring people needed to be protected from loan sharks. Opponents argued that preventing adult workers from deciding what to do with their wages was not a legitimate public purpose. Later, Illinois courts even blocked attempts by employers to prevent the use of wage assignments by their employees.[80] In many other states, however, courts ruled that restrictions on wage assignments did not violate due process.[81] In 1911, the US Supreme Court ruled that restrictions on wage assignments did not inherently violate the US Constitution, essentially leaving the issue to states to regulate as they chose.[82] Like small loan legislation, restrictions on wage assignment were part of a broader anti–loan shark campaign in the early twentieth century.

Unrestricted wage assignment increases bankruptcy in two ways. First, it tends to increase the supply of credit. Second, it keeps the cost of collection low, so it tends to increase the rate at which creditors seek to collect unpaid debts. The collection effort itself tends to push borrowers to seek bankruptcy protection. Contemporary observers believed the latter effect dominated the former.[83] There is no state-by-state summary of wage assignment law, though some aspects of it are included in the information on wage garnishment discussed below.

If the debtor defaulted and there was no wage assignment, the creditor could obtain a favorable court judgment and have the state-designated officer of the court (often the sheriff) execute the judgment. A judgment could be executed by seizing and selling some of the debtor's property, even though the property was not used to secure the debt.

EXEMPTIONS

Since 1839, states had restricted the ability of creditors to seize property in collections. States typically defined both a homestead exemption and a personal property exemption. During the 1920s, most states defined the homestead exemption in dollars, which averaged $2,070 with a maximum of $8,000 in the 1920s. (For a list, see table 2A.1 of the appendix to chapter 2.) A few states specified the homestead exemption in terms of a quantity of land. About two-thirds of states defined personal exemptions in dollars, with exemptions averaging $656 with a maximum of $2,000, but thirteen states exempted only an itemized list of personal assets, such as family Bibles, items of clothing, and tools.

In the nineteenth century, states in the West and the South generally had higher exemptions than states in the Midwest and East. Western states initially adopted high exemptions to attract settlers. Southern states increased exemptions after the Civil War. Unlike usury rates, states changed exemptions infrequently before the last quarter of the twentieth century. Even then, states with historically generous exemptions remained relatively generous, while few states that were historically stingy became generous.[84]

Again, under the 1898 Bankruptcy Act, bankrupts were allowed to keep any assets exempted under state law. Higher exemptions encouraged debtors to choose bankruptcy. During the 1920s, states with the most generous property exemptions (highest quartile) had personal bankruptcy rates that were about double the rates in states with the least generous exemptions (lowest quartile).[85]

GARNISHMENT

Garnishment allowed a creditor to go after assets that were in the possession of a third party. Garnishment could be applied to bank accounts or other assets; however, because many debtors had no assets beyond what the state declared exempt, it was most often used to obtain a share of any wages that had not yet been paid to the debtor. When a worker defaulted, garnishment was (and is still) the most important of the traditional creditors' remedies.

Creditors, especially retailers who sold on credit, lobbied for easy garnishment procedures and low exemptions. Labor organizations and large employers lobbied for restrictions on garnishment procedures and for high exemptions. Large employers found garnishment to be an expensive nuisance. Beyond the loss of wages, workers feared garnishment because they feared they would be fired because of a judgment.[86]

During the first decades of the twentieth century, state garnishment laws varied widely in terms of both wage exemptions and procedures. Some states allowed garnishment to proceed as soon as a creditor filed a claim to garnish—even before a hearing took place, and sometimes even before the debtor was served notice. In other states, a court judgment was required before garnishment started. In some states, only 50 percent of wages were exempt. As noted above, assignment laws also varied. There is enough extant information to classify the whole set of wage execution laws as *pro-creditor, pro-debtor,* or *intermediate* in thirty states.[87] Pro-creditor laws did not appear to leave enough for the support of the average wage earner's family; intermediate laws left an adequate amount for the support of a family; pro-debtor laws were ones in which wages were generally not subject to garnishment.

Recall that petitioning for bankruptcy halted other collection actions. That included garnishment. State law on garnishment was important to bankruptcy because a wage earner in default could choose between allowing garnishment or filing for bankruptcy.[88] A debtor who filed for bankruptcy kept future income but lost any assets in excess of the state-defined property exemptions. A debtor who allowed garnishment kept assets but lost a fraction of future income, determined by the wage exemption defined in the state's law. For the worker in default, the choice of whether to declare bankruptcy or leave creditors to use state garnishment law depended on what percentage of wages were subject to garnishment and how likely it was that creditors would actually collect using the state's garnishment procedures. All other things equal, pro-creditor garnishment and wage execution law increased the likelihood that a worker in default would choose to file for bankruptcy.

Contemporary observers were mindful of the direct effect of garnishment on bankruptcy. The 1905 *Annual Report of the Attorney General* laid the blame for Alabama's high wage earner bankruptcy rate on its garnishment law: "[Because of] a state statute affecting the right to attach or garnish wages or salary of the laboring class, hundreds of poor unfortunates with liabilities in many instances less than $500, have been driven to seek relief under the federal law as a matter of preservation."[89] It was not just Alabama. Georgia, Maine, Oregon, Tennessee, and Virginia had pro-creditor garnishment, and already in 1920, they had some of the highest personal bankruptcy rates in the nation. (Refer back to figure 1.3.) During the 1920s, states with pro-creditor garnishment had personal bankruptcy rates that were nine times larger than states with pro-debtor garnishment law.[90]

While it is possible to categorize garnishment laws, it is not possible to categorize states as pro-creditor or pro-debtor overall in the 1920s because the various laws were not coordinated. Only Colorado took a strictly pro-creditor stance: no small loan law, the highest usury limit, low personal exemptions, and pro-creditor garnishment law. Louisiana was the only state with a pro-debtor stance: a small loan law, a usury limit of 5 percent, personal exemptions over $2,000, and intermediate garnishment law. Usury laws, property exemptions, and wage execution laws evolved separately. Each had its own set of interest groups, its own legal history, and its own economic history.[91]

The laws were not codetermined, but they did interact in their effect on bankruptcy. As discussed in the introduction, the bankruptcy rate is the product of three component rates that correspond to steps along the path to bankruptcy. Specifically, the bankruptcy rate is the product of the rate of indebtedness, the rate of default among the indebted, and the rate at which people in default file for bankruptcy. Usury law affects the rate of indebtedness, while garnishment law affects the rate of filing among those in default. Because garnishment is farther along the path to bankruptcy, pro-creditor garnishment has the potential to amplify the impact of a law that increased the supply of credit, such as a small loan law.

To examine the interaction of passage of a small loan law and garnishment law on the bankruptcy rate, we use regression analysis. We include data for 1899 to 1932. In addition to accounting for garnishment law, the small loan law, and property exemptions in a state, we account for social and economic conditions that affected the rate of indebtedness and rate of default during these decades. (See the appendix to chapter 1 for the details of our regression methods in general and the appendix to chapter 2 for a description of our sources for social and economic control variables for this period. Table 2A.2 shows the regression results.)

The regression results are striking. Small loan laws caused the gap between the high-bankruptcy states and low-bankruptcy states to grow. When a state with pro-creditor garnishment passed a small loan law, it could expect the law to increase the bankruptcy rate by about 1.5 per 10,000 people in the state, during the decades when the mean bankruptcy rate was just over 1 per 10,000. If a state with pro-creditor garnishment had a very low usury rate on small loans, the usury law kept a lid on the bankruptcy rate by preventing people from obtaining access to credit. After a small loan law raised the usury limit, the personal bankruptcy rate shot up to among the highest rates in the country.

Interestingly, after a state with pro-debtor or intermediate garnishment passed a small loan law, it was unlikely to experience an increase in bankruptcy because of the law. In fact, states with pro-debtor or intermediate garnishment could expect a *decline* in bankruptcy petitions of about 0.8 per 10,000 people after passage of a small loan law. Of course, this is measured relative to the bankruptcy rate that we expect to see after accounting for other changes, including the common factors that were increasing rates everywhere. Recall that bankruptcy was, on average, only about 1 per 10,000; although the size of the coefficient is small, the effect of the small loan law was quite important.

Consider Missouri as an example. Missouri had intermediate garnishment and got a small loan law in 1927. The rate of growth in Missouri's personal bankruptcy rate averaged 40 percent per year from 1921 to 1926, but it fell to 6 percent per year from 1927 to 1930. Two things were probably going on. The first is what the Russell Sage Foundation hoped would happen. The availability of small loan laws appears to have helped some "honest debtors" who were having problems paying by giving them access to a legal way to avoid default. Second, the passage of small loan laws probably slowed the growth of small loans for a short while. Note how, in figure 2.2, the growth in the prevalence of small loan debt in the sample of Missouri bankrupts was rapid both before and after the small loan law was passed, but flat between 1926 and 1928. It seems likely that during the months before and after the law went into effect, fewer people were able to secure small loans as some illegal lenders exited the market and others sought to meet the licensing requirements. (Effects reported in this paragraph are from specification (3) of table 2A.2.)

Changes in the Political Economy of Bankruptcy Law

The widespread use of bankruptcy law to provide a fresh start transformed the political economy of bankruptcy legislation. The changing use of the law caused beliefs about the purpose of the law to change and led to the evolution of new organized interest groups.

In the late nineteenth century, John Lowell and Jay Torrey emphasized that honest bankrupts should be discharged so that they could resume their productive roles in society. Judge Lowell and Torrey were talking about business owners. Torrey went so far as to argue that the bankrupt business owners should receive a discharge, so that they are not "forced into competition with the great army of day laborers and salaried workers."[92] After the law went into effect, people began to apply the same logic *to* "the great army." Kenesaw Mountain Landis, a federal judge in Chicago and the first commissioner of Major League Baseball, was renowned for his treatment of bankrupts. It was said that when the "professional bankrupt" came before him "he pointed the way to restitution or jail," but "when the clerk or the laborer [came] as bankrupt, beset by loan sharks," Judge Landis scourged the loan sharks "as the money changers were scourged in the Temple." It was even claimed that Landis "may reach into his pocket and toss the money demanded to the loan shark as he would toss a dog a bone, and then tell the frightened and wondering bankrupt that he is free of all obligation and privileged to leave the court."[93] The story may be apocryphal, but it illustrates how the distinction between the treatment of honest and dishonest debtors, which had been central to the way people interpreted business bankruptcy, grew to include personal bankruptcy.

Although it is possible to find portrayals of personal bankrupts as irresponsible spendthrifts, they were often portrayed as victims of unscrupulous loan sharks. For the person hounded by loan sharks, "there is one door of escape which always stands ready and open for the harassed debtor, but in the nature of things he only takes advantage of it as a last desperate remedy. That is, the Bankruptcy court."[94] In 1927, the Russell Sage Foundation traced 20 to 30 percent of all the bankruptcies in St. Louis, Kansas City, and Topeka to loans sharks.[95] Austin Carey, president of the Retail Credit Men's Association of Memphis, claimed, "It is these companies that usually force the debtor into bankruptcy."[96] Just as bankruptcy was the means to restore honest business owners to productive business, it became accepted as the means to restore honest workers to productive labor.

Because personal bankrupts seldom had assets to liquidate, perceptions of the primary function of bankruptcy changed. To the nineteenth-century advocates, the primary function of bankruptcy law was the fair distribution of assets. Soon after the 1898 act was passed, Judge Addison Brown declared, "The most fundamental element in every system of bankruptcy has been to provide for and regulate the distribution of the bankrupt's property among his creditors."[97] A 1915 decision written by Justice James Clark McReynolds presented a similar view: "It is the purpose of the Bankrupt Act to convert the assets of the bankrupt into cash for distribution among creditors."[98] In contrast, by the mid-1920s when personal bankruptcy cases were surging, the discharge of debtors was more prominent in decisions. In 1925, Justice George Sutherland wrote that "a proceeding in bankruptcy has for one of its objects the discharge of the bankrupt from his debts. In voluntary proceedings . . . that is the primary object."[99] Also in 1925, F. Regis Noel, lawyer and chronicler of the bankruptcy legislation, asserted, "[Bankruptcy] is now regarded not as a crime, but as a misfortune, not as a disgrace, but as a malady which needs the soothing remedy of sympathy and encouragement."[100]

As the use of the law changed, interest groups evolved. First, the National Convention of Representatives of Commercial Bodies, which had been formed specifically to seek bankruptcy legislation, disbanded. Thereafter, the National Association of Credit Men (NACM) filled the void. The NACM was formed just two years before Congress enacted the bankruptcy law by the men who worked in the credit departments of wholesalers and manufacturers in 1896.[101] The NACM supported the convention, opposed attempts to repeal the law, and lobbied in favor of amendments that its members believed would improve the law. The association eventually changed its name to the National Association of Credit Management, and it continues to be active in lobbying for bankruptcy legislation in the twenty-first century.

The NACM did not represent the interests of the retailers who provided credit to consumers. The NACM viewed consumer credit and personal bankruptcy as problems because retailers who were too liberal with credit were more likely to fail to pay their creditors. The NACM, unlike the Sage Foundation, believed that personal bankruptcy was caused by irresponsible retailers. The secretary of the NACM wrote that "those who sell to the consumer must understand that they have the remedy in their own hands and are in a position at any time to curtail credit."[102] Retail credit managers lamented that the 1898 act had been written "at a time when the retailer sold almost entirely for cash and it is due to this fact and the lack of organization upon a national scale that his interests were not taken care of."[103] In 1912, retail credit men organized their own association, the National Retail Credit Association, to try to ensure that in the future their interests would be taken into consideration.[104]

Bankruptcy lawyers quickly became another important interest group. The Committee on Commercial Law of the American Bar Association began to lobby Congress against repeal and for amendments to the 1898 act almost as soon as the law was enacted.[105] In 1905, the committee declared: "[I]f there is anything that the American Bar Association would seem committed to as part of the permanent jurisprudence of the United States, it is a bankruptcy law embodying the essential features of the present law."[106]

In 1920, the Committee on Commercial Law began to draft amendments to reduce fraud in business bankruptcy. The 1926 amendments increased the number of causes for which a discharge might be denied and "increased the number of criminal offences and the punishments of those directly or indirectly associated with any fraud in connection with going into and through bankruptcy."[107] Both the drafting and enactment of the amendments were widely attributed to the cooperation of the ABA and the National Association of Credit Men.[108]

There is no record of retail creditors being consulted on the 1926 amendments. Yet, in the 1930s, when the National Retail Credit Association had more than 1,300 credit bureaus and was serving more than 150,000 retail credit providers,[109] it was part of the lobby that resulted in the major changes that are the subject of chapter 3. The Committee on Commercial Law did consult with bankruptcy referees, and in 1926, the referees formed their own association to "obtain a greater uniformity in bankruptcy practice and, by discussion of questions of administration, find ways of expediting the handling of cases and reducing the expenses."[110] The referees would have a profound effect on changes to the law in the 1930s and the 1970s.

By the 1920s, both Republicans and Democrats accepted bankruptcy as an essential element of the American legal system. The questions were about how the law should operate, not about whether the law should exist. As Congress considered the 1926 amendments, there was no real threat of a repeal. Congressman Thomas Blanton (D-TX) wanted the law repealed, but unlike in the past, other Democrats did not join him. Congressman Andrew Jackson Montague (D-VA) declared that he had worked with Congressman Earl C. Michener (R-MI) on the bill and that "[t]here has not been a semblance of partisanship in the consideration of the bill.[111] The bill was passed by the House 277 to 17.[112] Democrats voted 113 to 17 in favor of the amendments. Both the House and the Senate accepted the conference report without a roll call vote.[113] The criticisms the Democratic Party had traditionally leveled against bankruptcy law no longer reflected the reality of bankruptcy in the 1920s.

The authors of the 1898 act designed it for John Ellman, an insolvent businessman. They did not design it for Jasper C. Glascock, who was a typical petitioner for bankruptcy in June 1928. Glascock was a forty-year-old[114] railroad brakeman for the Chicago, Burlington, and Quincy (CB&Q) Railroad.[115] He had assigned several weeks' salary, totaling $196, to Majestic Finance, Salary Purchasing Company, and Ideal Credit

Company, all operating in downtown St. Louis. Though his wage assignments were recent, much of his $1,129 in unsecured obligations was not. He owed $275 in medical bills dating to 1920, when he had been living with his brother Nathanial in Hannibal and working as a laborer in the cement industry.[116] Despite the fact that he still owed money for a Maytag washing machine that he purchased on installment in the spring of 1928, it had probably been repossessed. It was not listed among his $62 in household goods. He reported that he had $80 in wages due from the railroad, and his lawyer included the notation that the wages due were exempt from collection under Missouri law. Glascock was quickly discharged of his debts. He was still working as a brakeman for the CB&Q Railroad in 1929.[117] The 1898 act had provided him—and tens of thousands of consumers like him—with a way to retain his job and his accrued wages without sacrificing any more of his assets.

Bankruptcy would change significantly in the 1930s and again in the 1970s. In both eras, it would become more amenable to debtors who were insolvent despite earning steady wages, especially if they wished to retain their assets.

Appendix to Chapter 2

Chapter 2 discusses developments in personal bankruptcy and consumer credit in the early 1900s, including installment debt and small cash loans. The first section below explains how we identify these two types of debt among the many debts owed by the bankrupt. The text of chapter 2 also summarizes our regression analysis of the impact of changes in state laws that limited the interest rate charged on small cash loans on the personal bankruptcy rate. The second section below gives details.

Debts of Personal Bankrupts

In figure 2.2, we use the debt schedules submitted by the petitioners for personal bankruptcy in the Missouri sample to estimate the extent to which installment debt and small loan debt were available and utilized by debtors. The appendix to chapter 1 contains general information about the Missouri sample.

Installment debts are the debts identified by the debtor as being secured by household goods or automobiles. Personal bankrupts in the sample for these years reported 1,324 secured debts, of which 591 (44.6 percent) were identified as installment debt. Small loan debt is secured or unsecured debt owed to local "finance companies" rather than to banks, savings and loans, or other traditional financial institutions. Personal bankrupts in the sample reported 50,468 unsecured debts, of which 2,257 (4.2 percent) were owed to banks (or credit unions or savings and loans) and 590 (1.1 percent) were owed to small loan or finance companies. Of secured debts, 16 (1.2 percent) were owed to small loan or finance companies.

Regression Analysis of the Impact of Small Loan Laws

Chapter 2 explains that one of the innovations in consumer credit during the 1920s was the expansion of small cash loans. Many states passed versions of the Uniform Small Loan Law developed by the Russell Sage Foundation. The small loan law defined a relatively high usury rate for small loans for working men from licensed lenders. The small loan laws aimed to displace loan sharks with licensed lenders, and they raised the usury limit to make licensed lending profitable. The first column of table 2A.1 shows whether a state passed a small loan law. If the state passed a small loan law, the table also gives the date of its passage.

Information on small loan laws passed prior to 1930 comes from a study of the political economy of passage of the laws.[118] Information on laws passed later come from a separate history of them.[119] The two sources differ about the date of passage of the small loan law in Missouri. We code it as passing in 1927.[120] The remaining columns of table 2A.1 describe the other state collection laws discussed in chapter 2. We compiled information on homestead exemptions, personal property exemptions, and garnishment law variables for earlier work.[121] Our original source of information on state laws governing garnishment before and during the Great Depression was a study conducted by the Bureau of Labor Statistics and the Russell Sage Foundation.[122] As explained in the text, there are three categories of garnishment: pro-creditor, pro-debtor, and intermediate. There is no information on garnishment in several states, so there are 899 state-years included in the regressions. Homestead and personal property exemptions come from scholarly legal studies and contemporary sources.[123]

In chapter 2, we utilize the regression framework as described in the appendix to chapter 1. The dependent variable is the bankruptcy rate in state s and year t. Sources and methods for the calculation of bankruptcy

	Small loan law?	Homestead exemption	Personal exemption	Garnishment law
	(Year Passed)	($)	($)	
AL	No	2,000	1,000	Pro-creditor
AR	No [A]	2,500	700	Pro-debtor
AZ	Yes (1919)	4,000	n/a	Not Ranked
CA	No [A]	5,000	[C]	Pro-debtor
CO	No [A]	2,000	200	Pro-creditor
CT	Yes (1919)	1,000	[C]	Not Ranked
DC	No	0	700	Not Ranked
DE	No	0	250	Not Ranked
FL	Yes (1925)	[B]	1,000	Pro-debtor
GA	Yes (1920)	1,600	1,600	Pro-creditor
IA	Yes (1921)	[B]	[C]	Not Ranked
ID	No	5,000	1,300	Not Ranked
IL	Yes (1917)	1,000	400	Pro-creditor
IN	Yes (1917)	600	1,200	Pro-debtor
KS	No	[B]	[C]	Pro-creditor
KY	No [A]	1,000	[C]	Pro-creditor
LA	Yes (1928)	2,000	[C]	Intermediate
MA	Yes (1911)	800	100	Intermediate
MD	Yes (1918)	0	100	Pro-debtor
ME	Yes (1917)	500	[C]	Pro-creditor
MI	Yes (1921)	1,500	850 [D]	Pro-creditor
MN	No [A]	[B]	0	Pro-creditor
MO	Yes (1927)	1,500	400	Intermediate
MS	No	3,000	250	Not Ranked
MT	No	2,500	[C]	Not Ranked
NC	No	1,000	500	Pro-debtor
ND	No	8,000	1000 [E]	Pro-debtor
NE	No	2,000	500	Not Ranked
NH	Yes (1917)	500	200	Not Ranked
NJ	Yes (1915)	1,000	200	Intermediate
NM	No [A]	1,000	500	Not Ranked
NV	No [A]	5,000	2200 [F]	Pro-debtor
NY	No [A]	1,000	250	Intermediate
OH	Yes (1913)	1,000	250 [G]	Intermediate
OK	No	5,000	C	Not Ranked
OR	Yes (1913)	3,000	275	Pro-creditor
PA	Yes (1915)	0	300	Pro-debtor
RI	Yes (1923)	0	C	Not Ranked
SC	No	1,000	800 [H]	Pro-debtor
SD	No	5,000	750	Not Ranked
TN	Yes (1925)	1,000	[C]	Pro-creditor
TX	No	5,000	[C]	Pro-debtor
UT	Yes (1917)	2,000	[C]	Not Ranked
VA	Yes (1918)	2,000	2,000	Pro-creditor
VT	No [A]	1,000	[C, I]	Not Ranked
WA	No	[B]	500	Pro-debtor
WI	Yes (1927)	5,000	400	Not Ranked
WV	Yes (1925)	1,000	200	Not Ranked
WY	No	2,500	1,250	Not Ranked
Average		**655**	**2,073**	**21 Not Ranked** **12 Pro-creditor** **6 Intermediate** **12 Pro-debtor**

Notes: [A]Passed after 1930. [B]Homestead exemption defined in acres. [C]Personal exemption itemized. [D]Decreased from 850 to 500 in 1932. [E]Increased from 1000 to 1500 in 1932. [F]Increased from 2200 to 3200 in 1932. [G]Increased from 250 to 1000 in 1932. [H]Decreased from 800 to 500 in 1932. [I]P Established dollar amount equal to 400 in 1932. *Sources*: Hansen and Hansen, "Crisis and Bankruptcy"; also see appendix to chapter 2.

rates are also in the appendix to chapter 1. The regression analysis covers 1899–1932. On average, there were about 1.9 personal bankruptcies per 10,000 people each year (standard deviation about 2.3). There are three vectors of independent variables in the regressions: *Files*, *InDefault*, and *InDebt*.

ELEMENTS OF *FILES*

Exemptions and garnishment laws are the main determinants of the final choice on the path to bankruptcy, choosing to petition for bankruptcy once in default. For the regression analysis here, we measure homestead and personal property exemptions relative to average weekly manufacturing wages.[124] In states that did not pass a small loan law by 1930, the average homestead exemption was about 142 times weekly wages, with a standard deviation of about 102. In states that passed a small loan law by 1930, the ratio of the homestead exemption to the weekly wage was about 152 (with standard deviation about 228) before passage but only about 60 (standard deviation about 85) after it. The decline is caused by a combination of changes to homestead exemptions during the Depression (see table 2A.1) and increases in real wages during the period. In states that did not pass a small loan law during the period, the ratio of the personal property exemption to weekly wages averaged about 27 (standard deviation about 29). In states that passed a small loan law by 1930, the ratio of the personal property exemption to the weekly wage was about 45 before passage and about 22 after it.

ELEMENT OF *INDEFAULT*

To capture unemployment, a main cause of default, we include the business failure rate. The business failure rate is the ratio of the number of business failures to the number of business concerns as compiled by Dun and Bradstreet.[125] Business failures are firms that discontinued with some loss to creditors. In states that did not pass a small loan law during the period, the business failure rate averaged about 1 (standard deviation about 0.5). In states that passed a small loan law by 1930, the business failure rate was about 1.1 (with standard deviation of about 1.1) both before and after passage.

ELEMENTS OF *INDEBT*

Again, the primary variable of interest in the vector for determinants of the indebtedness rate is whether a state has a small loan law in effect during year t. As additional proxies for the supply and demand of credit we include the number of bank locations per 10,000 people, weekly manufacturing wages (in 1984 dollars),[126] and the share of the labor force employed in manufacturing.[127] Bank locations per 10,000 people proxies the supply of bank credit, as opposed to the supply of installment and small loan credit. There were about 3.5 banks per 10,000 people (standard deviation about 2) in states that did not pass a small loan law by 1930. In states with a small loan law, it averaged about 2 both before and after the law (standard deviation about 0.8). Manufacturing wages proxies income of the group most relevant to small loan lenders and installment lenders. The mean was about 23 (standard deviation about nine) in states that did not pass a small loan law by 1930. In states with a small loan law, it averaged about 15 (standard deviation about 5) before the law and about 28 (standard deviation about 7) after the law. The share of the labor force in manufacturing proxies the number of small loan lenders. The mean was about 22 (standard deviation about 8) in states that did not pass a small loan law by 1930. In states that passed a small loan law, it averaged about 26 (standard deviation about 9) before the law and about 34 (standard

TABLE 2A.2. **Determinants of the bankruptcy rate, 1899–1932**

	OLS		FE
	(1)	(2)	(3)
Pro-creditor garnishment law	1.256**	1.185**	
	(0.495)	(0.473)	
Pro-debtor garnishment law	-0.006	-0.189	
	(0.259)	(0.374)	
Passed SLL by 1932	0.163	-0.144	
	(0.295)	(0.341)	
After SLL	-0.647*	-0.544	-0.747**
	(0.331)	(0.425)	(0.349)
Pro-creditor* after SLL	1.577**	1.485**	1.482**
	(0.733)	(0.691)	(0.637)
Observations	899	899	899
R-squared	0.445	0.492	0.521

The passage of small loan laws increased the personal bankruptcy rate only in states with pro-creditor garnishment. Notes: * $p<0.10$, ** $p<0.05$, *** $p<0.01$. Standard errors are in parentheses and clustered at the state level. Constant and year effects included in all specifications. Also included in specifications (2) and (3) are additional controls for social and economic conditions; see text for details. *Source:* See appendix to chapter 2.

deviation about 9) after the law. We make all inflation adjustments using the consumer price index for all urban areas.[128]

As emphasized in the text and as discussed in the appendix to chapter 1, pro-creditor garnishment law amplifies increases in bankruptcy caused by changes in the elements of *InDebt* and *InDefault*. Small loan laws and garnishment law interacted with each other to influence the bankruptcy rate. To capture this, we interact pro-creditor garnishment with an indicator for passage of a state small loan law. Small loan laws increased bankruptcy only in states with pro-creditor garnishment. The text of the section on small loan laws illustrates the point with simple averages of the bankruptcy rate across states with and without small loan laws, and before and after passage of the laws.

RESULTS

The regression results supporting our conclusions appear in table 2A.2. For conciseness, table 2A.2 suppresses the coefficients on the other control variables included in the regressions. In specification (3), there are 403 observations of state-years for states that did not pass a small loan law during the period. For states that passed a small loan law during the period, there are 310 state-years before passage and 186 after passage.

Results reported in the text rely on the fixed effects results in specification (3) of table 2A.2. The key results are as follows. When a state with pro-debtor garnishment passed a small loan law, the law caused a *decline* in bankruptcy petitions of about 0.75 per 10,000 people relative to the bankruptcy rate that would otherwise be expected in that state. This was an important decrease during a period when the mean bankruptcy rate was just over 1 per 10,000. In contrast, when a state with pro-creditor garnishment passed a small loan law, the law caused an *increase* in the bankruptcy rate of about 1.5 per 10,000 people in the state.

CHAPTER THREE

An Emphasis on Workout rather than Liquidation

In the 1920s, the Koplar Company built several properties in St. Louis, including the Embassy Apartments and the Congress Hotel-Senate Apartments. Koplar financed the construction with mortgage bonds brokered in 1925 and 1926 by Greenbaum & Sons Investment Company. Greenbaum sold $2.56 million in 6.5 percent serial bonds to the public.[1] Deeds of trust on the properties secured the bonds.

In 1931, Koplar defaulted on the principal payments on both properties. In 1932, it also defaulted on the interest payments. The trustee filed foreclosure suits in federal court. He tried to negotiate an out-of-court agreement with bondholders, but he was unsuccessful.[2] On June 9, 1934,[3] Koplar filed a petition to reorganize under an amendment to the Bankruptcy Act that went into effect on June 1.[4]

In January 1937,[5] the court approved Koplar's plan to create two new companies, one to manage each property and the second to issue new bonds. The original bonds were exchanged dollar for dollar of outstanding principal. The interest rate on the new bonds was 2 percent per year for 1938. Interest would rise over time to 4 percent. Bondholders further agreed to accept additional debt, rather than to foreclose again, if income from the properties did not cover interest payments at any time before maturity. The plan disallowed payment of any kind to the Koplar Company, unless it was specifically authorized by the trustee of the deed of trust on the new bonds. Within a few months of the approval, the bankruptcy trustee distributed about $8,100 to the general creditors of the Koplar Company, a stipulation that was part of the plan of reorganization. The court closed the case on September 24, 1937. As of November 2017, the Koplar Company was still active in real estate development in St. Louis.[6]

The Koplar Company was fundamentally sound but temporarily insolvent. During the crises that dominated the early years of the Great Depression, it could not effect a private agreement with its many creditors to modify the payments on its bonds. It seems likely that many of Koplar's creditors needed cash themselves. In 1933, Congress amended the 1898 Bankruptcy Act to provide a new way for corporations like Koplar to reorganize their finances and to avoid liquidation of their assets. During the Depression, Congress also enacted amendments to the bankruptcy law that provided procedures for unincorporated businesses and farmers to try to avoid liquidation. Finally, advocates convinced Congress that many consumers would also prefer to avoid liquidation and restructure payments. Thus, Congress added Chapter XIII to bankruptcy procedures as part of the 1938 Chandler Act.

It is tempting to view the changes in bankruptcy law during the Depression as responses to increases in bankruptcy rates. Bankruptcy is generally regarded as a countercyclical phenomenon, and a rapid increase in bankruptcy is viewed as one of the defining features of the Great Depression.[7] Yet a close look at bankruptcy during the Great Depression shows that one of its most noteworthy features is its diversity. Personal bankruptcy responded to the Depression and the recovery differently than business bankruptcy. Nationally, the bankruptcy rate did not increase sharply after the crisis began in late 1929. Instead, it leveled off. Virtually all of the increase in bankruptcy at the beginning for the Depression came from business bankruptcy.

The Depression and Business Bankruptcy

The first months of the Great Depression were staggeringly difficult for businesses. Although the Federal Reserve was established in 1913, among other things, to "furnish an elastic currency," each of the regional Federal Reserve Banks conducted its own policy until the Banking Act of 1935 enhanced coordination. The independence of the early regional Federal Reserve Banks inhibited a coordinated response to interregional banking crises. During the trio of crises in 1930, 1931, and 1932, one-quarter of all banks closed. Many were unable to reopen. The banking crises disrupted relationships between banks and businesses because they disrupted the market for banker's acceptances, a form of short-term commercial paper used especially by wholesalers.[8] The banking crises also caused trade credit to collapse.[9] The trade credit extended to retailers by wholesalers and manufacturers was much more important to most businesses than direct bank credit.[10] Distressed wholesalers and manufacturers needed cash for their own survival. They did not negotiate new terms for trade credit, as they might have done in normal circumstances. Instead, in 1930, trade creditors, especially the ones located in the major trade hubs of the upper Midwest where the regional Federal Reserve Banks were more conservative, tried to collect. They directed efforts to collect at their customers who were nearby, minimizing court costs, and at higher-quality customers, maximizing payoffs. The assets and liabilities of the typical commercial failure were 75 percent larger in the early 1930s than at any other time from 1900 to 1960.[11] Although the tight-money regional Federal Reserve Banks of the upper Midwest became more accommodating in 1931,[12] the damage to credit markets and the economy took years to repair.

Unsurprisingly, business bankruptcy rose at the onset of the Great Depression. Petitions by businesses, including merchants, manufacturers, and professionals, peaked in 1932 at about 21,000—almost one-third more than in 1929.[13] As the Depression wore on, new business formation fell. As new business formation fell, business bankruptcy filings fell precipitously. In 1935, courts saw fewer business filings than they had in 1929. The recession of 1937–38 did not register on business bankruptcy filings. Even with the reduced number of total business concerns, the business bankruptcy rate stayed low. In fact, the business bankruptcy rate during the "double dip" was 2 filings per 1,000 firms, which was about the same as it was *during* World War I.

In 1941, total business bankruptcy filings were below 5,000. They fell to about 500 in 1946. During the 1950s, less than 1 of every 7 bankruptcy petitions was filed by a business. Business filings did not rise to prewar levels again until the 1970s. During the Great Depression and World War II, the transformation of bankruptcy from a tool mainly for businesses to a tool mainly for consumers was completed.

The Depression and Personal Bankruptcy Rates

The growth in the number of personal bankruptcy petitions began to slow before the Great Depression began. As business bankruptcy and unemployment rose, incomes fell. But personal bankruptcy filings leveled off. Then they dipped. As consumer credit began to flow after 1933, personal bankruptcy grew again. It fell as the double dip began, and it grew as the domestic economy responded to the war abroad.

The response of personal bankruptcy to the Depression was not the same in every state. The personal bankruptcy rate *fell* in ten states after 1929. In thirty-eight states and the District of Columbia, the average annual rate of growth in the personal bankruptcy rate was lower in 1929–32 than it was in 1921–28. The personal bankruptcy rate grew between 1928 and 1932 in only ten states.

The common federal bankruptcy law again produced dramatically different outcomes in different states, depending on the broader legal context. Just as pro-creditor garnishment amplified the effect of the increase in the supply of credit caused by the passage of small loan laws in the 1920s (see chapter 2), it amplified the effect of a decline in income after 1929. States with pro-debtor garnishment laws had lower rates of personal bankruptcy before the Depression and experienced little increase in bankruptcy during the Depression, as shown in figure 3.1. In contrast, states with pro-creditor garnishment laws had high rates of bankruptcy before the Depression. When the Depression hit, it was almost entirely consumers in these few states that sought the protection offered by the federal bankruptcy law. They used the law to avoid losing part of their income, some of their assets, or, in some cases, their treasured employment.

To examine the differences in the response of a state's bankruptcy rate to the decline in income during the early Depression, we again use regression analysis. We use data for 1920 to 1932. In addition to income, we again account for many of the other things that can influence the components of the bankruptcy rate through the rate of filing (including the value of property exemptions in a state), the rate of default (such as measures of unemployment and social capital), and the indebtedness rate (including measures of access to credit in a state). The regression analysis shows that, by itself, growth in state income per capita was not related to the level of the personal bankruptcy rate in the typical state. In particular, a decline in income of 1 percent had no meaningful effect on the

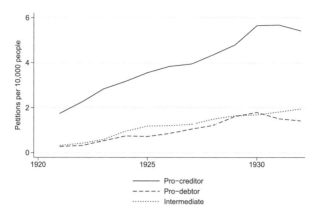

FIG. 3.1. States with pro-creditor garnishment law saw steeper increases in bankruptcy during the 1920s and had bigger spikes in personal bankruptcy as the Great Depression began. *Source*: See appendix to chapter 3.

bankruptcy rate in states with pro-debtor or intermediate garnishment law. Economic decline and the personal bankruptcy rate are strongly and positively related only in the states with pro-creditor garnishment law. In those states, higher growth in the 1920s kept bankruptcy relatively low, and the decline in growth early in the Depression increased bankruptcy. In states with pro-creditor garnishment, a decline in income of 1 percent during a year increased the bankruptcy rate by about 4 per 10,000 people that year. A switch from pro-debtor to pro-creditor garnishment would have moved a state from the bottom quartile to the top quartile in terms of the wage earner bankruptcy rate. To put it another way, the regression results imply that, if all states had enacted pro-creditor garnishment laws, the personal bankruptcy rate in the average state in 1930 might have been 30 percent higher, or 3.4 instead of 2.6 per 10,000 persons. (See the appendix to chapter 3 for details about variables measuring social and economic determinants of indebtedness and default, and see the appendix to chapter 1 for a discussion of empirical strategies. The main conclusions in this paragraph are based on regression specification (2) in table 3A.1 in the appendix to chapter 3.)

The regression analysis cannot be carried forward to the end of the Depression because state data were not published. The Department of Justice published national breakdowns of personal and business bankruptcy from 1933 to 1945, but it did not publish state- or district-level breakdowns of personal and business bankruptcy. (See the appendix to chapter 1 for more information about gaps in the published data.) However, the relationship between state garnishment law and bankruptcy rates is consistent across the interwar and postwar periods, so it is not surprising that there was no spike in total petitions for personal bankruptcy during the recession of 1937–38. Moreover, during the double-dip, relatively few workers lost their employment in pro-creditor states, where unemployment was most likely to result in use of the bankruptcy law. Unemployment in 1937–38 was much larger in states with pro-debtor or intermediate garnishment, but unemployment in those places was not likely to lead to bankruptcy.[14]

The Depression and Bankruptcy Law

As mentioned in the introduction, Congress passed the first major changes to the 1898 Bankruptcy Act during the Great Depression. Efforts to reform bankruptcy law began before the Depression did. They culminated in 1938 with the Chandler Act. Before that, a wide-ranging 1932 bill bundled three proposals. The first proposal aimed to reduce fraud and increase efficiency by jettisoning the system of creditor control established by the 1898 act. Congress never voted on it. The second aimed to provide alternatives to liquidation for businesses and farmers. Congress passed it in 1933. The third suggested an alternative to liquidation for consumers. Congress eventually created one, but not until 1938.

Since the 1898 Bankruptcy Act went into effect, the attorney general had reported the number of cases closed for wage earners, farmers, professionals, manufacturers, and merchants. But the only distinction between these groups as far as the law was concerned was that farmers and wage earners could not be made involuntary bankrupts. All of the groups had the same remedies available: liquidation or composition. For all practical purposes, liquidation was the only viable option. The amendments of the 1930s not only provided viable alternatives to liquidation, but they tailored different alternatives to meet the needs of different groups of people.

Reducing Fraud, Increasing Efficiency

Allegations of fraud committed by debtors, by referees, and by trustees began almost as soon as the 1898 act went into effect.[15] Several amendments, such as the ones passed in 1926 (see chapter 2), tried to curb fraud.

According to the attorney general, the 1926 amendments made it possible "to reach beyond the bankrupt and to prosecute attorneys and other persons conniving with him."[16] Though fraud cases declined 50 percent the year after the amendments,[17] not all fraud stopped. In early 1929, a grand jury indicted eleven New York attorneys on charges of bankruptcy fraud associated with business bankruptcy cases.[18] (Because personal bankruptcy cases seldom involve assets, corruption is not much of a problem in personal bankruptcy.) The report of the grand jury led legal associations in New York City to petition the US Court for the Southern District of New York to investigate the administration of bankruptcy.[19] Judge Thomas D. Thacher granted the petition and, at the request of the petitioners, appointed William J. Donovan to lead the investigation.

The Donovan Report indicted the bankruptcy law itself.[20] It concluded that creditor control had failed. It recommended replacing the system of creditor control with the administrative system known as "officialism" that was previously rejected in the debate over the 1898 act. Under officialism, as practiced in the United Kingdom, government officials examined petitioners for bankruptcy.

Donovan's investigation was still underway when the Depression began. The Donovan Report was released in March 1930. Shortly after Donovan filed his report, President Hoover appointed Judge Thacher as solicitor general. After Thacher's arrival in Washington, the Justice Department ordered a complete review of bankruptcy law. Thacher oversaw the review, and Lloyd Garrison, who also worked on the Donovan Report, directed it. The Commerce Department and Yale Law School participated, generating several reports on the causes and consequences of bankruptcy.[21] The national review was ongoing as the banking crises of 1930 and 1931 caused the contraction of trade credit discussed above. The Thacher Report was completed in December 1931 and released to the public the following February.

Not surprisingly, the Thacher Report repeated the recommendations of the Donovan Report. It declared that the 1898 act had been "carefully drawn and thoroughly considered," but it concluded that creditors could no longer be relied on to take charge of the management of bankruptcy cases because social and economic conditions had changed greatly.[22] It recommended that "to correct the fundamental weakness of the act in permitting bankrupts to obtain its benefits without adequate, and often without any, inquiry into their conduct, it is proposed to create a staff of examining officials, appointed under civil service rules."[23] Hoover, who sought to root out waste and inefficiencies while serving as secretary of commerce in the 1920s, endorsed the change.[24]

The recommendations of the Thacher Report reached Congress in early 1932 as the Hastings-Michener bill.[25] Regarding case administration, the bill proposed creating ten examiners under the attorney general and an unspecified number of supervisors to serve under the examiners. Hearings began in April 1932. In addition to extensive testimony by Garrison, the committee heard testimony on the bill from representatives of business associations, lawyers, and referees.

Associations representing creditors generally supported the creation of the examiners. The general counsel for the National Association of Credit Men testified that the association supported the new system of administration.[26] The president of the First National Bank of St. Louis declared that the "best thing in the whole business is the administrators and examiners."[27]

Legal professionals, on the other hand, strongly opposed the creation of examiners.[28] Recall from chapter 2 that lawyers had become an important interest group in bankruptcy by the 1920s. The rise in petitions during the 1920s increased their stake; their fees increased by a factor of five over the decade. In 1929, bankruptcy referees organized an association. At the 1932 hearings, Jacob M. Lashly, chairman of the Bankruptcy Committee of the American Bar Association, denied the claims that the current system was failing and that other countries had better systems. He argued that the body of legal decisions that had been built up around the Bankruptcy Act "must not be destroyed or abandoned in favor of theoretical and untested innovations."[29] He also warned that the new system could pose a broader threat: "We feel that the concentration of power in the executive department . . . would result in what has been termed a new bureaucracy, a concentration of power in the administrative machinery of the country, which at this time is undesirable."[30] Lashly found an ally in Senator Sam Bratton (D-NM), who believed that the system of administrators would inevitably expand beyond the original vision of the system: "The unbroken history here is when you start a system it grows. It never decreases. If we start with 200 I predict in five years it would multiply two or three times."[31] Senator Bratton warned that a growing bureaucracy would eventually need to be funded by the public, rather than by bankrupts and their creditors.

The Hastings-Michener bill was not reported out of committee. Its sponsors seemed to have been more concerned with getting the ball rolling than with having the bill enacted. Hastings declared that he had "no notion that we will come anywhere near having the bill ready to report to the present Congress."[32]

In the final weeks of his presidency, Hoover recognized that the proposal to reform the administration of bankruptcy was dead. He pleaded with Congress to take action on alternatives to liquidation, which was a far less contentious part of the bill.

Business Workouts

On March 3, 1933—the day before President Franklin Roosevelt's inauguration—Congress passed an amendment to prevent the liquidation of businesses and farms, which Hoover called "futile and destructive."[33] Congress added "Chapter VIII: Provisions for the Relief of Debtors" to the Bankruptcy Act. There were three key sections: Section 74 provided composition and extension for businesses; Section 75 provided for agricultural composition and extension; and Section 77 provided for railroad reorganization.

The idea of providing businesses with an alternative to liquidation had ample precedent. As discussed in chapter 2, the original 1898 act provided for composition; however, few businesses attempted it. Adjustment bureaus provided businesses services to affect private workouts, and they had become popular, but creditor distress during the Depression made private workouts hard to achieve. In 1933, the need to expand the use of composition and extension of debt, or "readjustment," was "proving more urgent every day."[34] Section 74 allowed debtors to offer a plan of extension and to do either a composition or extension without actually being labeled a "bankrupt."

Section 75 created conciliation commissioners to assist farmers who wanted to attempt composition or extension, but it was generally regarded as unsuccessful because creditors with secured claims (that is, mortgage holders) seldom agreed to loan modifications.[35] The 1934 Frazier-Lemke Act gave farmers a bypass. A farmer who was unable to accomplish a composition or extension could offer to pay the appraised value to the mortgage holder over an extended period. Even if the mortgage holder rejected the offer, foreclosure was stayed for five years, during which time the farmer could continue to occupy the land in exchange for a reasonable rental payment. The farmer retained the option of buying the property at the appraised value.

The Supreme Court deemed the Frazier-Lemke Act unconstitutional because it went too far in depriving the mortgage holders of their property rights.[36] Congress revised the law by reducing the stay to three years and including a way for the creditor to force a public auction. The revised law was upheld.[37] Justice Louis Brandeis wrote both decisions. The first decision emphasized that the power of Congress to enact bankruptcy laws was constrained by the Constitution, and particularly by the due process and takings clauses of the Fifth Amendment. The second decision reaffirmed the primacy of the Fifth Amendment, but it emphasized that Congress had the right to alter property rights, even of secured creditors. The constitutionality of any particular law turns on "whether the legislation modifies the secured creditor's rights, remedial or substantive, to such an extent as to deny the due process of law guaranteed by the Fifth Amendment."[38] The Supreme Court concluded that the revisions to Frazier-Lemke sufficed.

Section 77 added railroad reorganization to the bankruptcy law. Since the 1840s, railroads and some other quasi-public corporations could reorganize through equity receiverships.[39] Courts appointed receivers to manage insolvent railroads while reorganization plans were developed. Reorganization plans usually involved infusions of cash from shareholders and reductions in fixed payments to bondholders. Courts consistently emphasized the primacy of the public interest in the continued operation of the railroad. But reorganization through equity receivership was difficult. For instance, a railroad needed an ancillary receivership in each federal court district where it operated. Incorporating receivership into bankruptcy simplified the process. In 1934, Congress extended the option to reorganize to the Koplar Company in St. Louis, or any corporation, through Section 77b. Corporate reorganization became a critically important tool for businesses, and its history is well known.[40] Because business bankruptcy was never a large fraction of bankruptcy cases after the Depression, the remainder of this book focuses on personal bankruptcy.

Wage Earner Workouts

Personal bankruptcy, then known as "wage earner" bankruptcy, was not central to the matters of case administration covered in the Donovan Report, and Thacher himself was no fan of personal bankruptcy. Soon after arriving in Washington, he made clear his belief that personal bankrupts were living beyond their means. He seemed to favor expunging personal bankruptcy from the law, not reforming it: "A law which tolerates injustice is bad, but a law which encourages such practices on the part of hundreds of salaried people is a corrupting influence on the community which should not be tolerated."[41] However, Garrison's investigation concluded that personal bankruptcy was a problem that needed to be addressed and that unemployment and illness, rather than imprudent installment buying, oftentimes caused it. Garrison was convinced that consumers wished to repay their debts, that they were often driven to loans sharks in their attempts to repay legitimate debts, and that many would be able to repay if given sufficient time and a respite from garnishment and wage assignment. He seemed to have convinced Thacher that wage earner workouts were worth trying.

Although it has been asserted that wage earner workouts were invented during the Depression,[42] they were, in fact, not new. Before 1930, the state of Nebraska and the city of Boston created court-supervised alternatives to liquidation for consumers. In 1917, Nebraska created a "poor man's receivership." The idea behind the Nebraska law reflected the discussion of the relationship between garnishment law and personal bankruptcy emphasized in the Thacher Report and in chapter 2 above: "[M]any of these persons would have paid their debts in full if they could have done so without being tormented by collectors or penalized by costs in suits commenced and prosecuted against them by their numerous creditors."[43] In Nebraska, both debtors and creditors appeared before the court, at which time the court determined the weekly or monthly amount that it thought was appropriate for the debtor to pay. A court order directed the debtor to pay that amount to the court clerk, who distributed it to creditors.[44] In 1927, the Boston Poor Debtor Court introduced a similar plan.[45]

Neither local workout plan made its way into the Thacher Report. The Thacher Report and the Hastings-Michener bill drew recommendations for workout procedures for consumers from the out-of-court solutions that employers and creditors had devised. Garrison explained that, in the course of his investigation, manufacturing firms told him about their solutions to the problem of employee garnishment. The employers encouraged employees in difficulty to come to them. "[T]he employer would work out a system whereby a certain small percentage of the man's wages would be held out by the employer and distributed by him pro rata among the creditors."[46] Retail credit men's associations tried similar plans for consumers who owed their members. Several private companies specialized in effecting "wage earner amortizations."[47]

Garrison visited the American Amortization Company of Chicago. Its process worked as follows. A worker or an employer asked for its assistance. The company examined the worker's finances to assess the viability of a payment plan. If it appeared that the worker's debt burden was not too high and a plan was viable, the company contacted all of the worker's creditors, offered each participation in the plan, and requested that each refrain from collection activities. The worker/debtor paid the company 50 cents per creditor and a commission of 4 percent of the total debt.

The American Amortization Company was formed in 1929. By May 1931, it had handled over 600 cases.[48] Eighty-five percent of the 600 workers stuck to their plans. Garrison argued that the company's success indicated that most workers would rather pay their debts than have them discharged in bankruptcy. He did not claim that the high rate of success was indicative of what would occur under bankruptcy. He realized the amortization company was able to reject cases when it believed the ratio of debt to wages was too high.

Crucial to the success of any type of wage earner workout plan was the willingness of every creditor to forgo garnishment or other collection remedies. If all creditors agreed to the plan, they all were eventually paid. If one creditor tried to collect, the worker filed for bankruptcy, and none of them got anything. Garrison argued that bringing wage earner workouts into bankruptcy law eliminated the problem of an uncooperative creditor because the automatic stay prevented creditors from acting. Moreover, the law could require every creditor to accept a plan, so long as the plan paid the creditor more than it would get in liquidation. The wage earner workout provision in the Hastings-Michener bill allowed "a wage earner [to] file a petition alleging that he is insolvent or unable to meet his debts as they mature, but is able to make future payments sufficient to amortize the balance of his indebtedness . . . over a period of not more than two years."[49]

The bill would have made the workout plan mandatory for many debtors. It required judges to suspend discharge if debtors did not turn over to the court enough assets to pay at least half of the debts they owed. The debtor with a suspended discharge would be required to turn over to the trustee any nonexempt assets and any income, "excepting a reasonable allowance for the living expenses of himself and his dependents" for two years before earning a discharge of any amount the debtor still owed.[50]

Organizations representing retailers, of course, supported wage earner workouts and the suspended discharge. The National Retail Credit Association, which ran credit bureaus that served more than 100,000 stores, and the American Retail Federation testified in favor of the bill. Organized labor, including the United Brotherhood of Carpenters and Joiners of America, the National Federation of Federal Employees, the United Mine Workers of America, the Railway Mail Association, and the American Federation of Labor, also supported the proposal for workouts.[51] A representative of railway unions supported Garrison's view that wage earners wanted to pay. He testified that if wage earners had "a simple and inexpensive process, without the stigma of bankruptcy, under which they could have adequate time to meet their debts with protection against their creditors, large social benefits would result."[52] The other labor organizations sent similar letters in support of both workout and suspended discharge. They repeated that their members were honest debtors who would use the law to avoid loan sharks and the stigma of bankruptcy. They thought the suspended discharge would discourage dishonest debtors from using the law. One of the few amendments they suggested was to distribute the costs of administration between the debtor and the creditor(s), rather than passing the fees entirely onto the debtor.[53]

Bankruptcy lawyers did not oppose wage earner workouts on principle, but they did not see profit in it. Jacob M. Lashly, chair of the Bankruptcy Committee of the American Bar Association, believed that Garrison overestimated the demand for workouts by wage earners and that it was best left to private companies. He worried that "the machinery of it would likely be troublesome and expensive, difficult of management by the judicial officer, and the fruits of it would not be sufficiently worthwhile to justify setting up the system."[54]

Some members of Congress opposed incorporating wage earner workout into bankruptcy law because they saw it as a radical extension of the role of the federal government. Although Congressman Michener had put his name on the bill, he was one of the skeptics, noting: "It places upon the federal government or agencies thereof the duty of working out every unfortunate wage earner's financial condition."[55] While Michener was concerned that the government would be responsible for every wage earner in financial difficulty, Edmund Dryer, who had served as a referee in Birmingham, Alabama, since 1908, believed that the proposal would turn the court into a collection agency for creditors. Dryer was particularly concerned by the suspended discharge, which could force people into repayment plans. Dryer noted the irony of corporations, organized by people to take advantage of limited liability, raising "hue and cry" over a worker's decision to use the bankruptcy law rather than to allow his or her wages to be garnished. "Under this proposed bill," he argued, "they want to work him for two years after his bankruptcy and make him pay their debts by his labor." To Dryer it was clear that it was "the main purpose of that bill not to let a wage earner get his discharge" and to tell the worker "either go into servitude or stay out of bankruptcy court."[56] One witness believed that the founding fathers would roll over in their graves at the thought of an American citizen having to go before a government official to "explain to the court how much he needs for food and shelter and clothing for his family."[57]

The conflict over adding wage earner workout to bankruptcy law boiled down to this: Is the purpose to enable people to pay their debts and avoid the stigma of bankruptcy? Or is the purpose to make the courts a collection agency for creditors? The conflict was not resolved when the proposal for wage earner workout was abandoned in 1934 or when it was taken up again in 1937, which we turn to next. In fact, the same conflict emerged during every subsequent "bankruptcy crisis." Chapter 6 focuses on this theme.

Michigan, Ohio, and Wisconsin enacted wage earner receivership plans after the publication of the Thacher Report.[58] Congressman Walter Chandler revived the effort to incorporate it into federal bankruptcy law after he was elected to Congress in 1936. Congressman Chandler (D-TN) had previously been a city attorney for Memphis, Tennessee, where he helped to create a wage earner workout plan for city workers who faced garnishment.[59]

Chandler's plan was similar to the one described in the Thacher Report and the Hastings-Michener bill. Following the pattern set in compositions and extensions, petitioners seeking a workout instead of liquidation were not "bankrupts" but simply "debtors." Debtors made payments to a trustee, who then made payments to the creditors. The debtor could receive a discharge after following the plan for a specified period (which Chandler lengthened to three years from the two years in the Hastings-Michener bill), even if they had not paid the full amount of the debt. There were two substantial differences between the Hastings-Michener bill and the Chandler bill. Chandler wanted to require the consent of a majority of creditors in number and value, which was again similar to composition and extension, but he did not want to include a suspended discharge to force debtors into repayment plans.

Chandler brought Valentine Nesbit to testify before Congress. Nesbit was a bankruptcy referee in Birmingham, Alabama. He was appointed in 1933 to administer Section 74 cases. Recall from above that Congress had anticipated that sole proprietorships and partnerships would use Section 74; however, the language of the law said that it could be used by "any person excepting a corporation." Essentially, the wording of Section 74 repeated the wording of the original 1898 act that opened the door for personal bankruptcy in the first place. The primary difference between Section 74 and the later wage earner workout proposals was the level of involvement of the court. In Section 74, the debtor submitted a plan, the creditors voted on it, and the bankruptcy referee simply supervised the meetings and approved the plan. In proposals to add wage earner workout to bankruptcy law, the court determined the debtor's ability to pay and the payments the debtor would make, and it facilitated the distribution of payments to creditors.

Nesbit's second case under Section 74 in Birmingham was filed by five employees of Southern Bell Telephone and Telegraph.[60] Nesbit improvised. He established procedures much like the wage earner workout proposals in the Thacher Report and the Hastings-Michener bill. Nesbit called a meeting of the creditors, put the debtor under oath, and asked "what his rent is, what his grocery bill is, and the light, water, and gas, his coal bill, his clothes bill, the doctor's bill, and what his family consists of." Nesbit tabulated the expenses, subtracted them from the debtor's wages, and paid the "surplus" to creditors on a pro rata basis. If the debtor had secured debt, Nesbit tried to make sure that it was paid within eighteen months, but he did not have specific principles on which he divided the payments between secured and unsecured creditors. Nesbit credited any usurious payments to loan sharks against the amount owed to them. Originally, he required the debtor to make the payments directly to creditors, but eventually he hired young lawyers and several bookkeepers to collect and distribute the payments.[61] Michener later noted that Nesbit was "conducting a very laudable project down there, most of it, in my judgment, entirely without the law." Menalcus Lankford, a referee from Norfolk, Virginia, testified that he had developed essentially the same procedures to handle petitions brought by consumers under Section 74.[62] Nesbit's and Lankford's testimonies showed that the courts could succeed at wage earner workout plans.

The National Retail Credit Men enthusiastically endorsed Chandler's proposal, as they had the proposals in 1933–34. Its representative claimed that the wage earner workout plan could free up $500 million in delinquent accounts and could increase the revenue of retail merchants by $10 million to $25 million annually.[63] His testimony was not well received in Congress. Congress members regularly blamed retailers for excessive lending to consumers.[64]

Labor unions did not actively lobby when Chandler reintroduced the idea of wage earner workout. Representatives of the manufacturers and wholesalers upstream from retailers actively opposed Chandler at first. Their opposition probably stemmed from Chandler's decision to proceed with a wage earner workout bill independently of a general revision of the Bankruptcy Act.[65] The National Association of Credit Men belonged to a relatively new interest group, the National Bankruptcy Conference, which was formed in 1932. By early 1937, it was working on recommendations for general revisions.

Interest Groups and Politics during the Depression

The "radical and revolutionary provisions" for officialism that were contained in the Thacher Report and the Hastings-Michener bill left many bankruptcy professionals "profoundly disturbed."[66] Robert A Cook, a lawyer from Boston, noted that "in the past the Bankruptcy Committees of various nationally known organizations had happily cooperated [with Congress], with the result that the bills previously introduced had represented the thoughts of these national organizations."[67] In 1932, the nationally known organizations had been left out of the process. The organizations responded by forming the National Bankruptcy Conference. The conference included representatives from the American Bar Association, the Commercial Law League of America, the National Association of Referees in Bankruptcy, and the National Association of Credit Men. The National Retail Credit Men were not included.

In 1935, the conference submitted a draft bankruptcy bill to Congress. The bill intended to make the bankruptcy law, which had been amended many times, into a more harmonious whole. It retained creditor control but suggested several changes in administration to improve efficiency; for example, it reduced some of the time limits for action by interested parties and expanded the jurisdiction of referees. It included versions of everything introduced in the emergency relief measures, but it consolidated alternatives to liquidation into two categories: "arrangement" and corporate reorganization.[68] "Arrangements" included composition and extension.[69] A single procedure for arrangement would be available to everyone: wage earners, small businesses, and even corporations could choose to use it. The National Bankruptcy Conference version did not allow the court to supervise or to revise the plan, and it did not provide the possibility of a discharge after the plan had been completed.

At the beginning of 1937, as Chandler was bringing particular referees to testify in support of his vision of wage earner workouts, the National Bankruptcy Conference was revising its bankruptcy bill. In July 1937, it completed the work. Congress passed the Chandler Act in 1938. The Chandler Act revised corporate bankruptcy in Chapters X and XI. It incorporated wage earner workout, largely as envisioned by Garrison and Chandler, into bankruptcy law as Chapter XIII. According to Senator Joseph O'Mahoney (D-WY) , the Chandler Act made "the machinery of the Federal courts available to small businesses *and individuals in the same manner* as to railroads and large corporations" (emphasis added).[70]

By the end of the 1930s, the recasting of the role of bankruptcy law in economic life was complete. Even the creditors who had written the 1898 act saw distributing the assets of the bankrupt for the benefit of creditors as "a secondary object." In 1939, the National Association of Credit Men told its members: "[B]ankruptcy legislation is primarily for the benefit of the bankrupt."[71] Before the Depression, judges and legislators began emphasizing the benefits of discharge. During the Depression, workout became the "new concept of bankruptcy" according to Michener. Every victim of "financial evil days" was entitled to "seek the aid" of the bankruptcy law to "regain his financial equilibrium."[72]

Because there was widespread acceptance of the need for bankruptcy law and substantial agreement about its purpose, bankruptcy no longer held the partisan and ideological significance that it had in the late nineteenth century. Even though amendments of the 1930s fundamentally changed the scope and function of bankruptcy law, there were few roll call votes on bankruptcy in the 1930s, and none of substance.[73] Instead of partisan speechifying and numerous roll call votes, Congress held many—many—hearings. At these hearings, interest groups, old and new, lined up to try to influence the bankruptcy legislation. Bankruptcy remained largely nonpartisan until the turn of the twenty-first century.

The 1898 Bankruptcy Act had done little to promote workouts, but its structure made possible the growth of private workouts through adjustment bureaus and wage amortization companies. Bureaus used the threat of bankruptcy to promote creditor cooperation. They told creditors that, if they cooperated, they could eventually all receive at least partial payment; however, if they proceeded with individual collection efforts, the debtor would have no alternative but to file for bankruptcy, in which case, each creditor would probably receive nothing. The success of the bureaus suggested a way to incorporate workout directly into the bankruptcy law. Congress readily amended the law for businesses and farmers, but it hesitated to incorporate workout procedures into personal bankruptcy. One Congressman, Walter Chandler, with an assist from his hand-picked witness Nesbit, was the driving force behind the years-long struggle for Chapter XIII.

Ironically, the struggle to rewrite bankruptcy law was followed by a period in which the law was almost irrelevant. In 1940, after procedures for Chapter XIII had been available nationwide for more than a year, there were seventeen states where they were not used at all. Beyond the states where these procedures had been "invented," they had only caught on in a few places. During World War II, personal bankruptcy petitions filed under all chapters declined substantially. The decline was not surprising. The first step in the path to bankruptcy is borrowing. In 1941, President Roosevelt authorized the Federal Reserve to regulate consumer credit to keep the lid on interest rates and inflation. Then, wartime rationing made most consumer durables unavailable anyway. Bankruptcy declined because borrowing and lending declined.

When pent-up demand met a postwar expansion in consumer lending, personal bankruptcy rates caught up and then surpassed their pre-Depression levels. States with pro-creditor garnishment again had high personal bankruptcy rates. But Chapter XIII still did not catch on in most places. Chapter 4 explains why.

Appendix to Chapter 3

The regression analysis in chapter 3 follows the analysis of the determinants of personal bankruptcy rates from the 1920s, covered in chapter 2, into the Great Depression.

Regression Analysis of Impact of Great Depression

The focus of the regression analysis in chapter 3 is that economic conditions interact with state garnishment law to influence the bankruptcy rate. See the appendix to chapter 1 for a description of the empirical approach. The regression analysis in this chapter comes directly from our published work.[74]

The dependent variable is again the personal bankruptcy rate in state *s* and year *t*. For a description of the sources and methods for the calculation of bankruptcy rates, see the appendix to chapter 1. The regression analysis covers 1920–32. On average, there were about 1.9 personal bankruptcies per 10,000 people each year (standard deviation about 2.3). As shown in figure 1.1, the personal bankruptcy rates rose quickly as per capita income declined at the start of the Great Depression. In this chapter, we show that the increase came largely from states with pro-creditor garnishment law. There are three vectors of independent variables: *Files*, *InDefault*, and *InDebt*.

ELEMENTS OF *FILES*

Many of the elements of *Files* in the regressions underlying chapter 3 are the same as those described in the appendix to chapter 2. They are state homestead and personal property exemptions and the characteristics of state garnishment law. The characteristics of garnishment law are not known for about one-third of states (see table 2A.1), so there are 358 state-years included in the regression that we use for our main results. In this chapter, we measure exemptions relative to income per capita in the state and year.[75] The value of exemptions is shown in table 2A.1. Per capita income (in 1920 dollars) averaged $570 (with standard deviation of about $200).

ELEMENT OF *INDEFAULT*

In chapter 3, the main way that we capture the likelihood of default is with the growth rate of real income. Per capita income fell 2.3 percent in the average state-year (standard deviation 10.8). We additionally control for unemployment, which we proxy with the business failure rate (see appendix to chapter 2). In the average state-year, there were 10.6 business failures per 1,000 business concerns (standard deviation of about 4.5).

We also include church membership.[76] States with larger congregations of a religious denomination have greater private social safety nets in this period. About 43 percent of the population belonged to a church (standard deviation about 9). Finally, because more like-minded people may be more likely to construct a strong private social safety net, we include a Herfindahl index of concentration of church membership. The index averaged 0.2 (standard deviation about 0.1).

ELEMENTS OF *INDEBT*

As indicators of the overall supply of credit during this period, we include the maximum interest rate that could be charged if the rate was not stated in a contract,[77] the ratio of bank loans to state income,[78] the number of automobile registrations,[79] and the share of the population that is urban.[80] The maximum interest rate averaged 6.3 percent (standard deviation about 1.3). The average loan-to-income ratio was about 400 (standard deviation about 130). On average, there were about 17 registered vehicles per 100 people in a state (standard deviation about 8). About 47 percent of the population in the typical state lived in an urban area (standard deviation about 20).

TABLE 3A.1. **Determinants of the personal bankruptcy rate, 1920–32**

	OLS	FE
	(1)	(2)
Pro-creditor garnishment	9.868**	
	(2.393)	
Pro-debtor garnishment	-16.758**	
	(2.459)	
Real income growth (%)	0.881	-0.008
	(8.847)	(7.29)
Pro-creditor * growth		-0.413**
		(6.791)
Observations	274	358
R-squared	0.556	0.339

During the Great Depression, personal bankruptcy rates spiked in states with pro-creditor garnishment but not in states with pro-debtor garnishment. The dependent variable in this table is defined as filings per 100,000 people rather than filings per 10,000 people. References to the coefficients in the text have been multiplied by 10. Notes: * p<0.10, ** p<0.05, *** p<0.01. Standard errors are in parentheses and clustered at the state level. Constant and year effects included in both specifications. Additional controls for social and economic conditions are included; see text for details. *Sources*: Hansen and Hansen, "Crisis and Bankruptcy"; also see appendices for chapters 2 and 3.

RESULTS

Table 3A.1 shows the main results of the regressions. Specification (1) of table 3A.1 shows that the difference between pro-creditor and other states is statistically significant and large relative to the average state's bankruptcy rate, even when we include controls for other variables that affect the bankruptcy rate (that is, elements of the *Files*, *InDebt* and *InDefault*). For conciseness, the table suppresses the coefficients on the other control variables included in the regressions. Specification (2) shows that, in a fixed effects framework, changes in real income do not have a statistically significant effect on the personal bankruptcy rate in states with pro-debtor garnishment. The personal bankruptcy rate responded to the onset of the Great Depression only in states with pro-creditor garnishment law. In pro-creditor states, a one percentage point decrease in growth in a state resulted in an increase in the bankruptcy rate of about 4 per 10,000 people in that state.

Personal Bankruptcy after World War II

In 1942, Wendell T. Hall began work as a red cap, or baggage porter, for the Kansas City Terminal Railroad Company in Union Station, Kansas City. Though he lived in an apartment in the city, he hoped to build a house in the country for his family. Sometime during the 1940s, he bought about twenty acres of property north of Kansas City with a seller-financed mortgage. Then, in 1948 and 1949, he or one of his family members saw at least three different doctors. In early 1949, Hall was unable to make the payments on his mortgage, and he relinquished the property to the seller-mortgage holder. On April 20, 1949, he petitioned for an extension of time to pay his remaining creditors under Chapter XIII of the federal bankruptcy law.[1]

At the time he filed his petition, Hall still owed $270 in medical bills. He owed $418 on furniture purchased in 1947 from Gorman's, a local department store, and $70 on open accounts at other department stores. He had used his 1936 Buick to secure several notes, mostly from Union Finance Company. He still owed $70 on the notes, but the car was worth just $50. It was "not in condition to drive."

Under Hall's Chapter XIII "wage earner's plan," the railroad sent payments directly to the trustee appointed by the court. Hall's secured creditors (Union Finance Company and Gorman's) received full payment in three installments ending in June 1950. His unsecured creditors had to wait until October 1952, but they also recovered their claims. Over forty months, the railroad turned over $1,220, about 15 percent of his pay, to make good on his $880 in debt. Of the $340 difference between his payments and his debts, the trustee used half to pay for car repairs and for medical expenses incurred by Hall after he filed. The other half (equal to almost 20 percent of his original debt) went to the attorneys, the trustee, the referee, and other court fees.

Chapter XIII gave consumers the option to use the bankruptcy law to avoid liquidation by paying their debts under new terms. As discussed in chapter 3, Congress created Chapter XIII in 1938. Soon after, World War II dramatically reduced the number of personal bankruptcy petitions. The return to normalcy after the war provided the first real opportunity to observe how many debtors would choose repayment over liquidation. Hall's case was not too unusual in the Federal Court for the District of Western Missouri, where just over 10 percent of petitions for personal bankruptcy were filed under Chapter XIII. Yet, Western Missouri was an unusual district. The bankruptcy referee working in Kansas City in 1949 encouraged debtors to use Chapter XIII. In contrast, because most bankruptcy referees did not particularly favor its use, most districts had no Chapter XIII cases in 1949. Changes in local legal culture—in particular, a change in the bankruptcy referee—determined much of the geographical spread of Chapter XIII.

The return to normalcy also put the personal bankruptcy rate back on its prewar trend. As in the years before the Great Depression, expanding access to consumer credit was the primary force behind rising bankruptcy rates, and state collection laws determined the extent to which the increase in consumer credit was reflected in the state's bankruptcy rate.

Referees and the Use of Chapter XIII

Recall from chapter 3 that Chapter XIII was a significant innovation of the Chandler Act. For the first time, bankruptcy law in the US gave the consumer in default a choice. A consumer could choose between liquidation under Chapter VII and a repayment plan under Chapter XIII. Both options stopped other collection efforts, such as garnishment. With the traditional Chapter VII option, the debtor retained future earnings in exchange for giving up any nonexempt assets. With Chapter XIII, the debtor retained assets in exchange for giving up part of future income.

Advocates for repayment plans, such as the bankruptcy referee Valentine Nesbit, who had testified before Congress during hearings on the

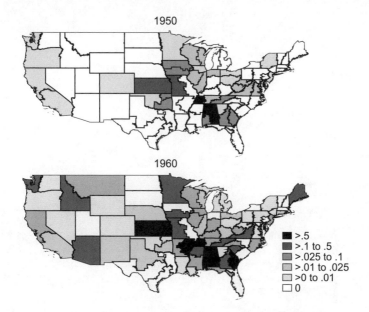

FIG. 4.1. Variations in the share of petitions filed under Chapter XIII across districts were large and inconsistent in the 1950s and 1960s. In states with multiple districts, there were differences within the state. In some states (e.g., Missouri), the differences persisted over time. In many states (e.g., Arkansas, the Carolinas, Iowa, and Virginia), differences emerged over time. An extreme example was Indiana: In 1950, no Chapter XIII cases were filed in its Southern District, but a number were filed in its Northern District. In 1960, the pattern was reversed. Map constructed by Matt Davis. *Source*: See appendix to chapter 4.

Chandler Act, believed that there was strong demand among debtors for Chapter XIII. Whether they were correct was not immediately clear because World War II reduced bankruptcy rates to an extraordinarily low level. After the war, it quickly became clear that the number of debtors who would use Chapter XIII was substantial but geographically uneven.

About 16 percent of all petitioners from 1946 through 1965 sought to use Chapter XIII. Figure 4.1 shows that almost all petitions under Chapter XIII during the period came from a small number of places. In 1950, petitioners were more likely to choose Chapter XIII over Chapter VII only if they lived in one of three federal court districts—two in Alabama and one in Tennessee. These states had among the highest bankruptcy rates in the country because of their pro-creditor collection law. Ten years later, only four additional districts saw 50 percent or more of filers choosing Chapter XIII. Throughout the 1950s and 1960s in most districts, less than 2.5 percent of petitioners used a repayment plan.

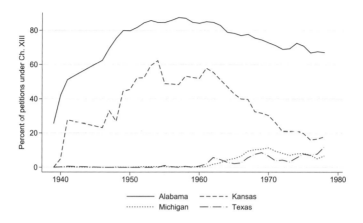

FIG. 4.2. Only Alabama had a consistently high share of all petitions filed under Chapter XIII. In other states, such as the examples here, the use of Chapter XIII petitions prior to 1979 was not closely correlated with changes in the benefits of using them. Instead, it reflected the influence of particular referees who encouraged lawyers to convince debtors to pay. *Source*: See appendix to chapter 4.

As mentioned before, the geographical spread in the use of Chapter XIII during the 1950s, shown in figure 4.1, did not result in an upward trend in the national average. The share of all petitions filed under Chapter XIII fluctuated from a high of almost 22 percent in 1953 to a low of 12 percent in 1960. Figure 4.2 shows the rise and decline of Chapter XIII in four states from the passage of the Chandler Act through 1979. (The bankruptcy law was substantially rewritten in 1978; see chapter 5.) In Alabama and Kansas, two early adopters of Chapter XIII, its use peaked before 1960 and declined steadily thereafter. Use of Chapter XIII caught on in Michigan and Texas around 1960, though its use peaked at only 10 percent of cases.

We use regression analysis to measure the extent to which the geographic and temporal patterns in the use of Chapter XIII responded to the likely determinants of demand for it. (The regression results are in table 4A.1 of the appendix to chapter 4.) We expect the share of bankruptcy cases filed under Chapter XIII to be higher where the benefits of Chapter XIII relative to Chapter VII were higher, and we expect use of it to be lower where its costs relative to Chapter VII are higher. We can measure one type of relative cost and two types of relative benefits: the value of property exemptions, the ability of debtors to repay, and the supply of future credit.

The relative benefits of using Chapter XIII varied inversely with the generosity of the property exemptions allowed by the state under Chapter VII liquidation.[2] In the late twentieth and early twenty-first centuries, exemptions influenced chapter choice, but the size of the effect was small. A state with an unlimited homestead exemption would have been required to lower the exemption to $15,000 to encourage a meaningful increase in the use of repayment plans.[3] In contrast, the regression analysis shows that, during the years after World War II, the homestead exemption did not influence chapter choice at all. Moreover, Chapter XIII was used more in states with *larger* personal exemptions, which is the opposite of what debtors acting in their own best interests would have chosen, all other things equal.[4]

The benefits of Chapter XIII varied positively with the ability to repay. Therefore, we expect that a "wage earner" in a place with high average income was more likely to devise and complete a Chapter XIII repayment plan than a similar wage earner in a place with low average income. Again, the regression analysis shows that the pattern in the use of Chapter XIII is not consistent with what debtors would rationally choose. The state-to-state variation in the use of Chapter XIII was *negatively* associated with income, suggesting repayment plans were more likely to be imposed where ability to pay was lowest. Unemployment and recession are negatively associated with ability to repay, but they are positively correlated with use of Chapter XIII.

In a similar vein, we expect a wage earner in a place where income was growing quickly would have higher ability to repay than a wage earner in a place where income was growing more slowly. However, the regressions show no meaningful association between the use of Chapter XIII and change in real income per capita within a state.

Chapter XIII benefited debtors if fees for management of the repayment plan were lower than fees for liquidation. This was unlikely. The trustee charged a commission of 10 percent on funds handled under either repayment or liquidation. The courts did not report statistics on attorney and administrative fees by chapter during the postwar period. However, the average administrative expenses and fees across all cases closed were unrelated to the use of Chapter XIII. In comparison, recently, lawyers' fees in filings with repayment plans were more than three times larger than filings for liquidation.[5]

Finally, choosing Chapter XIII sent a positive signal to creditors, potentially preserving access to credit in the future. However, creditors in more recent times did not respond to the signal by offering more credit to debtors who chose repayment.[6] In the decades following World War II, no more filers used Chapter XIII in states that enjoyed a greater access to credit. If anything, debtors were less likely to use Chapter XIII where mortgage lending grew.

Overall, then, historical patterns in the use of Chapter XIII are not systematically related to its costs or benefits. Of course, it is possible that the use of Chapter XIII following World War II reflects costs and benefits that we cannot measure. We cannot measure the reasonableness of Chapter XIII plans, the option value of choosing Chapter XIII, or the social benefits of choosing Chapter XIII.

The benefits of Chapter XIII varied inversely with the share of income the court required in the repayment plan. Chapter XIII required debtors to use all of their income above basic living expenses to pay creditors, but until 2005 there was no standard definition of "basic living expenses."[7] Debtors presented a plan, which the court could approve or reject. The courts never reported information about the ratio of payments to income under Chapter XIII. The creditor's point of view—not the debtor's—was represented. In 1946 and 1947, the courts reported only the amount of debt owed and the amount paid by filers who chose Chapter XIII. In nearly every district with more than a handful of Chapter XIII cases, creditors were paid in full under Chapter XIII. (In contrast, they received only token dividends under Chapter VII.) This pattern does suggest that where Chapter XIII repayment was used, the plans were feasible or flexible.

Debtors using Chapter XIII preserved the option of using Chapter VII later, either by filing a petition to convert the current case to Chapter VII or by completing repayment and filing again later if circumstances changed. A debtor who chose Chapter VII and received a discharge could not use the bankruptcy law again for at least six years. Preserving the option to file later probably caused people to delay filing as long as possible,[8] and some lawyers mentioned it as a benefit,[9] but its importance is not easily measured with available data.

Lastly, recall from chapter 3 that the creators of Chapter XIII believed that choosing it would have lower social costs than using Chapter VII. Social costs, or bankruptcy stigma, took several forms. To the extent that a person internalized a belief that default and bankruptcy were morally wrong, using the bankruptcy law to avoid paying caused psychological discomfort. To the extent that the belief was widely shared, the bankrupt lost his or her good reputation or status in the community. Advocates for Chapter XIII believed that social costs were large and that many consumers wanted to avoid the stigma of bankruptcy. In the hearings on the Chandler Bill, the referee Valentine Nesbit was particularly adamant that the language of Chapter XIII must mirror the language of its predecessor, Section 74. The petitioner who sought relief under Chapter XIII was simply a "debtor," not a "bankrupt." However, as discussed at greater length below, it is unlikely that such perceptions of stigma ever drove decisions about filing for bankruptcy, much less decisions about chapter choice.

In sum, the measurable benefits to debtors of using Chapter XIII do not account for the variation in chapter choice across space or over time.[10] The inability of state-level differences to explain much of the variation in Chapter XIII should, perhaps, not be surprising given that the share of petitioners using Chapter XIII varied considerably from one district to another even within a state. Congress was aware of the differences highlighted in figure 4.1.[11] In 1966, Chapter XIII accounted for 72 percent of personal bankruptcy cases in the Western District of Tennessee, but only 18 percent in the Middle District. It accounted for 69 percent of personal bankruptcy cases in the Southern District of Georgia, but only 18 percent in Georgia's Northern District. The only state with uniformly high use of Chapter XIII was Alabama. Over the course of the 1950s, the Southern District of Alabama caught up to the Middle and Northern Districts.

In some states, differences between districts persisted over time. For example, filers in the Western District of Missouri were always more likely to use Chapter XIII than filers in the Eastern District. However, in many states, including Arkansas, the Carolinas, Iowa, and Virginia, differences emerged over time.[12] An extreme example is Indiana: In 1950, there were no Chapter XIII cases filed in the Southern District, but its use was relatively high in the Northern District. In 1960, the pattern was reversed.

Demand by debtors for the procedure probably did not influence decisions about chapter choice. Of course, most debtors do not make decisions about bankruptcy on their own. They seek the advice of lawyers.

Today, the factors that influence the profits that lawyers make explain more of the variation in chapter choice than the factors that influence the well-being of debtors.[13] Race also figures prominently: Repayment plans are used more often in states with larger shares of blacks.[14]

Controlling for other factors, lawyers are more likely to direct people they believe to be black toward repayment rather than toward liquidation.[15] Consequently, "African Americans disproportionately use a type of bankruptcy that requires greater repayment of debt, costs more in legal fees, and takes longer."[16] Historically, little is known about race and chapter choice, though some reports suggest that the trend may be long-standing. During the Great Depression, about half of the debtors using an early debt-repayment procedure in Alabama were black, even though blacks made up only about one-third of Alabama's population.[17] In one 1960s sample of bankrupts, blacks were significantly overrepresented among the bankrupt, but the racial breakdown by chapter is not known.[18] Our regression analysis indicates a negative but small and statistically weak correlation between the share of whites living in a state and the use of Chapter XIII in the state. The most statistically robust evidence comes from the years immediately following World War II. Between 1946 and 1955, when the share of nonwhites in a state rose by one percentage point, the share of petitions filed under Chapter XIII went up on average of 0.4 percentage points, or just 8 percent of the average share of cases filed under Chapter XIII. (Again, see table 4A.1 of the appendix to chapter 4.)

When lawyers consider how to advise clients, they consider how the judge is likely to respond to a petition. The preferences of judges regarding chapter choice shape the advice that lawyers offered to clients. Today, the outcomes of repayment plans, including the dismissal of cases and the ability to obtain discharge of debts, vary considerably from one bankruptcy judge to another, reflecting differences in judicial ideology.[19] In the three decades after Congress established Chapter XIII, the preferences of the judge-like referee drove the adoption of Chapter XIII and the extent of its use.

The preferences of the referee were important because Chapter XIII cases entailed more work for referees and lawyers than Chapter VII cases. Because creditors seldom elected trustees in personal bankruptcy cases (see chapter 2), the referee appointed one. Through this choice of a trustee, the referee held significant sway in the system of administration of Chapter XIII cases.

The referees in Birmingham followed the lead of Valentine Nesbit. Clarence W. Allgood plugged the local system at the annual meeting of the National Conference of Referees in 1940. The most important feature of a successful administration of repayment plans was, in his opinion, "the trustee and the functioning of the trustee's office."[20] In Birmingham, a single trustee, with the assistance of four clerks, administered all of the Chapter XIII plans. Allgood noted that the cooperation of employers was also important for efficient administration. Employers in Birmingham deducted the court-approved amounts from the debtors' pay and sent them to the trustee.

One referee from Kansas City, Henry Bundschu, said that he had attended the meeting of referees specifically to hear Allgood talk about the administration of wage earner cases. Both Kansas City, Missouri, and Kansas City, Kansas, joined Birmingham and Montgomery, Alabama; Knoxville, Tennessee; Norfolk, Virginia; and Atlanta, Georgia; as early adopters of Chapter XIII (see figure 4.1). These courts employed the Birmingham system. They used one or two trustees who specialized in Chapter XIII cases. These trustees developed forms for standardizing the development of plans, collected wages directly from the employers, and made payments to creditors at specific times.[21] Certainly, the administration of Hall's case followed the Birmingham system.

The referees who adopted Chapter XIII in its first years promoted its spread. They were evangelical. Several spoke at the annual meeting of the Referees' Association or authored papers in its journal. They praised the benefits of Chapter XIII and described the procedures that they had developed to make it run efficiently.[22]

Lawyers were not altogether opposed to the additional work that Chapter XIII cases required. Yet, Lin Twinem of the Consumer Bankruptcy Committee of the American Bar Association agreed that referees were the key because "if a referee is sincerely interested in Chapter XIII, he can develop a good Chapter XIII program."[23] Twinem believed that Chapter XIII was unlikely to spread unless judges appointed new referees: "The [referees] that have been on the bankruptcy court for a long time have a very definite feeling against Chapter XIII."[24]

One of the new referees, Charles Pomeroy, introduced the use of Chapter XIII in Maine in 1952. By 1966, Chapter XIII filings there were 52.6 percent of personal bankruptcy cases, more than twice the national average. Pomeroy's successor, Richard E. Poulos, knew that attorneys recognized his preferences. "The attorneys are pretty gun shy." If they are representing a client who filed a case under Chapter VII, but that "looks on its face as if it should be under XIII, they usually approach the court either in advance or come to the bench and explain on the record that the client has been fully advised of the Chapter XIII procedures."[25]

Poulos added that, if the efforts of the attorney were not successful in getting the client to switch to Chapter XIII, Poulos would interrogate the debtor himself.

Although referees in Maine, Minnesota, Southern Iowa, and other districts successfully encouraged the use of Chapter XIII, referees elsewhere found it more difficult. Harold Bobier became a referee in Genesee County, Michigan, in 1963. Bobier educated lawyers about Chapter XIII and encouraged them to discuss plans with their clients. Like his counterpart in Maine, he was not averse to intervening to persuade the debtor to choose Chapter XIII. During one hearing, Bobier explained the option value of Chapter XIII to a debtor: "One of the most valuable aspects of it to you personally is that you do preserve the right to go into bankruptcy, you see, at a later time if you have a financial calamity."[26] He told the debtor that, if there was insurance that provided similar protection, he would not be able to afford the premiums. The referee in Flint, Michigan, also "believed very sincerely in the use of Chapter XIII, and in the encouragement of its use."[27] But, as figure 4.2 shows, the referees in Michigan never succeeded in convincing more than about 10 percent of petitioners to choose Chapter XIII.

As the referees in Michigan struggled to "convert" their districts to Chapter XIII in the 1960s, its use began to decline in places where it was previously widely used. Chapter XIII use declined even in Kansas and Alabama. Advocates for its continued expansion took their case to Congress in 1967. The hearings reprised the debate over the Hastings-Michener bill in 1932. Recall from chapter 3 that the central issue in 1932 was whether debtors should be required to repay at least part of their debts through a process of "suspended discharge." The debate over this requirement and other parts of the consumer workout proposal caused a delay at a time of economic crisis. Congress postponed the creation of Chapter XIII to 1938. In 1967, two bills sought to amend the bankruptcy law to require petitioners to repay if they could. The bills did not attempt to reanimate "suspended discharge," but instead they required petitioners for Chapter VII liquidation to show that a repayment plan would not provide "adequate relief." The bills would instruct a referee to dismiss a petition that, in his opinion, failed to persuade that a repayment plan was infeasible. After a dismissal, the debtor could choose to forgo any bankruptcy protection or to file a second time under Chapter XIII.

The debate over the bills showed that, almost 70 years after the passage of the 1898 Bankruptcy Act, the proper role of bankruptcy law was

still not settled. Was bankruptcy, including Chapter XIII, a law for helping unlucky debtors? Or was bankruptcy a law that, through high exemptions and easy discharge, encouraged debtors to avoid paying their
creditors? Members of Congress and witnesses who believed the former argued that since repayment plans had many benefits for the debtor
compared to liquidation, referees and lawyers should simply do their
jobs and make Chapter XIII work. People who believed the latter argued that because repayment plans were economically and ethically su-
perior, debtors with a steady income should be required to try to meet
their obligations.

The proposals to make Chapter XIII the default option for personal
bankruptcy failed in 1967, which was a time when consumer debtors won
considerable protections in both Congress and the courts. (See chapter 5 for more information.) But the underlying disagreement was not
resolved. It emerged again in the 1980s and gained prominence in the
1990s and early 2000s. In 2005, proponents of required repayment made
significant inroads. (See chapter 6 for details.)

The Second Run-Up in Consumer Bankruptcy

In 1945, total nationwide bankruptcy filings were at an all-time low of
10,200. In 1960, there were more than 110,000 petitions. From the long-
run perspective of figure 1.1, personal bankruptcy simply returned to the
pattern that the war had interrupted. But at the time, the rapid increase
alarmed people. People offered two competing explanations for the increase in bankruptcy rates. One explanation was that a decline in the
stigma of bankruptcy caused more people to choose it. The other explanation was that increased access to consumer credit was allowing more
people to fall more deeply into debt and, therefore, become potential
bankrupts.

Stigma

Earlier concern about declining stigma appeared in the Thacher Report,
but the concern was stifled by the length and severity of the Great Depression. In the late 1950s and the 1960s, concern came from all parts of
civil society—from the bar, from academia, and from the media. Critics claimed that a change in beliefs about the morality of debt, default,

and bankruptcy was the fundamental cause of the increase in personal bankruptcy.[28] In 1959, Fred C. Fields, an Oklahoma attorney, observed that "the moral courage that has so long been dominant in our wage earners began to deteriorate. . . . [Now] the bankrupt just simply lacks the moral courage to deny himself a few luxuries and make an honest effort to liquidate his obligations."[29] In 1963, *Time* magazine echoed Fields's sentiments: "Once upon a time, when both morals and money were harder, bankruptcy was bad. Wastrels used to be bailed out by their better-off relations in order to save the family name from the stigma. But in these days of looking-glass economics, bankruptcy is growing more and more fashionable as a way to settle one's debts and land some more credit."[30] According to this view, a decline in the stigma of bankruptcy influenced a consumer's decision at every step on the path to bankruptcy. Declining stigma made a debtor in default more likely to file. It made a debtor more likely to "choose" default over belt tightening. Finally, a decline in the stigma of bankruptcy made a consumer more willing to take the risk of borrowing in the first place.

Changes in tastes and preferences, including changes in stigma, can be important elements of choice and drivers of demand. But measuring change in stigma is difficult. Perhaps the most straightforward way to measure it is to ask people. A Gallup poll taken in the 1960s found that the stigma of bankruptcy was still strong. Nine out of ten people in the US said they would feel "disgraced" or "rather die" than file for bankruptcy.[31]

An indirect way to measure a change in the stigma of bankruptcy is to measure changes in things that probably contribute to stigma's decline. Stigma is transmitted through social networks. A decline in social connectivity may reduce the enforcement of social norms, making defaulting on a loan or filing for bankruptcy less socially costly, in addition to possibly being financially beneficial.[32] Social connectivity also could work in the opposite direction. Even within a strong social network, news of a filing within the network can increase the probability that others in the network believe that "[i]t's okay for people like me to use the bankruptcy law if I need it." Stigma falls within the network. Moreover, information about the benefits of the automatic stay or the helpfulness of the discharge can also be passed along a social network. Finally, specific information, including information about local procedures and referrals to lawyers, can spread across a social network. When attitudes like stigma and information like referrals are passed along a social network, they are collectively called "social spillovers."

If the recent history of the bankruptcy rate within a defined geographic area influences the bankruptcy rate there today, then social spillovers probably occurred. Falling social connectivity explained some of the rapid increases in bankruptcy in the 1980s, 1990s, and 2000s,[33] but social spillovers were more important.[34]

It requires highly detailed geographic information to separate the information effect from the stigma effect and to determine whether the mechanism of transmission of spillovers is impersonal (information) or interpersonal (stigma). Stigma and impersonal information (such as attorney advertising) can be transmitted through networks as large as a district or a county, but households are more likely to interact and share actionable information in small neighborhoods. Furthermore, stigma effects can last for a long time, but the value of specific information gained from conversations with neighbors depreciates quickly. In the 1950s and 1960s, as in the 2000s, the information effect dominated.[35] If a decline in stigma was not the primary reason for the increasing bankruptcy rate after World War II, it was unlikely to have caused an increase in demand for credit by households.

Household Debt

The causes of the second run-up in the personal bankruptcy rate were similar to those of the first. Increases in the supply of personal credit pushed bankruptcy rates up, especially in states with pro-creditor collection law. As in the 1920s, household debt grew rapidly in the 1950s and 1960s.[36] Outstanding consumer credit per person grew more than 400 percent. At the same time, real GDP per capita increased about 30 percent.[37]

Along the path to bankruptcy, default increases with the share of income that goes to payments on debt. In 1962, households with installment debt were devoting 10 percent of income to payments.[38] Seven percent of households made payments in excess of 30 percent of income. Across all households, payments on debt increased from 11 percent of income in 1949 to 22 percent in 1966.[39]

The increase in indebtedness and the debt burden could arise from an increase in demand for credit, from an increase in supply of credit, or from a combination of the two. As discussed above, the patterns in bankruptcy data suggest that the contemporary explanation—that declining stigma of bankruptcy caused an ever-increasing demand for consumer credit—is unlikely. More direct evidence comes from interest rates. Although data on the interest rates that consumers paid are not very complete for this period,[40] a contemporary survey found that finance charges fell at most types of lenders during the 1950s, and consumer finance charges rose, modestly, only at commercial banks.[41] That survey did not take into account the fact that interest rates on many consumer loans were highly regulated before the late 1970s. As discussed in chapter 2, usury laws are typically binding. Most consumer credit transactions during this period were made at the highest legal rate.[42] Hence, it is likely that outstanding consumer debt rose because the supply of credit increased.

One cause of the increase in the supply of consumer credit was the removal of restrictions placed on it during World War II. In 1941, President Roosevelt used the War Powers Act to authorize the Federal Reserve to regulate consumer credit. The Fed used its Regulation W to set minimum down payments and maximum repayment periods and to require the licensing of businesses that provided installment credit for small personal loans and particular consumer durables.[43] The minimum down payments and maximum repayment periods varied for different categories of goods. The goods covered by Regulation W changed over time and ranged from passenger planes and automobiles to household appliances. The regulation covered both credit issued at the sale of an item and rollovers of loans made previously. Consumer debt decreased from $9.2 billion in 1941 to $4.9 billion in 1943. Over the same two years, installment credit fell from $5.9 to $1.8 billion.[44] Consumer credit did not surpass $9 billion again until 1947, when the Fed relaxed the regulation.[45] That is why Hall, the bankrupt red-cap whose case was featured in the introduction to this chapter, was able to buy his furniture on installment in 1948. The Fed again invoked Regulation W to restrict consumer credit during the Korean War, but never used it in that way again after 1952.

Ironically, the attempts to restrict credit during World War II and the Korean War may have contributed to innovations in consumer credit products by retailers.[46] Rural retailers had long offered open accounts or book credit.[47] Customers paid off such accounts on a regular basis. Urban department stores offered such convenience "charge accounts" to good customers.[48] At first, charge accounts were not covered by Regulation W because the debt was not secured. But many stores responded to Regulation W by allowing more customers to carry balances.[49] The Fed fought this subterfuge by extending Regulation W. It required stores to convert long overdue charge accounts to installment loans or to freeze the accounts. Most stores complied with the regulation by using the charge plate, which had evolved at the end of the 1920s to reduce errors in accounts and to track accounts.[50] Other stores continued evasive maneuvers. Some began to "serially liquidate" charge accounts, closing one account while transferring balances to a new account. Yet others began to allow customers to pay off charges flexibly. Charge account sales fell far less than installment sales early in World War II and even grew toward its end.[51]

After the war, department stores waged "Charge it!" ad campaigns, and they competed for customers by offering "easy credit." By 1949, about 75 percent of stores offered revolving credit with modern characteristics.[52] Revolving credit accounts offered purchases, up to a predefined limit, without down payment and with flexible repayment. Stores levied a service charge on unpaid balances. It seems likely that Hall's unsecured account at Montgomery Ward was revolving credit. In the 1950s and 1960s, department stores became ever more generous about credit limits and began charging interest on unpaid balances. Eventually, many stores created their own credit subsidiaries or contracted with the consumer finance companies that had made installment lending possible. Manufacturers followed suit, offering revolving credit that encouraged repeat buying and repeat borrowing.[53]

Figure 4.3 shows the changes in the supply of credit from the perspective of the creditors owed by households in Maryland when the households filed for personal bankruptcy. The left panel of the figure shows the relative size of the major groups of creditors listed by filers.[54] The right panel shows the share of debt owed to each group of creditors. In 1945, department stores represented only about 3 percent of the creditors listed by the bankrupt. By 1965, the representation of department stores had more than doubled. The amount of debt owed by the bankrupt to department stores rose from less than 1 percent of their debts in 1945 to just over 5 percent of all debts in 1965. It is not possible to identify revolving credit from other unsecured credit owed to department stores. It seems likely, however, that many bankrupts obtained revolving credit from department stores. They certainly obtained revolving credit

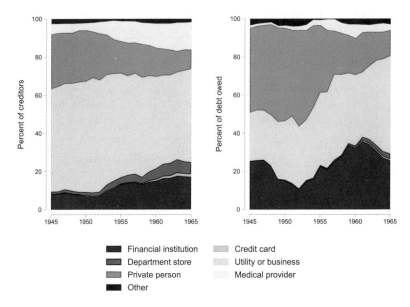

FIG. 4.3. Immediately after World War II, utilities, independent businesses, and private persons dominated the list of creditors and the amounts of debt owed by the bankrupt in the Maryland sample. In the 1950s, financial institutions and medical providers took on greater importance. In the 1960s, department stores and credit cards emerged as significant creditor interest groups, though the amount of debt owed to them remained small. *Source*: See appendix to chapter 4.

from the earliest general-purpose cards. Diner's Club, American Express, and BankAmericard all appear among the creditors of the bankrupt soon after their introduction.[55] (The expanding role of credit cards in bankruptcy is the focus of chapter 6.)

As consumers spent and borrowed more from department stores, they spent and borrowed less from small specialty stores.[56] Overall, the number of commercial businesses that had extended credit to bankrupts fell over the period. At the same time, households increasingly had access to utility services that were billed on unsecured open accounts. From 1945 to 1965, the output of utility industries rose by 500 percent.[57] Except during the Korean War, household expenditures on natural gas, water, sewer, electricity, and telephone services all grew at a steady pace.[58] As households used these services, they became indebted to the providers. On average, bankrupts owed twice as much money to commercial businesses and utilities in 1965 than they did in 1945, even though the number of commercial creditors was smaller.

In addition to medical providers, utilities, and department stores, banks also supplied credit to households. Consumer loan departments grew during the New Deal in response to Federal Housing Administration (FHA) guarantees on home improvement loans.[59] After World War II, banks expanded these departments. In 1945, banks and other financial institutions, such as credit unions, were only about 5 percent of the creditors listed by bankrupt households. By 1965, nearly 20 percent of the creditors listed on bankruptcy documents were banks or financial institutions. The amount of debt owed to banks by bankrupt households "only" doubled because each bankrupt owed a relatively small amount to banks.

Most bank loans, like other installment loans, were secured by the item that the loan was used to acquire. Similarly, many personal finance companies—like the one used by Hall—made secured loans. In 1951, the year before the Fed stopped using Regulation W to control consumer credit, about 32 percent of households had some kind of installment debt. By 1962, 50 percent did. The share of households with installment debt held steady until the stagflation of the late 1970s.[60] Figure 4.4 shows that nearly all bankrupt households in Maryland, no matter when they filed, owed some debt that was secured.

While a bankrupt was more likely to hold secured debt than the representative household was, a bankrupt was not more likely to hold mortgage debt. In the 1950s, the share of Maryland's bankrupt households

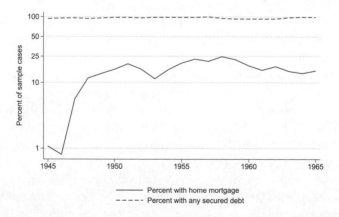

FIG. 4.4. Nearly all bankrupts in the Maryland sample had some secured debt. The share with home mortgages peaked at 25 percent in the late 1950s, just as the bankruptcy rate was reaching its pre-Depression level. *Source*: See appendix to chapter 4.

with mortgages tracked the share of all households with them.[61] By the late 1950s, at the same time that the bankruptcy rate returned to its prewar peak, the share of Maryland filers with mortgages peaked at 25 percent. The Maryland bankrupts seem typical of bankrupts in general. In Utah, 23 percent of a 1963 sample of filers had mortgage debt.[62] The same year, 26 percent of filers in Genesee County, Wisconsin, "were purchasing real estate."[63]

Variation in Bankruptcy across States

The increase in the supply of mortgages and consumer credit during the postwar period, especially credit issued by retailers and other commercial businesses, surely put more households on the path to bankruptcy. At the national level, the growth rate in bankruptcy was similar to the growth in mortgage lending and consumer credit. At the state level, the relationship was not so direct. The bankruptcy rate rocketed past its prewar peak in states with pro-creditor collection laws. It grew moderately elsewhere. The personal bankruptcy rate had been over 25 per 10,000 people in Alabama for ten years when, in 1960, it reached 5 per 10,000 in the median state. (Once again, refer to figures 1.2 and 1.3.)

Faster growth in the supply of credit did not cause the high growth of personal bankruptcy in states with pro-creditor collection law. In fact, between 1945 and 1965, there was slightly *less* consumer credit issued by banks in the states where it was easiest to collect.[64] Although state-level data on consumer credit extended by finance companies or retailers do not exist on a yearly basis, there is little reason to expect that banks were less aware of collection law than other creditors.

From 1945 to 1970, the bankruptcy rate in the average state went up by 9.2 per 10,000. In states with pro-creditor garnishment, it went up by 19.4 per 10,000. We again use regression analysis to examine the extent to which pro-creditor garnishment in a state interacted with rising amounts of mortgage and consumer credit to cause increases in personal bankruptcy. Because of some limitations in the data, we use data from 1946, 1960, and 1970, and we examine the change within the state between the years. (For more details about the limitations and methods, see the appendix to chapter 4. Regression results appear in table 4A.2.)

The regressions show the average increase of $270 in mortgage lending by banks (in 1984 dollars) nudged the bankruptcy rate up by 0.5 per

10,000. Consumer credit issued by banks rose by $38 per person, which pushed the bankruptcy rate *down* by about 1 per 10,000. Neither form of bank lending predicts the trajectory of the bankruptcy rate particularly well.

The change in the number of retail establishments, a proxy for retail lending, is a better predictor of the increase in the bankruptcy rate, even after taking into account the difference in the share of state population living in urban areas. Because of the rise of department stores, the average number of retail establishments per 1,000 people fell by 3.7. In states where it fell by only 2.7 (states that had a higher concentration of stores per person in 1970), the increase in the bankruptcy rate was about 2.5 per 10,000 higher (about 25 percent of average) than in the typical state. If a state with a higher concentration of retail outlets also had pro-creditor garnishment, the bankruptcy rate was higher still.

The measured relationship between the growth in the supply of credit and the bankruptcy rate are imprecise because the gaps in the data leave us with a small number of observations. Yet the pattern for the postwar period is clear, and it is consistent with patterns from the 1920s. In the 1920s, new forms of consumer credit, such as legal small loans, increased indebtedness in many places but increased the bankruptcy rate primarily in states with pro-creditor garnishment. From 1945 to 1965, creditors, and especially retailers, such as the local and national department stores where Hall shopped, made installment loans and extended revolving credit to consumers. When a consumer defaulted, the collection law in the state was the most important determinant of his or her decision to file a bankruptcy petition.

The second run-up to a peak in the bankruptcy rate in the 1950s and 1960s was largely a return to the trend of increasing personal bankruptcy that had begun before the Great Depression. Differences in state collection laws continued to play a prominent role in explaining differences in bankruptcy filing rates. However, the strongly pro-creditor collection laws in Alabama and elsewhere did not survive the scrutiny of the consumer rights movement of the 1960s. Before 1970, Congress and the Supreme Court limited the ability of states to enforce their pro-creditor collection laws. Chapter 5 shows how this movement reduced the variation in state rates.

Chapter 6 continues the story of the evolution of Chapter XIII. Because of the success of Chapter XIII in the districts where referees championed it, repayment plans gained broad support. Support did not translate into consensus about its role in the bankruptcy system. While many legal professionals and scholars, and even some creditor interest groups, argued that debtors should simply be further encouraged to use it, others argued that debtors should be *required* to repay unless they could demonstrate that it would not be feasible. The debate continued through the end of the twentieth century and into the beginning of the twenty-first.

Appendix to Chapter 4

Chapter 4 first describes the uneven geographic and temporal variation in the use of Chapter XIII after World War II. It concludes with an analysis of the impact of the postwar expansion of consumer credit on the bankruptcy rate.

Regression Analysis of Use of Chapter XIII

The text of chapter 4 explains that variation in the use of Chapter XIII in the decades after its creation depended on the preferences of the local bankruptcy referee. Chapter XIII was used by a significant number of bankrupts only when and where referees favored it.

The regressions in this part of chapter 4 differ from the others in *Bankrupt in America* because they do not describe the path that leads to the debtor's decision to use the bankruptcy law in the first place. Instead, they describe the determinants of the use of the particular wage earner workout procedures of Chapter XIII of the bankruptcy law.

The relevant dependent variable is the percent of cases filed under Chapter XIII in state s and year t. In the published statistics on bankruptcy described in the appendix to chapter 1, filings under Chapter XIII are reported from 1939–41 and from 1946 onwards. (Recall that Chapter XIII was introduced in 1938.) We begin the analysis in 1946. In addition, some independent variables are not available for 1956–65. We therefore consider 1946–55 and 1966–78 in separate regressions. There are 449 state-years in the regressions covering the decade immediately after World War II, and there are 663 state-years in the regression covering the mid-1960s to the mid-1970s. About 4.4 percent of bankruptcy petitions were filed in Chapter XIII in the earlier period, and about 11.5 percent of petitions were filed under Chapter XIII in the later period.

The relevant vectors of independent variables measure the costs and benefits of repayment under Chapter XIII relative to liquidation under Chapter VII. In the text, we discuss the following costs and benefits: state laws governing property exemptions in collections, the debtor's ability to repay, and future supply of credit. In addition, historical and modern sources suggest that blacks are overrepresented in Chapter XIII.

STATE LAWS

We include the real value of homestead and personal exemptions (in 1984 dollars). The exemption laws are from a comparison of summaries of collection laws compiled by the National Association of Credit Management,[65] studies advocating for bankruptcy reform,[66] and studies of a federal law limiting states' exemptions.[67] From 1946–55, homestead exemptions averaged $55,600 (standard deviation about $14,000); from 1966–78, they averaged $30,800 (standard deviation about $16,000). From 1946–55, personal exemptions averaged about $3,800 (standard deviation about $4,000); from 1966–78, they averaged about $2,200 (standard deviation about $2,400).

ABILITY TO REPAY

Income per capita comes from the Bureau of Economic Analysis (BEA),[68] and the months of recession in each fiscal year is calculated using National Bureau of Economic Research (NBER) dating.[69] From 1946–55, real income (in 1984 dollars) averaged about $6,400 (standard deviation about $1,500); from 1966–78, it averaged about $11,400 (standard deviation about $2,200). In the earlier period, there was an average of 2.7 months of recession per fiscal year. In the later period, there were 2.2 months of recession per fiscal year.

SUPPLY OF (FUTURE) CREDIT

Statistics on the supply of credit by state are available only for bank credit. There are estimates from 1955 and earlier,[70] and there are estimates for 1966 and later.[71] The supply of mortgage credit is measured as residential (1–4 family) mortgage lending per capita, and other consumer credit is measured as all other consumer loans per capita.[72] Mortgage lending per capita averaged $370 in the earlier period (standard deviation $390) and $630 in the later period (standard deviation $320). Consumer credit per capita averaged $29 in the earlier period (standard deviation $23) and $93 in the later period (standard deviation $23).

RACE

For 1969 and later years, we take the share of whites in the population from the Survey of Epidemiology and End Results (SEER).[73] For earlier years, we interpolate from the census.[74] Whites comprise about 81 percent of the population in the earlier period (standard deviation about 14) and about 87 percent in the later period (standard deviation about 14).

RESULTS

Table 4A.1 shows the regression results. Specifications (1) and (2) show OLS regressions (cross-section time-series) and specifications (3) and (4) show fixed effects regressions. Because some supply of credit variables are not available for 1956–65 (see above), the odd numbered specifications include observations for 1946–55, while even numbered specifications include observations for 1966–78.

The results show that the use of Chapter XIII is not well explained by the variables capturing its benefits and costs. Larger homestead exemptions do not encourage use of Chapter XIII. Larger exemptions of personal property should encourage liquidation and discourage use of Chapter XIII, but exemptions of personal property are not closely related to use of Chapter XIII. In specification (1), there is a positive relationship, not the expected negative one. In the fixed effects regressions, changes in the real value of exemptions do not have a statistically measurable effect on the use of Chapter XIII.

Higher income per capita indicates greater ability to repay, which we expect to be positively correlated with use of Chapter XIII. But in OLS specifications (1) and (2), income per capita is negatively associated with use of Chapter XIII. An increase in per capita income within a state is not associated with greater use of Chapter XIII (specifications 3 and 4). More months of recession in a year would make it more difficult to repay and therefore is expected to decrease use of Chapter XIII, recessions have a positive influence on use of Chapter XIII in the OLS specifications (specifications 1 and 2). In the fixed effects specifications, differences in recession-months is not associated with use of Chapter XIII within the state.

Preservation of credit relationships may motivate the use of Chapter XIII, so we expect mortgage and consumer credit per capita to be positively correlated with use of Chapter XIII. They are not.

TABLE 4A.1. **Determinants of the share of petitions filed under Chapter XIII, 1946–78**

	1946–55	1966–78	1946–55	1966–78
	OLS		FE	
	(1)	(2)	(3)	(4)
Homestead exemption (10,000s of $1984)	-0.091	-0.239	-0.113	0.029
	(0.094)	(0.197)	(0.239)	(0.218)
Personal exemption (10,000s of $1984)	0.001**	0.001	-0.002	0.002
	(0.001)	(0.001)	(0.001)	(0.001)
Income per person (1,000s of $1984)	-4.522*	-2.551**	0.254	0.022
	(2.509)	(1.086)	(0.646)	(0.356)
Months of recession in year	0.343*	1.302**	-0.035	0.029
	(0.194)	(0.528)	(0.064)	(0.162)
Whites/population	0.012	-0.186	0.052	-0.404
	(0.149)	(0.160)	(0.119)	(0.671)
Mortgage lending per capita (1,000s)	6.847	-2.790	-5.566	-5.840
	(6.196)	(6.468)	(3.489)	(6.423)
Consumer credit per capita (100s)	2.900	1.381	1.590	-2.675
	(4.143)	(6.728)	(2.524)	(4.332)
Pro-creditor foreclosure	5.218	16.359*		
	(4.897)	(8.980)		
Pro-creditor foreclosure* mortgage per capita	-11.780	-15.311	2.642	3.714
	(7.630)	(11.206)	(2.855)	(5.663)
Observations	489	663	489	663
R-squared	0.206	0.297	0.190	0.103

Proxies for the benefits and costs of using Chapter XIII do not consistently explain changes in the share of bankruptcy cases filed under it. Notes: * $p<0.10$, ** $p<0.05$, *** $p<0.01$. Standard errors are in parentheses and clustered at the state level. Constant and year effects included in all specifications. Additional controls for social and economic conditions are included; see text for details. *Source*: See appendix to chapter 4.

SUPPLEMENTAL RESULT: STATE FORECLOSURE LAW

Although it is not discussed in the text of chapter 4, we also considered whether debtors in the postwar period, like more modern debtors,[75] were motivated to choose Chapter XIII to keep their homes after they defaulted on a mortgage and the mortgage holder initiated foreclosure proceedings. Debtors are more likely to choose to use the bankruptcy law to protect their homes if the state law makes foreclosing easy for creditors. Information on the creditor friendliness of foreclosure law captures the ability of a creditor to foreclose without a judge's order in 1957 and comes from a legal history of the subject.[76] About 60 percent of the observations in the regressions are of states with pro-creditor foreclosure law.

Pro-creditor foreclosure is positively associated with use of Chapter XIII, but only in the late 1960s and 1970s, not in the 1950s and early 1960s. The result is driven by the inclusion of Alabama and Tennessee in the regressions. Because pro-creditor garnishment law interacts with the growth of consumer credit to drive up personal bankruptcy rates, we expect pro-creditor foreclosure law to interact with the growth of mortgage credit to drive up the use of Chapter XIII. It does not.

Regression Analysis of Impact of Growth in Consumer Credit

The final section of chapter 4 argues that return to normalcy in credit markets after World War II resulted in a return to "normal" increases in personal bankruptcy rates. Chapter 4 emphasizes the role of innovations in retail credit, especially the revolving credit accounts that led, eventually, to general-use credit cards.

The regression analysis for chapter 4 uses specifications similar to those in chapters 2 and 3. The analysis is more limited than the analysis in other chapters because data for both independent and dependent variables are incomplete. First, as explained in the appendix to chapter 1, the number of personal bankruptcies by district was not published for 1948–59. In graphs showing long-run trends, we estimate them by linear interpolation. To avoid using many constructed observations in the regression analysis, we model the *change* in the personal bankruptcy rate between 1946–60 and 1960–70 in specification (1) of table 4A.2. This gives us 100 observations. The average change in the bankruptcy rate is about 2.6 per 10,000 people (standard deviation about 9.6).

However, specification (1) omits some important but unavailable data on bank-issued consumer credit. As noted in discussion of the regressions in table 4A.1, there is a decade-long gap in statistics on bank credit at the state level. Specification (2) therefore models the change in the personal bankruptcy rate between 1946 and 1970. There are just 49 observations. The change in the bankruptcy rate averages about 9.2 (standard deviation about 6.5).

We include *Files* and *InDebt*, defined in differences, and we interact measures/proxies of the amount of credit extended with state garnishment laws to measure their influence on the personal bankruptcy rate. Variables representing the likelihood of default are not included; during this period, long-run differences in these variables are not meaningfully large.

ELEMENTS OF *FILES*

We control for the creditor friendliness of garnishment by including an indicator of whether wage exemptions were at or below 75 percent, which is the exemption level that become the federal minimum after a 1968 law. (See chapter 5.) Half of states had pro-creditor garnishment law. The wage exemption data used here are from annual summaries of collection laws compiled by the National Association of Credit Management.[77]

TABLE 4A.2. **Determinants of changes in personal bankruptcy between 1946, 1960, and 1970**

	1946, 1960, 1970	1946, 1970
	(1)	(2)
Pro-creditor garnishment	2.414*	10.286*
	(1.249)	(5.421)
Difference in retail est./1,000 pop.	0.038	2.519
	(0.455)	(2.131)
Pro-creditor* difference in retail est.	0.332	2.686
	(0.566)	(2.447)
Difference in mortgage lending per capita (1,000s)		1.926
		(6.883)
Pro-creditor* diff. in mortgage lending		-0.522
		(7.953)
Difference in consumer credit per capita (100s)		-3.069
		(6.353)
Pro-creditor* diff. in consumer credit		-3.351
		(8.324)
Observations	100	49
R-squared	0.106	0.415

The growth in personal bankruptcy after World War II is weakly but positively correlated with the number of retail outlets per capita, and the effect is stronger in states with pro-creditor garnishment. There were changes in exemptions in garnishment during this period. Notes: * p<0.10, ** p<0.05, *** p<0.01. Standard errors are in parentheses and clustered at the state level. Constant included in both specifications. *Source*: See appendix to chapter 4.

ELEMENTS OF *INDEBT*

To the best of our knowledge annual, state-level data on retail credit extended or outstanding are not available. To proxy the supply of retail credit, we use the number of retail establishments per 1,000 people in the state. The number of retail establishments comes from a compilation of census and other data.[78] The source of population data is described in the appendix to chapter 1. Because of the rise of department stores after World War II, the average number of retail establishments per 1,000 people declined by about 3.7 (standard deviation about 1.6).

The supply of credit to consumers by banks is measured by residential (1–4 family) mortgage lending by banks per capita and bank consumer loans per capita.[79] Mortgage credit per capita increased by $270 between 1946 and 1970 (standard deviation about $250). Consumer credit increased by $380 (standard deviation $220). The supply of credit is greater in cities (compared to rural areas). For this period, the percentage of the population that lives in urban areas is from census data, and so it is interpolated for 1946.[80] The share of the population living in urban areas increased by about 13 percentage points (standard deviation about 8). Because there were more department stores in urban areas than in rural areas, there is correlation between retail establishments per capita and this variable, which reduces the standard errors.

RESULTS

Because of the limited number of observations, the explanatory power of the regressions in table 4A.2 is low in comparison to the results presented in the appendices to the other chapters. The coefficient on procreditor garnishment law is the only statistically significant coefficient. The coefficients on the elements of *InDebt* are not precisely estimated. However, the overall pattern is consistent with the patterns for other periods. From 1945–78, the best predictor of the change in the bankruptcy rate at the state level is whether the state has pro-creditor garnishment. Increases in the supply of retail credit pushed up the bankruptcy rate, especially in states with pro-creditor garnishment. The text reports full marginal effects from specification (2) of table 4A.2. The coefficients on the difference in bank credit, as well as the coefficients on the interactions between pro-creditor garnishment law and bank credit, have standard errors that are larger than the point estimates.

CHAPTER FIVE

The Renegotiation of the Relationship between Consumers and Their Creditors

William Henry Nayers was earning $1,500 a year working as a bus driver for the Town of Scarborough, Maine, in the spring of 1963 when Days Jewelry Store in Portland garnished his pay in an effort to recover the $57 he owed from a purchase made the previous June. To stop the garnishment, Nayers filed for personal bankruptcy protection under Chapter XIII on May 13, 1963.[1] He reported about $1,700 in debts. Nayers paid $15 per week on his repayment plan until he paid $1,700. However, after fees, his creditors got only $991. After three years of payments, Nayers filed a new bankruptcy petition, this time under Chapter VII. At the end of 1967, the court discharged Nayers's remaining debts.

Nationally, the personal bankruptcy rate was about ten times higher in 1960 than it had been in 1950. In the 1960s, two groups sought change. The first group believed that unscrupulous creditors were taking advantage of a combination of poor workers and archaic collection laws to drive people like Nayers into a sort of debt peonage. The group sought reform of the laws governing consumer credit and collection. The second group believed that the bankruptcy law itself was the problem: Access to an easy discharge promoted excessive indebtedness. They sought bankruptcy reform. Both movements bore fruit, but not at the same time.

Changes to collection laws came first. In 1968, Congress enacted the Consumer Credit Protection Act (CCPA), which promoted "Truth in Lending" and placed restrictions on garnishment. In 1969, the Supreme

Court ruled in *Sniadach v. Family Finance Corporation* that prejudgment garnishment (that is, garnishment without a judge's order) violated the Fourteenth Amendment's due process clause. Thus, by 1970, Congress and the Supreme Court had combined to restrict the use of garnishment throughout the US.

Reform of bankruptcy law moved more slowly. As discussed in chapter 4, people were already raising concerns about increasing bankruptcy rates in the 1950s. Congress did not pass legislation to create a commission to study bankruptcy until 1968. The commission was not established until 1970, and it did not present a report until 1973. It took another five years to enact the Bankruptcy Reform Act of 1978.

The timing is crucial to how the story ends. Because the CCPA and the decision in *Sniadach* reduced creditors' ability to garnish easily, creditors were less likely to pursue garnishment. Because creditors were less likely to garnish, debtors were less likely to file for bankruptcy protection. By the time the Commission on the Bankruptcy Laws of the United States presented its report in 1973, the bankruptcy rate was no longer regarded as a problem. None of the recommendations made by the commission was directed at reducing the bankruptcy rate. Instead, its recommendations focused on improving administration, increasing uniformity throughout the US, and encouraging debtors to choose repayment plans over liquidation. Ultimately, the effort to reform bankruptcy law, which began to address concerns about the rapid rise in consumer bankruptcy, culminated in the enactment of a law that was widely regarded as friendly to debtors.

Protecting Consumers from Creditors

In the late 1950s and early 1960s, consumer advocates voiced new concerns about the combination of easy credit and unrestricted garnishment of wages. They argued that misleading advertisements for easy credit lured in low-income workers, especially black workers. Easy garnishment then enabled creditors to force repayment, again especially from black workers. They argued that the system of consumer credit led to both high rates of bankruptcy and to civil unrest.

The consumer advocates of the 1960s took up themes emphasized by past reformers. Like the Russell Sage Foundation earlier in the century, they portrayed creditors as predators of desperate and unsophisticated borrowers. As discussed in chapter 2, the Russell Sage Foundation focused on abuses by small loan agencies, or "loan sharks." In the 1950s and 1960s, reformers focused on the retailers who sold on credit and then relied on garnishment to collect. The *Washington Post*, for instance, reported that there were 47,877 wage garnishments in the District of Columbia in 1957, when the population of the city was about 763,000.[2] The *Post* attributed the large number of garnishments in D.C. to the combination of an "antique law" and merchants who sold on easy credit. It noted that a large share of the garnishments came from a few stores. In fact, it traced 3,882 garnishments to Hollywood Credit Clothing.[3] The District of Columbia was not unique. In 1968, one judge in Washington State labeled garnishment "a remedy run amuck."[4] A study in the *Washington Law Review* found that Seattle district justice courts processed more than 15,000 garnishments in 1966.[5]

Maine, where Nayers lived, was also a high-garnishment state. He filed his bankruptcy petition after Days Jewelry Store opened garnishment proceedings against him. Days was a multistore chain in Maine that sold radios, personal electronics, and other conveniences. Their regular ads in the *Portland Press Herald* emphasized their easy-to-use charge accounts, promising, "Easy terms" and "Never an added charge for credit."[6]

Advocates for reform argued that unrestricted garnishment gave retailers like Days Jewelry a reason to offer easy credit. For instance, George Ranney, vice president of Inland Steel, suggested that the ability to garnish wages easily "may well lead to the extension of credit to wage earners in situations where credit more reasonably might be withheld."[7] Moreover, Clive W. Bare, a bankruptcy referee in the Eastern District of Tennessee, stated that "too many loans are being made not on the basis of the debtor's character, integrity, or ability to pay, but solely because the lender or creditor knows that if debtors do not pay, their wages can be attached."[8] Easy garnishment and easy credit reinforced each other.

As discussed in previous chapters, easy garnishment caused higher bankruptcy rates when credit was expanding. Although the connection between garnishment and bankruptcy was recognized earlier in the century, new and systematic studies made it salient to policymakers in the 1960s.[9] The studies showed that indebted workers were not just worried about losing some of their wages; they worried that they might lose *all* of their wages. They worried that they might be fired if a creditor initiated garnishment proceedings. Many employers did not want to deal with the inconvenience and expense of satisfying demands to garnish an employee's wages.[10] Some employers made it a policy to fire an employee who had wages garnished more than a certain number of times.[11]

Critics of garnishment noted a relationship between race, easy credit, and unrestricted garnishment. In its report on garnishment in the District of Columbia, the *Washington Post* suggested that "nine out of ten wage attachments are against poor Negroes earning roughly $30 to $60 a week."[12] More formal studies tended to come to the same conclusion: Blacks were overrepresented in both garnishment and bankruptcy. Retailers in New York attracted customers from low-income communities with misleading offers of easy credit; thus, blacks and Hispanics were likely to have higher levels of debt at any given level of income.[13] In four Wisconsin cities, blacks were overrepresented among both garnishments and bankruptcies.[14] Surveys of people who had filed for bankruptcy showed that blacks were overrepresented in five of six districts.[15]

While filing for bankruptcy was one way that an individual consumer could respond to easy credit and easy garnishment, reformers argued that riots were the collective response. Otto Kerner, who successfully campaigned for governor of Illinois in 1960–61 on the issue of credit reform, also chaired the commission that President Lyndon Johnson established to investigate the series of riots that took place in the US during the 1960s. The *Report of the National Advisory Commission on Civil Disorders* cited credit and collection methods as contributing factors causing the riots.[16]

The Consumer Credit Protection Act

Kerner's 1960 platform for governor emphasized restricting garnishment and wage assignment.[17] Illinois was not alone. At least twenty states changed their garnishment laws between 1954 and 1964, most of them increasing the amount of wages that were exempt from collection.[18] The most important change, however, was the shift from state to federal regulation of the market for consumer credit.

In 1960, Senator Paul Douglas (D-IL) introduced a "Consumer Credit Labeling bill."[19] As the name of the bill implied, Senator Douglas believed that deceptive advertising was misleading consumers. He proposed that businesses be required to disclose total finance charges and simple annual interest. Consumers would then be able to shop and compare terms and rates. Thus, they could avoid being saddled with higher payments than they had anticipated. Douglas's bill evolved into a broader "Truth in Lending bill," but its provisions were not passed until 1967, a year after Douglas left the Senate.

Senator William Proxmire (D-WI) sponsored the 1967 bill. The House had its own bill on truth in lending, along with several alternatives. Representative Leonor K. Sullivan (D-MO) chair of the Subcommittee on Consumer Affairs of the House Committee on Banking and Currency, introduced the main alternative. The Sullivan bill, which was also called the "Consumer Credit Protection bill," included the provisions on truth in lending. It also established a Consumer Finance Commission, gave greater responsibility to the Federal Reserve to regulate lending to consumers, and prohibited entirely the garnishment of wages.

Sullivan's subcommittee held extensive hearings on her bill. President Johnson's special assistant for consumer affairs, Betty Furness, voiced the president's support for truth in lending but argued that the additional provisions in the Sullivan bill, including its prohibition of garnishment, needed further study. Furness suggested that, while garnishment might be used unfairly against some low-income individuals, it might be an appropriate remedy for those with higher incomes.[20] Proponents of prohibiting garnishment, like Congressman Frank Annunzio (D-IL) countered that "many merchants and lenders now use garnishment as a sword, rather than a shield, and in fact, they extend credit or money to poor credit risks simply because the person is employed and subject to garnishment."[21] Annunzio also argued, vehemently, that garnishment allowed creditors to pass on the costs of collection to all citizens by using the court. He noted that a few states already prohibited garnishment, and the effect was positive. For example, Texas and North Carolina did not have garnishment and had low rates of bankruptcy.

Bankruptcy referees testifying at the hearings concurred. Bare testified that "between 60 and 70 percent of bankruptcy filings are the direct result of wage garnishments."[22] Estes Snedecor, from Portland, Oregon, declared, "The one overriding cause precipitating consumer bankruptcies is the garnishment or threat of garnishment of wages coupled with an unrealistic wage exemption."[23] Sullivan summed it up: "What we know from our study of this problem is that, in a vast number of cases, the debt is a fraudulent one, saddled on a poor ignorant person who is trapped in an easy credit nightmare, in which he is charged double for something he could not pay for even if the proper price was called for, and then hounded into giving up his pound of flesh, and being fired besides."[24]

The concerns raised by the earlier Kerner Commission on race riots also appeared in the hearings on the CCPA. Sargent Shriver, director of the Office of Economic Opportunity, suggested that "the system of consumer credit to which this bill addresses itself has been a major contributor to the frustrations and despair which finally led to the tragic upheavals which have recently rocked Newark, Detroit, and so many other cities."[25] Shriver argued that reform of the market for consumer credit was not just a remedy for the high rates of bankruptcy, but it was also essential to promote social justice and prevent civil unrest.

The Consumer Credit Protection Act of 1968 ultimately resembled the Sullivan bill much more than the bills put forward by Douglas and Proxmire. It contained four sections. The first section covered truth in lending. The second section aimed to undermine loan sharks and their connections to organized crime. The third section contained the provisions on garnishment. It did not prohibit garnishment, but it created a national minimum for wage exemptions. The debtor was entitled to keep the greater of either 75 percent of disposable income or thirty times the minimum wage per week. This section also prohibited the termination of employment because of a single garnishment. The fourth section of the law established a Consumer Finance Commission that would recommend reforms in the future.

The law did not require states to pass enabling legislation to change their garnishment laws. Instead, it prohibited any court official (federal, state, or local) from engaging in an activity that was in violation of the law. In other words, court officials were supposed to ensure that garnishment proceedings left the wage earner with at least 75 percent of disposable income or thirty times the minimum wage. The secretary of labor was given jurisdiction to enforce the law.

Considerable evidence suggests that the law was effective. First, although it was not required, most of the states that had less generous exemptions than the law required did raise exemptions to the federal minimum.[26] Second, the secretary of labor actively enforced the law. The secretary sued employers who terminated employees because of garnishment,[27] and he sought injunctions against court officials who failed to comply with the wage exemptions in the law.[28] In one case, a judge in

Hamilton, Ohio, had sent letters to local businesses telling them that he planned to follow Ohio law rather than federal law; he was stopped.[29]

The court cases brought to enforce the CCPA resulted in rulings that defined the limits of the law. The exemption applied only to unpaid wages still in the possession of the employer; it did not apply to wages once they had been deposited in a financial institution.[30] Furthermore, the exemption did not apply to wage assignments, in which the debtor agreed to have the employer withhold a portion of his or her wages and make payments to the creditor directly.[31] Wage assignments would not be restricted until the 1980s.

Sniadach v. Family Finance Corporation

Not all of the restrictions on garnishment that were recommended during congressional hearings made it into the CCPA. One of the recommendations that was left out was a prohibition on prejudgment garnishment. In prejudgment garnishment, the creditor can obtain wages before the debtor has a chance to be heard in court, and, possibly, even before the debtor knows about the creditor's claim. In the early 1960s, seventeen states and the District of Columbia allowed prejudgment garnishment.[32] The *Sniadach* case challenged its constitutionality.

Sniadach began when the Family Finance Corporation of Bay View, Wisconsin, instituted a garnishment action against Christine Sniadach, an assembly line worker at the Miller Harris Instrument Company. At the time the garnishment suit was filed, Family Finance asked the clerk of the Wisconsin court to issue a summons, which it immediately served on the debtor's employer. Miller Harris informed Family Finance that they had in their possession $63.18 that was owed to Sniadach. They said they would freeze half and set aside the other half for her. Under Wisconsin law, the lawyers for Family Finance had ten days to serve the original complaint and summons on Sniadach, after which she would have to go to court and win in order to receive any of her frozen wages. Sniadach's lawyers, who were from the NAACP Legal Defense Fund, argued that freezing wages before a court had ruled on the complaint was unconstitutional. It violated Sniadach's right to due process.

At around the same time that the CCPA went into effect, the Supreme Court ruled in favor of Sniadach. Writing for the majority, Justice William O. Douglas detailed the numerous hardships that can befall workers if prejudgment garnishment is allowed. Notwithstanding his claim that "[w]e do not sit as a super-legislative body,"[33] Justice Douglas cited extensively the testimony given at the hearings before the House Subcommittee on Consumer Affairs on the CCPA.

Like the CCPA, the *Sniadach* decision reflected a shift from the state to the federal level in the evolution of laws governing credit markets. Before the 1960s, most action in debt collection law, including garnishment and wage assignment laws, took place in state legislatures and courts.[34] Each state passed its own legislation, which its own courts interpreted. A wage assignment law that was deemed to violate due process in one state could be upheld in another. But in the 1960s, federal action reduced the variation in collection laws by moving the states that had few restrictions on garnishment closer to the states that placed greater restrictions on it.

The CCPA and Bankruptcy Rates

In the 1960s, the states that already restricted garnishment had an average of about 6 bankruptcies annually for every 10,000 people, while the states that had easy garnishment and were eventually affected by the changes to federal law had about 11 bankruptcies per 10,000 people per year. In the 1970s, the gap closed. Bankruptcy rose slightly in states where garnishment had long been restricted, and it fell slightly in states where the restrictions were new.

Figure 5.1 shows how state bankruptcy rates diverged before the CCPA and converged after it went into effect. As discussed in chapter 4, beginning right after World War II, the bankruptcy rate increased more quickly in the states with low wage exemptions in garnishment (the solid line) than in states with more generous exemptions (the dashed line). In 1967, bankruptcy rates peaked at an average of 13 per 10,000 people in low-exemption states. Rates averaged just over 7 per 10,000 people in high-exemption states. The vertical line at 1971 in figure 5.1 indicates the date that the CCPA went into effect. The fact that bankruptcy rates peaked before 1971 suggests that the bankruptcy rate may also have been affected by earlier Great Society legislation. We return to those laws in the next section.

We use regression analysis to measure the extent to which the CCPA was responsible for the decline in bankruptcy rates in the states that its restrictions affected. We include data from 1960 to 1979 in the

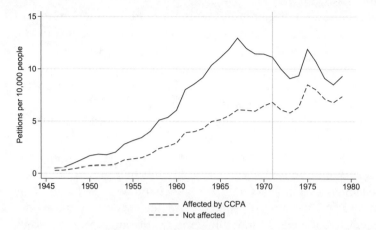

FIG. 5.1. In the 1950s and 1960s, bankruptcy rates rose faster in states where wage exemptions in garnishment were low (solid line). Rates began falling in low exemption states before the CCPA required that at least 75 percent of wages be exempt from garnishment beginning in 1971, indicated by the vertical line. After 1971, convergence between states accelerated. Excludes Alabama, which increased exemptions to 75 percent prior to passage of the CCPA. *Source*: See appendix to chapter 5.

regressions. As in chapters 2 and 3, in addition to accounting for changes in wage exemptions in garnishment, we account for other social and economic variables that affect the rate of indebtedness, the rate of default, and the choice to use the bankruptcy law. The regression results suggest that the CCPA had a large causal impact on bankruptcy rates. In states that had to increase their wage exemptions, a one percentage point increase in the wage exemption decreased the bankruptcy rate by 0.043 per 10,000 people. The regression coefficient seems small, but it translates into a large impact on the bankruptcy rate in the typical state that was affected by the CCPA. Exemptions rose an average of 28 percentage points in affected states, so the average increase in exemptions alone predicts a decline in the bankruptcy rate of 1.2 filings per 10,000 people—at a time when the filing rate in these states was about 13 per 10,000 people. That is, the garnishment provisions of the CCPA reduced filing rates in affected states by almost 10 percent. (See the appendix to chapter 5 for a description of the social and economic determinants of indebtedness and default that we include for this period. Table 5A.1 shows the regression results.)

Though the *Sniadach* decision was important from a legal perspective, regression analysis cannot cleanly separate its impact on the bankruptcy rate from the impact of the CCPA's garnishment provisions. That is because *Sniadach* was decided around the same time that the CCPA went into effect, and it affected several of the same states as the CCPA.

There is no evidence that the truth-in-lending provisions of the CCPA had any impact on markets for consumer credit.[35] The effects can be attributed entirely to the garnishment provisions.

Had the CCPA been in effect in 1960, peak bankruptcy in 1966 would have been lower and the increase in bankruptcy filings nationally would have been less dramatic. For instance, in the 1960s, Tennessee had the lowest wage exemption and the highest bankruptcy rate among the states that were affected by the CCPA (equivalently, the pro-creditor, low-exemption states). If Tennessee had been required to raise its effective rate of wage exemptions in garnishment from 25 to 75 percent before 1960, the bankruptcy rate in Tennessee may have been about 19 per 10,000, instead of 21. After accounting for the uncertainty surrounding the estimate of the effect of wage exemptions on bankruptcy, we can conclude that there probably would have been between 460 and 1,190 fewer petitions for bankruptcy annually in Tennessee. In Michigan, the CCPA required exemptions to increase by about 40 percentage points. Had the higher wage exemption been in effect in Michigan throughout the 1960s, the average bankruptcy rate there may have been 5.5 per 10,000 instead of 7.25, which translates to about 800 to 2,100 fewer filings each year. As a final example, if California had been required to allow wage exemptions of 75 percent rather than 50 percent, the bankruptcy rate may have been 14.5 instead of 15.6 per 10,000. This translates into a reduction in filings of as many as 2,833 annually because of California's large population. Adding up across the more than twenty states that were affected by the CCPA, if a 75 percent wage exemption had been the norm in every state during the 1960s, between 5,000 and 12,700 filings might have been averted *each year.* The gap between total filings in affected states and unaffected states would have been considerably smaller.

Great Society Programs and Bankruptcy

The CCPA is not often listed as a Great Society program, perhaps because it was not passed until the end of the Johnson presidency, and it was not implemented until after President Richard Nixon took office. However, President Johnson considered it important.[36] Like other Great

Society programs,[37] it addressed matters of both social and racial justice, and it transferred power from the state to the federal level. Former Senator Paul H. Douglas, who had introduced the original Truth-in-Lending bill, believed that the measure passed when it did because it provided an opportunity to continue the program of the Great Society without adding to the federal budget, which had become more of a concern due to the expansion of the war in Vietnam.[38]

Return to figure 5.1. Bankruptcy rates began to fall in low-exemption, high-bankruptcy-rate states soon after the implementation of President Johnson's major initiatives. Is it possible that the Great Society programs implemented in 1965–66 are responsible for the decline in bankruptcy from 1967 until the CCPA took effect?

Most of the early and large Great Society programs could not have caused a short-run decline in bankruptcy. They aimed to solve long-term problems in education, training, and housing. Even income generated through Great Society expenditures is unlikely to have dampened bankruptcy rates because expenditures made under the Economic Opportunity Act went to places with the lowest incomes.[39] Despite the high rates of bankruptcy in some states in the Deep South (such as Alabama), and despite reports of overrepresentation of blacks in bankruptcy, our regression analysis shows that during the 1960s and 1970s, bankruptcy was negatively but weakly correlated with state income and with the share of blacks in the state population.

Medicare and Medicaid, however, were two Great Society programs with the potential to reduce bankruptcy by reducing default. Medicaid was passed in March 1965, and Medicare was passed six months later. Medicare was implemented quickly. On July 1, 1966, the nearly 20 million Americans who were age sixty-five or older were immediately eligible. Almost all were enrolled on this date.[40] Within a year, bankruptcy began to decline in states with high bankruptcy rates. Because there was so little variation in enrollment rates between states, and because the decisions along the path to bankruptcy can play out over many months, the decline cannot be definitively attributed to Medicare. But what happened later is instructive. As eligibility requirements for Medicare were phased in, the share of the elderly population that was enrolled fell. Each one percentage point decrease in enrollment in a state is associated with an increase in the bankruptcy rate of 0.02 to 0.03 per 10,000.

In samples of bankruptcy case files from Maryland and Maine, people who filed after 1966 and who were eligible for both Medicare and Medicaid were far less likely to owe any medical debt than similar consumers who filed before the programs were in place. Historically, the elderly have been a small share of the bankrupt,[41] so Medicare's effect on the elderly alone cannot explain the overall decline in bankruptcy seen in figure 5.1. Instead, Medicare is more likely to have reduced bankruptcy by reducing the financial strain on younger people caring for aging parents. In the Maryland and Maine samples, people under sixty-five who filed in the years right after Medicare implementation were 8 percent less likely to owe medical debt than those who filed in the years right before.[42]

Medicaid affected bankruptcy differently. In states with more generous Medicaid eligibility, bankruptcy rates were slightly higher even after controlling for racial demographics. In Maryland and Maine, low-income filers under age sixty-five were 2 percent more likely to owe some medical debt than their higher-income counterparts after the implementation of Medicaid. Medicaid likely increased access to medical care, medical expenditures, and medical bankruptcy among a group already at high risk of default. Recent Medicaid expansions had similar effects.[43]

Bankruptcy Reform

Around the same time that Congress was voting on the CCPA in 1968, it also began considering the first bills to establish a commission to make recommendations for bankruptcy reform. The primary impetus for reform was the increase in bankruptcy rates following World War II. A secondary problem, exacerbated by the sheer volume of cases, was that the machinery of the 1898 act and its many amendments was outdated. One referee called it "a maze of confusion, complexity, frustration, injustice and inequality."[44] An influential Brookings Institution report concluded: "The mess is too bad to tinker with. We need a new bankruptcy act, a new organizational structure, a new personnel system, a new method of financing, and new records and procedures."[45] As if to demonstrate how intractable the problem would prove to be, Congress did not actually establish the Commission on the Bankruptcy Laws of the US until July 24, 1970.[46] The delay was not caused by disagreement over the need for reform. It was caused by a dispute over the membership of federal judges and bankruptcy referees on the commission.

Recall from chapter 2 that, under the 1898 act, federal district court judges appointed bankruptcy referees to manage most aspects of cases.

Debtors and creditors could appeal the referee's decision to the federal court. The decisions of referees were never final and their status was low. Yet the fees and expenses they earned could be large. In 1916, the attorney general wrote with astonishment that in the previous year one referee earned more than $15,000—more than the salary of the chief justice.[47] In 1940, the Administrative Office of the US Courts (AO) began to recommend that Congress make referees salaried court employees,[48] and Congress complied in 1946.[49] After the referees moved into the courts, the AO declared the system a success: "The dignity and prestige of the referees are enhanced."[50] Appointing referees remained a prime patronage opportunity for federal judges, and costs were contained— for a while.

Under the Referee Salary Act, Congress allowed the Judicial Conference to recommend the number of referees to be appointed,[51] as well as their salaries. Congress was responsible for appropriating funds. As filings rose after World War II, Congress failed to appropriate more funds for referees, preferring to increase the number of clerks to the referees instead.[52] On average, courts had a backlog of 436 cases in 1950, up from 200 in 1947. By 1960, the typical court's backlog exceeded 1,000 cases. At the end of 1967, the year that filings peaked, the average backlog was 2,051 cases.[53]

Referees and the Judicial Conference believed that, beyond the lack of appropriations, the backlog could be reduced by making the referee a more judge-like figure (reducing appeals to the district court judge) and by simplifying and clarifying rules and administrative procedures. Tweaking administrative procedures was by far the easier of the two. In 1963, the Judicial Conference promulgated guidelines for the administration of Chapter XIII cases.[54] In 1964, it held its first seminar for new referees.[55] In 1965, Congress authorized the Supreme Court to make rules for bankruptcy practice and procedure,[56] but in 1968, the rules were still being formulated, and the status of referees was still unchanged.

Against this backdrop, the Senate called for three bankruptcy referees but no federal judges to serve on a commission to study bankruptcy reform. The House called for a commission that would include three people appointed by the president and two people appointed by the chief justice of the Supreme Court. The House version allowed bankruptcy referees to serve, but it did not require any of the appointees to be referees. The House version eventually prevailed, but neither the president nor Chief Justice Warren Burger appointed a referee.

In 1971, the commission began to hold hearings, and it filed its report on July 30, 1973. Again, there was delay. The delay was not caused by an extended partisan debate on the floor, as had been the case with the 1898 act. As was the case in the 1930s, all the drama in the 1970s stayed in committee hearings and closed-door meetings.[57] From 1973 to 1978, there were only six roll call votes on bankruptcy in the House of Representatives. There was only one in the Senate. None involved any of the three major points of contention, discussed below.[58]

The first point of contention reprised the dispute over the membership of the commission: How powerful would bankruptcy judges be? Although the Supreme Court did not have the power to change their official status, it used the term "bankruptcy judge" instead of "bankruptcy referee" in 1973 when it issued its first Bankruptcy Rules. The commission recommended that bankruptcy judges remain adjuncts to the court with some expanded authority. The referees put forward their own bill lobbying for full Article III appointments and powers.[59] The House—ironically, since they had sided with the judges on commission membership—sided with the referees. The Senate and Chief Justice Burger sided with the commission. The compromise signed into law in 1978 gave bankruptcy judges many powers of an Article III judge, but not Article III status or lifetime appointment.[60]

The second point of contention was over how best to improve day-to-day administration. The commission noted the lack of uniformity between states and even between districts within a state. It noted the extreme differences in the use of Chapter XIII, described in chapter 4. It was troubled by differences in the extent to which debtors were allowed to waive their exemptions and to make "reaffirmation" agreements with creditors. In a reaffirmation agreement, the debtor agrees to repay debt that would be dischargeable, often with the expectation that the creditor would not cut off future credit. Like the Thacher Report, the commission wanted to go beyond establishing uniform rules for local courts. The commission recommended that Congress establish an administrative agency to handle most of the business of bankruptcy, including personal bankruptcy.[61] Bankruptcy judges would be freed from cumbersome administrative burdens and would deal with actual legal conflicts that arose in the course of bankruptcy proceedings. Instead of drawing international comparisons as the Thacher Report did, the commission compared the proposed system to the way in which the administration of federal taxation was divided between the Internal Revenue Service and the tax court. It argued that a comprehensive administrative agency would lower costs, increase the amount realized from the sale of assets, and provide more uniform treatment of debtors. The House agreed; the referees and the Senate did not. The compromise established a limited pilot of the US Trustee System as part of the Department of Justice. In 1986, the Trustee System was extended to all districts except ones in Alabama and North Carolina.

The third and final point of contention was about exemptions. The commission recommended uniform federal exemptions. The referees suggested a minimum exemption, along the lines of the minimum wage exemption in garnishment under the CCPA. The House sided with the referees, though details of the two proposals differed.[62] The Senate wanted to keep the right to determine exemptions in the states. The compromise established federal exemptions that were higher than exemptions in many states, but it allowed states to opt out and require their citizens to use the lower state exemptions.

Establishing federal exemptions was friendly to debtors in states with low exemptions, at least until those states opted out.[63] In fact, almost all of the changes to personal bankruptcy increased the net benefit of filing, though the Bankruptcy Reform Act of 1978 was not, in the end, as debtor friendly as the commission had wanted.[64] The most well-known change is that the 1978 Bankruptcy Act, known as the "Code," allowed spouses to file on a single "joint" petition. Previously, if both spouses filed, each was to file a petition and pay the filing fee.[65] Other pro-debtor changes in the Code included:

- Strengthening a debtor's ability to get and enforce the discharge by making the discharge self-executing, giving the bankruptcy court jurisdiction over whether a debt is dischargeable, and expanding the debts that could be discharged to include judgments in tort cases.[66]
- Providing increased protection of exemptions. For instance, it prohibited unsecured creditors from obtaining waivers of exemptions in the small print of loan agreements.[67]
- Requiring approval of the court for reaffirmation agreements.[68] This reduced the incentive of creditors to bully debtors into waiving discharge, while still retaining debtors' option to offer to reaffirm a debt in exchange for future credit.
- Prohibiting government agencies and private companies from discriminating

against a debtor who had filed for bankruptcy or had received a discharge for debts owed to it.[69]

Aside from these changes, personal bankruptcy in 1980 was not terribly different from personal bankruptcy in 1960. Households still had two options: liquidation and discharge or a repayment plan.[70] The names of the options were changed from Roman to Arabic numerals. Chapter VII became Chapter 7 and Chapter XIII became Chapter 13. Creditors' main wins were in codifying the nondischargeability of student loans and in making Chapter 13 more attractive. Chapter 6 discusses them.

By the time Congress turned its attention from the Great Society programs and from the protection of consumers in credit markets to rewriting bankruptcy law, the midcentury "bankruptcy crisis" had passed. The bankruptcy rate peaked in 1967 and was relatively stable for the next six years. The commission established to reform bankruptcy law did not find "any reason to believe that the number of such petitions is too high or ought to be reduced."[71] It lauded the work of the National Commission on Consumer Finance, which had persuaded Congress to restrict garnishment. We have confirmed the intuition of the commission: The CCPA lowered the rate of bankruptcy in many states, thereby lowering the national bankruptcy rate. Without strong opposition from creditors,[72] Congress passed a pro-debtor Bankruptcy Reform Act in 1978.

Appendix to Chapter 5

Chapter 5 argues that changes in federal law and court decisions that constrained states' autonomy by requiring minimum protections for debtors in collections resolved the post–World War II bankruptcy "crisis" by keeping a lid on the bankruptcy rate in the highest-rate states. By the time Congress considered the legislation that became the Bankruptcy Reform Act of 1978, the bankruptcy rate was no longer considered a problem, and Congress passed a set of pro-debtor reforms.

Regression Analysis of the Impact of the CCPA

The regression analysis for chapter 5 uses specifications similar to those in chapters 2 and 3. The dependent variable is the bankruptcy rate in state s and year t. We include data from 1960 to 1979 in the regressions. There are 950 state-years. We model the bankruptcy rate as a function of the determinants and/or proxies of its three component rates, which we divide into three vectors: *Files*, *InDefault*, and *InDebt*. (See the general description of regression methods and data on bankruptcy rates in the appendix to chapter 1.)

ELEMENTS OF *FILES*

The focus in chapter 5 is on the impact of the CCPA, which required courts to exempt at least 75 percent of wages in garnishment, on state bankruptcy rates. Some states already had high wage exemptions in garnishment and were unaffected by the CCPA. States that had exemptions lower than 75 percent of wages were affected by the law differentially. That is, the CCPA resulted in large increases in exemptions in some states, but only small increases in exemptions in other states.

We determine wage exemptions in garnishment before the CCPA by comparing reports for 1967,[73] studies of the effect of the CCPA,[74] studies prepared for Congress,[75] and summaries of collection laws compiled by the collections industry.[76] We use this information to construct the related variables indicating whether a state was affected by the CCPA and the required increase in the wage exemption. The following list summarizes our reconciliation for states for which the sources disagreed. An asterisk (*) indicates that we could not resolve disagreements between the sources, but our reading of them suggests that the wage exemption in the state was not much lower than the 75 percent the CCPA required. For these states, we code the required increase in exemptions as zero.

- CT: Not affected
- DE: Affected*
- MN: Affected
- NH: Affected*
- NJ: Not affected
- OH: Affected*
- AR: Affected*
- KS: Not affected

The average wage exemption in 1967 in states that already had high exemptions, and so were not affected by the CCPA, was about 84 percent of wages (standard deviation about 17). In states with low exemptions, it was about 50 percent of wages (standard deviation about 14). As noted in the text and shown in figure 5.1, the bankruptcy rate rose slightly in states that did not have to increase exemptions because of the CCPA. Before the CCPA, the bankruptcy rate in high exemption states was about 7 per 10,000 people (standard deviation about 7). After the CCPA, it was about 8 (standard deviation about 5). In contrast, before the CCPA, the bankruptcy rate in low exemption states was about 12 per 10,000 people (standard deviation about 7). After the CCPA, the bankruptcy rate in these states fell to about 10 (standard deviation about 5) as the effective exemption rose to the 75 percent minimum.

The vector *Files* also contains the value of the property exemptions in effect in each state in 1967 adjusted for inflation. We take the size of the homestead and personal property exemptions in collections in 1967 from a Brookings Institution study of bankruptcy.[77] We adjust to 1984 dollars. For states with unlimited homestead exemptions, we top-code this variable at $99,999. (The highest limited exemption is $12,500.) For states with personal property exemptions limited to only specific listed items (with no dollar values given), the personal property exemption is set equal to $100 (the smallest dollar-denominated exemption level).

In the years before the CCPA, the real value of the homestead exemption in states with high wage exemptions was about $45,800 (standard deviation about $98,000). In the years between passage of the CCPA and enactment of the Code, it was about $32,000 (standard deviation about $69,000). Before the CCPA, the homestead exemption in states with low wage exemptions was about $32,000 (standard deviation about $75,500). Between the CCPA and the Code, it was about $22,000 (standard deviation about $53,000).

Before the CCPA, the personal property exemption in states with low wage exemptions was about $2,300 (standard deviation about $3,200). Between the CCPA and the Code, it was about $1,600 (standard deviation about $2,200). In the years before the CCPA, the real value of the personal property exemption in states with high wage exemptions was about $3,000 (standard deviation about $2,500). In the years between passage of the CCPA and enactment of the Code, it was about $2,000 (standard deviation about $2,000).

ELEMENTS OF *INDEFAULT*

We include the number of months of recession during a fiscal year using the National Bureau of Economic Research business cycle dates.[78]

In the years between 1960 and the enactment of the CCPA, there were 1.4 months of recession per fiscal year on average. From the CCPA to the Code, there were about 1.6 months of recession per year.

To capture the offsetting effect of unemployment insurance and Great Society programs on the probability of default,[79] we include the number of recipients of public aid relative to the population. Recipients of public aid per capita is linearly interpolated and extrapolated from 1969 and 1979 estimates.[80] Before the CCPA, about 5 percent received benefits (standard deviation 2 percent). After the CCPA, about 15 percent received benefits (standard deviation about 9 percent). The percent receiving benefits did not differ statistically between states that were affected by the CCPA and states that were not.

ELEMENTS OF *INDEBT*

To the greatest extent possible, we include the same variables as in the analysis for chapters 2 and 3. The relevant usury rate is the highest rate that finance companies were allowed to charge on small, unsecured personal loans in 1971.[81] The usury rate in most states was between 20 and 30 percent and was, on average, about two percentage points lower in states with low wage exemptions. We control for state per capita income.[82] There are no income estimates for Hawaii, Alaska, or the District of Columbia during this period. Per capita income averaged about $10,000 (in 1984 dollars, standard deviation about $2,000) from 1960 until the CCPA went into effect, and it was about $12,000 (standard deviation about $2,000) from the CCPA until the Code. There was no statistically significant difference in per capita income between states that were affected by the CCPA and states that were not affected.

We include the share of whites in the population. For 1969 and later years, we take the share of whites in the population from SEER.[83] For earlier years, we interpolate from the census.[84] States unaffected by the CCPA have populations that are 83 to 84 percent white (standard deviation about 14.5), while states affected by the CCPA have populations that are about 92 percent white (standard deviation about 7).

The number of locations of commercial banks per 10,000 people in a state and the amount lent by banks to consumers for residential mortgages and other purposes are from the FDIC.[85] The number of banks per 10,000 people was about 1.8 (standard deviation about 0.7) in states with high wage exemptions prior to the CCPA. There were about 2 banks per 10,000 people (standard deviation about 0.7) in states with low wage ex-

TABLE 5A.1. **Determinants of the personal bankruptcy rate, 1960–78**

	OLS			FE
	(1)	(2)	(3)	(4)
After CCPA	7.651***	2.450*	0.162	
	(1.451)	(1.441)	(0.690)	
Affected by CCPA	2.170	3.028	2.448	
	(2.188)	(2.267)	(2.199)	
Affected* after CCPA	-1.601**	-2.230***	-1.367*	
	(0.753)	(0.779)	(0.810)	
Wage exemption in garnishment				-0.043**
				(0.019)
Observations	950	650	950	950
R-squared	0.269	0.292	0.284	0.899

The CCPA reduced the personal bankruptcy rate in states that had to increase protections for consumers and decrease protections for creditors. Notes: * p<0.05 ** p<0.01 *** p<0.001. Standard errors are in parentheses and clustered at the state level. Constant, year fixed effects and controls for homestead and personal property exemptions included in all specifications. Specification (1) is a baseline model without additional controls. Additional controls included in specifications (2)–(4); see text. Specification (2) limited to 1966–78 because some controls are not available. *Source*: See appendix to chapter 5.

emptions prior to the CCPA. Between enactment of the CCPA and the Code, the number of banks per 10,000 people grew by an average of 0.4 regardless of whether the state was affected by the CCPA.

The supply of credit to consumers equals the sum of residential real estate loans and unsecured loans to individuals.[86] The bank lending variables are measured on a per capita basis and are adjusted for inflation. The detailed FDIC state-level series on unsecured loans to individuals begins in 1966.

The modern series on the number of banks and the amount of bank loans begins in 1966, and so are included only in one specification.

RESULTS

Table 5A.1 shows regression results. For conciseness, the table suppresses the coefficients on the other independent variables included in the regressions and described above. In specifications (1)–(3), we use a difference-in-differences approach to measure the impact of the CCPA. These are cross-section time-series regressions estimated by OLS. In specification (4), we use a fixed effects approach, which accounts for both the differential effect of the law on states and controls for unobservable state differences. Please refer again to the appendix to chapter 1 for a discussion of the regression approaches.

In specifications (1)–(3), the variable "Affected by CCPA" equals one if a state was required to increase exemptions after the CCPA. The variable "After CCPA" indicates that the year is 1971 or later, when the CCPA was in effect. The controls included in the three specifications differ, as described above, but the results of the three specifications are consistent. After the CCPA, the personal bankruptcy rate fell by about 1.4 to 2.3 filings per 10,000 in states that were affected by it.

Specification (4) includes state fixed effects and captures the effect of the CCPA by including the size of the required change in a state's wage exemption. A one percentage point increase in the wage exemption decreased the personal bankruptcy rate by 0.043. In the text, we contextualize the importance of the pro-debtor reforms to garnishment in the CCPA by constructing a counterfactual to answer the question: What if the CCPA had been in effect beginning in 1960? To do this, we use the coefficient on *Wage exemption in garnishment* from specification (4) to estimate how much lower the personal bankruptcy rate would have been in 1960 if the CCPA had been in effect in that year. From those estimates, we calculate how many fewer bankruptcy filings there might have been in the typical year of the 1960s given the populations of states affected by CCPA.

We also considered whether bankruptcy rates responded to the debtor protections guaranteed by the *Sniadach* decision, but it has no measurable effect.[87] Of course, the timing of *Sniadach* and the CCPA were very close, and *Sniadach* affected many of the same states as the CCPA, so it is not surprising that we are unable to capture independently the effects of both changes.

The Triumph of the Consumer Creditor

Recall Glenda Clutch, whose case opened chapter 1. Clutch filed a bankruptcy petition in Maryland under Chapter 7 in December 2002. She was divorced and retired. Prior to her retirement, she taught public school in Virginia. The year before she filed, she had about $12,800 in income from a combination of alimony, Social Security, and pensions from the Virginia and Newport News retirement systems. After paying for Medicare supplement insurance, rent, and anticipated medical expenses each month, she had about $100 left for food, utilities, and liability insurance on her used car.

Clutch owed her largest debts to auto finance companies. She also owed some back taxes, and she owed ValuCity Furniture about $500. However, unlike most of the debtors who filed petitions for personal bankruptcy before the Bankruptcy Reform Act of 1978, Clutch did not list any other stores, any utility companies, or any medical providers among her creditors. From her bankruptcy documents, it appears that she paid all of her other bills with credit cards. She owed $5,200 to Discover, based in Greenwood, Delaware, and $1,400 on a card issued by Mellon Bank of New York.

The Bankruptcy Reform Act of 1978, described in chapter 5, was a debtor-friendly revision of bankruptcy law. It is therefore not surprising that the bankruptcy rate increased after 1978. What is, perhaps, surprising is the extent of the increase. Throughout the 1970s, the bankruptcy rate in the typical state hovered around 10 per 10,000 people. By 1990, it was about 25. By 2000, it was 50. There was a new personal bankruptcy "crisis."[1]

At first, most observers blamed this latter-day bankruptcy crisis on the 1978 bankruptcy law;[2] early dissenters from this view found the two recessions of the early 1980s to be important factors.[3] When, in the 1990s, the bankruptcy rate continued to rise, people looked for other explanations. Some returned to an argument put forth to explain the "bankruptcy crisis" of the early 1960s: Bankruptcy no longer carried much stigma.[4] Others emphasized demand-side factors that pushed households to take on more debt, such as the necessity of carrying a substantial mortgage to live in a neighborhood with good schools.[5]

Arguments emphasizing declining stigma or increased economic and social pressures to borrow tended to downplay the importance of the legal environment in shaping the decisions that debtors and creditors make along the path to bankruptcy. However, as chapters 1 to 5 show, legal changes mattered throughout the twentieth century. Each of the eras covered here thus far contained one or two significant legal changes that caused a change in the bankruptcy rate: the 1898 Bankruptcy Act and small loan laws (chapter 2), the 1938 Chandler Act (chapters 3 and 4), the 1968 Consumer Credit Protection Act and the 1978 Bankruptcy Reform Act (chapter 5). In contrast, in the years following the 1978 bankruptcy law, many legal changes buffeted debtors and creditors. Congress made the bankruptcy law less beneficial to debtors, and there were many other changes at both the national and state levels. They originated in legislatures, in courts, and in administrative agencies.[6] The most important legal changes increased the supply of credit and so increased bankruptcy. The increasing importance of banks that issue credit cards led to the changes in both the bankruptcy rate and the bankruptcy law.[7]

The first general-purpose credit cards in the US were issued in 1966. The cards were marginally profitable for banks until the Supreme Court's 1978 decision in *Marquette National Bank of Minneapolis v. First Omaha Services Corporation* and the changes in state law that followed it. The *Marquette* decision created a national market for credit cards, transforming cards into one of the largest and most profitable parts of American banking.[8] The *Marquette* decision made it possible for Clutch to borrow so easily on cards from out-of-state banks.

Credit Cards, *Marquette*, and Bankruptcy

The *Marquette* decision effectively ended usury restrictions on credit
card lending. Recall from chapter 2 that, for most of American history,
each state had a usury law limiting the maximum interest rate that lenders could charge. In fact, most states had multiple usury limits.[9] The applicable usury limit depended on who the lender was, who the borrower
was, what the loan was for, and whether there was a written contract for
the debt. As department stores and banks developed revolving credit
accounts (see chapter 4), most states created a category of usury limits
to regulate them. Unlike the fairly similar rates in the small loan laws
passed by states earlier in the century (see chapter 2), usury rates on revolving credit varied widely from state to state.

During the 1960s and early 1970s, most credit cards went to customers of the brick-and-mortar branches of issuing banks. Most of the card
lending stayed within the state, and lending per capita increased with
the state usury rate because higher usury limits made the cards profitable. Figure 6.1 shows that differences in the usury rate between states
in 1975 are highly correlated with the personal bankruptcy rate during
the 1970s. The usury rate that applied to balances on bank-issued credit
cards ranged from 10 to 24 percent. The median was 18 percent.[10] In
states with a usury rate that was above the median, the bankruptcy rate

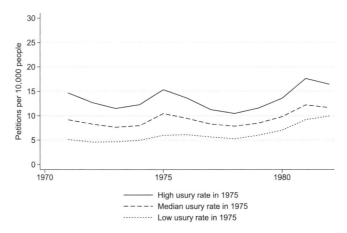

FIG. 6.1. Higher state usury limits increased state bankruptcy rates before the *Marquette*
decision. *Source*: See appendix to chapter 6.

averaged 12.7 per 10,000 from 1971 to 1978. The bankruptcy rate averaged just 5.3 in states with a usury rate below 18 percent in 1975.

We again use regression analysis to measure the extent to which the differences in the usury rates on credit cards explain the differences in bankruptcy rates. We use data from 1971 to 1990, and we control for other determinants of the rate of indebtedness, the rate of default, and the choice to file for bankruptcy. The regression results show that each percentage point increase in the usury rate was associated with an increase in the bankruptcy rate of about 0.7 per 10,000, or nearly 10 percent of the average bankruptcy rate. (See the appendix to chapter 6 for the details of our methods and for a description of our sources for social and economic determinants of indebtedness and default for this period. Table 6A.1 shows the regression results. The results in this paragraph and the next are calculated as the total marginal effect of a change in the usury rate for 1971–82 from table 6A.1.)

The regressions also show that the bankruptcy rate was most responsive to a larger supply of credit if the state offered few protections from garnishment. As discussed in chapter 5, the Consumer Credit Protection Act created a federal minimum wage exemption in garnishment. Restricting garnishment reduced bankruptcy in high-rate states. However, states that offered only the minimum protection from garnishment continued to have higher rates of bankruptcy. At the turn of the twenty-first century, differences in garnishment law still explained one-third of the difference in bankruptcy rates.[11] In the 1970s, the difference in the bankruptcy rate between high and low usury states in figure 6.1 is explained entirely by the difference in bankruptcy between states that offered only the federally required exemptions in garnishment and states that offered additional protections from garnishment.

Not long after issuing their first credit cards, a few midwestern banks began to use them to attract new customers. They sent credit card offers to people located in other nearby states.[12] In 1968, Fred Fisher, a resident of Iowa, received credit cards from First National Bank of Omaha and First National Bank of Chicago. Fisher used both cards. Later, when Fisher became aware that both banks were charging interest rates higher than the applicable usury rate in Iowa, he sued both companies in federal court.

At the same time the courts were deciding Fisher's case, First National Bank of Omaha established a subsidiary in Minnesota specifically to issue credit cards there. Minnesota allowed the annual fees that made cards profitable when usury rates—even high ones like Nebraska's—were binding. After some legislative and legal machinations, Marquette National Bank in Minnesota sued the subsidiary, First Omaha Service Corporation, in state court. Fisher lost in federal court, and Marquette lost in Minnesota's state supreme court.

However, the Minnesota Supreme Court did not fully embrace the findings of the Eighth Circuit in *Fisher*. The US Supreme Court took up the *Marquette* case and in 1978 established without a doubt that the usury law that applied in credit card lending was the law in the state where the bank was located. The *Marquette* decision applied to national banks, but state banks got similar privileges two years later.[13]

Two things happened after *Marquette*. First, many state legislatures raised or removed their state's usury ceilings. In 1978, New Hampshire and Oregon were the only states without a usury limit on credit cards when *Marquette* was decided. In 1980, Arizona joined them. In 1981, nine states eliminated usury on cards (Delaware, Illinois, Montana, Nevada, New Jersey, New Mexico, South Dakota, Utah, and Wisconsin). Between 1982 and 1985, three more states removed their usury limits (Idaho, North Dakota, and Virginia).[14] In the states that had previously capped rates on credit cards at 18 percent, the maximum rate went up to 21 percent on average. In states that had previously capped rates at less than 18 percent, the maximum rate went up to 19.6 percent. Even the states that had been the most permissive before the *Marquette* decision raised their usury rates on credit cards.

Second, after *Marquette*, banks located in states that did not raise usury limits began to look for ways to establish operations in states that had raised the limit. The first, and perhaps most famous, case was Citibank's opening of credit card operations in South Dakota. Under the Bank Holding Company Act of 1956, a bank could enter a state only if the state's statutes explicitly invited it to do so. South Dakota passed legislation inviting Citibank in March 1980.[15] Citibank got approval from the comptroller of the currency quickly, and it got Federal Reserve approval in January 1981. It opened its South Dakota operation the next month.[16] Also in 1981, MBNA became the first institution to specialize in issuing credit cards to consumers in any state.[17]

Data from the sample of bankrupts in Maryland shows that out-of-state credit cards spread quickly. Figure 6.2 shows that after the *Marquette* decision, cards issued from states that had removed their usury limits began to appear almost immediately among the creditors of the

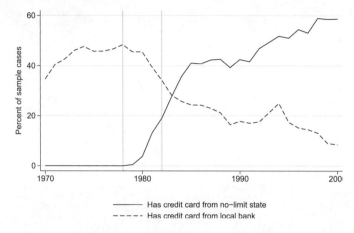

FIG. 6.2. Vertical lines show year of *Marquette* decision (1978) and year that many states removed their usury limit on credit cards (1982). In the 1970s, the share of personal bankrupts in the Maryland sample who listed credit card debt rose substantially. Most of the cards were issued by local banks. Immediately after the *Marquette* decision, cards from states that removed their usury limits begin to appear among the creditors of the bankrupt in Maryland and quickly become more prevalent than locally issued cards. *Source*: See appendix to chapter 6.

bankrupts.[18] Virtually none of the bankrupts in the sample who filed before 1978 had a card issued from outside the local market.[19] By 1982, 20 percent of filers in Maryland had cards from no-limit states.[20] By 1985, about 45 percent of filers in Maryland had cards from no-limit states, while only 30 percent had cards from banks in Maryland, the District of Columbia, Virginia, or West Virginia. Card holding continued to become more common among bankrupts, but growth after 1985 was entirely from out-of-area cards. (Though Virginia removed its usury limit in 1983, we always count cards from Virginia as locally issued cards in figure 6.2.)

Between 1980 and 1982, the real value of credit card lending doubled in the states that had removed their usury limits. At the same time, as figure 6.3 shows, card lending grew so slowly in other states that inflation reduced its real value.[21] Beginning in 1982 and intensifying in the mid-1980s, states passed general statutes removing restrictions on interstate banking,[22] but the growth in credit card lending remained concentrated in states without usury limits. By the end of 1984, 70 to 80 million people in the US held bank-issued cards. The average number of cards was 1.9.[23] By 1990, credit card lending per person was about 25 times higher than it had been in 1970.[24]

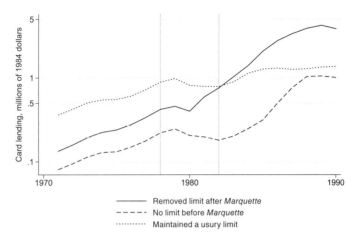

FIG. 6.3. Vertical lines show year of *Marquette* decision (1978) and year that many states removed their usury limits (1982). Before *Marquette*, the real value of credit card lending was growing in all states, regardless of the usury limit. Inflation reduced the real value of lending. When growth resumed, it was much faster in states that had removed their usury limits on credit cards after the *Marquette* decision. *Source*: See appendix to chapter 6.

Because the *Marquette* decision broke the link between a state's usury rate and the supply of credit in the state, it also broke the link between the state's usury rate and its bankruptcy rate. After the *Marquette* decision and the subsequent changes in state law, a state's usury rate on credit cards ceased to predict its bankruptcy rate. The changes in the usury limits after *Marquette* never had a statistically significant impact on the bankruptcy rate in regression analysis. While bankruptcy rates in states with high usury limits had been more than twice the bankruptcy rate in states that had low usury limits before 1978, the gap was eliminated between 1982 and 1990. On average, after 1982 the bankruptcy rate in states that maintained any usury limit was 17.7 per 10,000, while it was 17.6 in states that removed the limit.

Without the mechanism of usury to link credit markets in a state to the state's bankruptcy rate, we cannot use regression of post-*Marquette* data to measure the impact of *Marquette* on bankruptcy. We can, however, use regression analysis to conduct a thought experiment. We ask, "What if a state's usury rates before 1978 had been the same as its rates after *Marquette*?" Consider the example of Arizona: Arizona's personal bankruptcy rate averaged almost 14 per 10,000 annually in the 1960s and 1970s, when its usury rate was 16 to 18 percent. Arizona's state legislature removed the state's usury cap in 1980. Assume, conservatively, that after 1980 the interest rate on revolving credit in Arizona was equal to the highest usury rate in the country. Regression analysis predicts that, had the usury rate in Arizona been as high from 1960 to 1978 as rates were allowed to go after *Marquette*, the bankruptcy rate there would have been about 19 per 10,000, an increase of 5 filings per 10,000 people or more than 30 percent. Between 2,200 and 4,400 more people probably would have filed in Arizona each year. Now consider Maryland, where the legislature increased the usury rate by six percentage points. The regression analysis predicts that the bankruptcy rate in Maryland may have doubled, from 2 to 4 per 10,000 people, meaning that annual filings may have increased by as many as 2,900. Finally, consider California. The California legislature increased the state's usury rate by a modest 1.2 percentage points after *Marquette*. Had that higher rate been in effect earlier, the bankruptcy rate might have gone up by about one filing per 10,000 people. In the large state of California, that means an additional 28,000 to 31,500 more people may have filed in California each year during the 1960s and 1970s. Across all states that increased or eliminated usury rates after *Marquette*, between 77,700 and 107,700 more people may have filed if the allowable interest rate on revolving credit had been as high before *Marquette* as it was after. Averaging across the eighteen states that increased usury rates after *Marquette*, bankruptcy filings would probably have been about 50 percent higher before *Marquette* than they actually were. To look at it another way, the increase in the supply of revolving credit on credit cards explains 20 to 30 percent of the increase in bankruptcy between the decades just before and just after *Marquette*.

To summarize, the *Marquette* decision resulted in the following: (1) cards issued from banks in states with high or no usury limits appeared all across the country, including among the debts of the bankrupt; (2) the bankruptcy rate increased everywhere; and (3) the bankruptcy rate in states with usury limits converged to the rate in states without usury limits. Taken together, these three things suggest that the deregulation of credit card interest rates increased consumer indebtedness, especially on the extensive margin. Whether the issuing bank was nearby or far away, unregulated interest rates allowed credit card companies to do more than increase the supply of credit to financially sound households during a period of high inflation. It gave them margin enough to expand the pool of households that could borrow. Women and minority customers got access to credit,[25] and banks could profit from offering cards to high-risk consumers.[26]

An increase in access to cards may have resulted from indiscriminate direct mail marketing of preapproved offers and low utilization of credit screening during the early period of growth.[27] Alternatively, it could have resulted from advances in information technology that allowed banks to tailor high-interest offers to high-risk borrowers. Banks established to enter the national credit card market in the 1980s were well aware of the potential for price discrimination.[28] It seems likely that the *Marquette* decision increased the bankruptcy rate mainly by expanding the supply of credit to first-time and high-risk card holders.[29]

The expansion of credit card debt gave rise to a new interest group. From 1970 to 2000, financial institutions and credit card companies became more prevalent among the creditors of the bankrupt in the Maryland sample. Figure 6.4 shows that, in 1970, about 25 percent of the bankrupts' creditors were financial institutions or credit card issuers.[30] In 2000, 37 percent of creditors listed were. The stakes of these creditors in bankruptcy grew. Through the 1970s and 1980s, the bankrupts in the

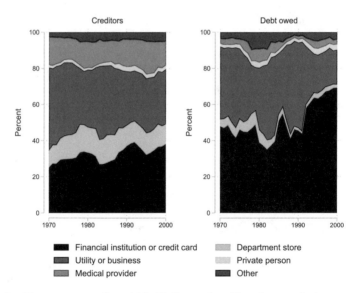

FIG. 6.4. From 1970–2000, financial institutions and credit card companies became more prevalent among the creditors of the bankrupt in the Maryland sample. Through the 1970s and 1980s, bankrupts owed about 40 percent of their debts to financial institutions and credit card companies. By the end of the 1990s, bankrupts owed 75 percent of their debts to financial institutions and credit card companies. *Source*: See appendix to chapter 6.

sample owed about 40 percent of their debts to financial institutions and credit card companies. By the end of the 1990s, they owed 75 percent of their debts to financial institutions and credit card companies.

During this period, and for the first time since the late nineteenth century, creditors, rather than legal professionals, played the leading role in shaping bankruptcy legislation. The legislation, however, was very unlike that of the creditor-authored 1898 Bankruptcy Act. Not surprisingly, creditors did not emphasize the role of *Marquette* and changes in usury laws in expanding access to credit as causes of increasing bankruptcy rates. Instead, they argued that an overly generous bankruptcy law and declining stigma were leading some consumers to declare bankruptcy even when they had the means to pay and that the costs of these discharged debts were ultimately borne by more responsible borrowers. Consequently, they argued that the law should be amended to require more debtors to repay their debts rather than obtain an immediate discharge. The argument was not new. As we have seen, creditors had advocated mandatory repayment plans since at least the 1930s. This time, however, creditors were able to marshal far more resources in support of their case than they had in the past.

Consumer Creditors Build Momentum

Changes in bankruptcy law after 1979 were designed by creditors, for creditors. In particular, consumer creditors aimed to make filing less attractive by building on a couple of "wins" that they had achieved during the debate over the Code in 1978.

Although the final section of chapter 5 emphasizes the pro-debtor changes to bankruptcy law in the Code, creditors did achieve two longstanding goals. First, the Code made student loans nondischargeable unless they had become due more than five years before the date of filing for bankruptcy or unless failure to discharge would create an "undue hardship." Creditors believed it was important to clarify the nondischargability of student loans in the bankruptcy law, even though they had successfully inserted a provision blocking the discharge of student loan debt into a 1976 amendment to the Higher Education Act. Second, as discussed several times in the preceding chapters, since at least 1932 consumer creditors and some bankruptcy referees had been pushing for changes to personal bankruptcy that would result in more repayment of debt. The Code included several provisions that made filing under Chapter 13 more attractive than filing under Chapter 7.[31] The Code encouraged filing under Chapter 13 by creating a "super discharge" that allowed some debts (for example, old tax debts) to be discharged in Chapter 13 but not Chapter 7 and by allowing residential mortgage debt to be included in the Chapter 13 plan. The Code opened Chapter 13 to "any individual with regular income" rather than just "wage earners," which allowed small business owners, professionals, and Social Security recipients like Clutch to use a repayment plan. These debtors could not use it before because they were not technically "employed by" a company. The Code protected codebtors from collection efforts while the repayment plan was in effect. Finally, the Code eliminated the requirement that creditors approve a Chapter 13 plan.

During and after the recession of 1980, associations of creditors began working together "in response to the alarming growth of bankruptcies following the passage of the Bankruptcy Act of 1978."[32] Much like the National Convention of Representatives of Commercial Bodies did almost one hundred years earlier, consumer creditors formed a larger association, which they called the National Coalition for Bankruptcy Reform. The coalition commissioned the Credit Research Center at Purdue University to conduct a study of consumer bankruptcy.[33] The study concluded: "15 to 30 percent of bankrupt debtors could repay all of their non-mortgage debts out of their future income, while as many as 37.4 percent of bankruptcy debtors could probably repay at least half of their debts out of future income."[34] They also estimated that these "potentially recoverable" debts amounted to more than $1 billion annually.[35] Moreover, they argued that the cost of these unpaid debts was ultimately borne by other consumers. When he testified before Congress, Robert W. Johnson, the director of Purdue's research center, emphasized, "What we are talking about is a wealth transfer from those who pay their debts to those who have chosen not to pay their affordable debts."[36] In addition to funding the research to sell Congress on their story, the coalition hired the Ogilvy & Mather advertising agency to publicize the results to a general audience.[37]

In 1981, with a draft of the Purdue study to support their arguments, the coalition put forward a proposal to amend the law. It also proposed lengthening the repayment period in Chapter 13 from three years to five years. It proposed amending the law to prevent "abuse" by creating a means test. A debtor who was capable of repaying some debts out of future income would be required to use Chapter 13. A debtor could use Chapter 7 only if he "cannot pay a reasonable portion of his debts out of anticipated future income."[38]

At congressional hearings, representatives from the National Coalition for Bankruptcy Reform, other creditor associations, some large retailers (such as Sears), and the Credit Research Center spoke in favor of the proposed changes. Opposition came from representatives of the Consumers Union, the National Bankruptcy Conference, and the National Conference of Bankruptcy Judges. The opponents of the changes had their own research: Phillip Shuchman of Rutgers Law School sampled 123 bankruptcy cases from Connecticut and concluded that only around 8 percent of filers might be able to "manage some payment."[39] The opposition was successful. As had been the case since the 1920s, the issues were decided in committee, and the differences voiced in committee hearings did not carry over to partisan conflict on the floor.[40]

The Supreme Court inadvertently gave the National Coalition for Bankruptcy Reform another opportunity to propose amendments when, in spring of 1982, it struck down a portion of the Bankruptcy Reform Act. Recall from chapter 5 that one of the most contentious issues in drafting the Code involved the status of bankruptcy judges (previously called referees). The Senate wanted to give them only slightly expanded authority. The House wanted to make them Article III judges. The compromise separated the Bankruptcy Court from the Federal District Court and made the position of bankruptcy judge a presidential appointment requiring advice and consent of the Senate, but with a limited term and not a lifetime term as required under Article III. The purpose of creating a separate court was to remove the judge from the daily business of case administration, thereby reducing the chance that the judge would hear evidence that would later be inadmissible and reducing the appearance that the judge was biased in the trustee's favor.

The Supreme Court ruled in *Northern Pipeline Construction Co. v. Marathon Pipe Line Co.* that the system of bankruptcy courts established under the Bankruptcy Reform Act of 1978 was unconstitutional. Bankruptcy matters do not fall under the exceptions to Article III in the Constitution,[41] so bankruptcy matters must be heard in a venue presided over by an Article III judge. As Congress debated how to create a constitutional system of bankruptcy judges, the National Coalition for Bankruptcy Reform took the opportunity to argue again that the Code had shifted the law too far in the direction of debtors.[42]

Amendments passed in 1984 resolved the issue with bankruptcy judges and added a series of other changes regarded as favorable to creditors.[43] But the coalition gained far less than it had sought. It did not get a means test for Chapter 7. To encourage debtors to choose Chapter 13, Congress amended the Code to allow the court to dismiss a case if the court suspected "substantial abuse." However, the law did not define "substantial abuse";[44] creditors could not press the court to dismiss on grounds of abuse; and the law stipulated, "There shall be a presumption in favor of granting the relief requested by the debtor." Another change ensured that bankrupts were informed about Chapter 13 by requiring clerks to provide notification about the various options to debtors in writing prior to filing. To reduce personal bankruptcy filings overall, Congress reduced federal exemptions, but by 1984, most states had opted out of the federal exemption scheme.[45]

The 1984 amendments did not increase the share of cases filed under Chapter 13. It averaged 21.1 across all states in fiscal 1984, fell to 20.3 in fiscal 1987, and was 21.5 in 1989. At the same time, the personal bankruptcy rate doubled, from 11.7 to 22.9 per 10,000, in the average state. Clearly, the coalition's attempt to make the discharge less attractive was no match for the expansion of consumer credit, especially through credit cards, which was working in the opposite direction.

Consumer Creditors Win the Story

Bankruptcy rates doubled again in the 1990s. In 1994, Congress created a new Bankruptcy Review Commission, but it restricted the commission to "improving, and updating the Code in ways which do not disturb the fundamental tenets and balance of current law" because Congress was "generally satisfied with the basic framework established in the current Bankruptcy Code."[46] The commission's 1997 report suggested numerous amendments but left the essential features of the law intact.

Four of the nine members of the commission dissented from its report, and creditors opposed the report even before the commission issued it.[47] The American Financial Services Association, a trade group representing both secured and unsecured consumer creditors, employed lawyers to draft a new bill.[48] This version got specific about a means test for Chapter 7: If a person with income above the state median filed for Chapter 7, the court would determine whether the filer had expected future income sufficient to cover necessary living expenses and, at the same time, make payments to creditors. Filers deemed to have sufficient income would be required to use Chapter 13. In addition, all filers would be required to participate in credit counseling.

In the 105th Congress, both the House and Senate passed a bankruptcy bill, and the House passed the conference report, but the Senate did not take it up. The 106th Congress passed a bill, but President Bill Clinton pocket-vetoed it in December 2000. Though the nature and timing of the delays varied, the 107th and 108th Congresses roughly repeated the performance of the 105th.[49] One roadblock to enactment was disagreement over details. Reaching agreement on how to restrict exemptions and on how to structure the means test was particularly difficult. External events presented a second type of roadblock.

As discussed in previous chapters, exemptions were always controversial. Ever since the 1898 act placed states in control of exemptions, some people had argued that it defeated the idea of a uniform bankruptcy law. They noted that some states seemed to have homestead exemptions intended to game the system. Others responded that state-determined exemptions made sense because of differences in economic conditions between states. The Bankruptcy Reform Act of 1978 created federal exemptions, but (again) states nullified that effort by exercising their option to opt out of them. Efforts in the 1990s to cap state exemptions also failed. Exemptions remained under state control.

The means test required the court to determine an allowance for necessary living expenses. But how? Chapter 13 already had a disposable income test, but it was not standardized. As one example of the types of details that needed to be resolved, consider the problem of choosing a source of data for a standardized means test. Some dissenters to the commission's report recommended using data from the Bureau of Labor Statistics (such as the Consumer Expenditure Survey), but the version of the means test under consideration at 1998 hearings used the more restrictive "necessary expense allowances" created by the Internal Revenue Service (IRS) as a benchmark.[50] Henry Hyde (R-IL), a conservative and chair of the House Judiciary Committee, opposed the use of IRS allowances and favored the flexibility of current law.[51] The hearings in 1998 included two days of testimony devoted to the means test issue alone.[52]

The external events that got in the way of enactment were diverse. Some bankruptcy bills failed to make it to the president because of attempts to inject debates about other issues, such as abortion and the minimum wage. Enactment was further delayed by the Clinton impeachment proceedings in late 1998 and early 1999, Senator Jim Jeffords's (VT) defection from the Republican Party in May 2001 (which shifted the balance of power in the Senate), and the terrorist attacks in September 2001.

A bill was finally enacted in 2005. The Bankruptcy Abuse Prevention and Consumer Protection Act (BAPCPA) provided much of what creditors wanted.[53] Filers were required to obtain credit counseling. If a filer's income was greater than the median income in the state, he or she had to pass a means test to use Chapter 7.[54] The means test compared the filer's income to IRS-defined necessary expenses. If the test showed that the filer could pay at least $100 a month, he or she could not use Chapter 7.

To appreciate fully the significance of the introduction of a means test into bankruptcy law, consider its historical precedents. When BAPCPA became law, consumer creditors achieved a goal they had been pursuing for almost three quarters of a century.

Recall from chapter 3 that in 1932 retail creditors supported the Hastings-Michener bill, which supplemented a proposal for wage earner workout with a "suspended discharge" that required debtors to repay 50 percent of their debts before they would be eligible to receive a discharge. The 1932 bill would have forced many debtors into a repayment plan. The retail creditors lost in 1932 because congressional members opposed to the suspended discharge believed it was unfair. Suspended discharge would force employees to repay debts owed to corporations, while bankruptcy law would still allow corporations to wipe out their debts. Congress further objected to turning the federal courts or government agencies into a collection agency. They believed that retailers could solve their own problems by extending consumer credit less liberally. Wage earner repayment was part of the Chandler Act, but the suspended discharge was not.

Recall from chapter 4 that in 1967 retail creditors tried again. They lobbied for amendments to the bankruptcy law that would have required debtors to pursue a repayment plan before becoming eligible for a discharge. Again, their proposal failed. Amendments in 1984 gave the court the power to force a debtor into a Chapter 13 repayment plan, provided the court believed that the debtor's use of Chapter 7 constituted (undefined) substantial abuse. Bankruptcy judges were not anxious to use this power.

Consumer creditors in the 1990s and early 2000s had advantages that their predecessors in the 1930s, 1960s, and 1980s did not. Democrats dominated Congress for most of the time from the Great Depression through the 1970s. Legislation passed during these years, including the Consumer Credit Protection Act, tended to protect consumers and restrict creditors. In contrast, from 1995 to 2005, Republicans controlled both houses of Congress in all but one year, and, in 2001, Republicans gained the White House. Republicans consistently supported creditors' bills. Some Democrats did strongly oppose them, which resulted in a larger number of roll call votes on bankruptcy than at any time since the turn of the twentieth century. Yet each Congress between 1997 and 2005 passed a version of the creditors' bills because moderate Democrats in the late 1990s and early 2000s also supported elements of the creditors' proposals and even served as cosponsors on bankruptcy bills. In the final vote on BAPCPA, 73 of 198 House Democrats voted *yea*. In the Senate, 18 of 43 Democrats voted with Republicans for the creditors' bill.[55]

Beyond the changed political environment, consumer creditors in the 1990s and early 2000s were able to create a more successful lobby than creditors in earlier periods. Mergers reduced potential conflicts of interest among different types of creditors and made it easier to speak with a single voice.[56] The Financial Services Modernization Act of 1999, which overturned Glass-Steagall restrictions on mergers between banks, insurance companies, and investment banks, accelerated the consolidation of the credit card market. The market share of the five largest credit card lenders increased from 27 percent in 1990, to 37 percent in 2001, and to more than 70 percent by 2010.[57] Card issuers, through their preexisting trade groups, again joined to form a new single-issue lobby. The new lobby took a name that was confusingly similar to the old lobby. They called themselves the National Consumer Bankruptcy Coalition. The American Financial Services Association (which, again, paid for the drafting of the 1981 bill) was part of the new coalition. But there were just nine members in all, including Master Card International and Visa USA.[58] The new coalition did not merely seek passage of particular legal language. It sought to flip the dominant narrative about the cause of rising bankruptcy rates.

Throughout this book, we emphasize the interdependence between bankruptcy law and the use of the law. Changes in the law caused changes in the way debtors used bankruptcy, and changes in the way debtors used bankruptcy caused changes in the law. Moreover, how the law changed depended on the narrative that was used to explain the changes in how debtors used bankruptcy. When personal bankruptcy overtook business bankruptcy in the 1920s, the narrative was that use of bankruptcy had changed because some consumer creditors used predatory practices. That narrative dominated until the late twentieth century. As a result, changes in the law throughout the twentieth century protected consumers from their creditors. It is important to note that the narrative was always contested. There were always people who believed that consumer behavior, not creditor behavior, caused high bankruptcy rates. In the lead up to BAPCPA, banks and credit card companies finally convinced both Congress and the public that consumers were to blame.[59]

The storyline followed the one established by the Credit Research Center in 1981. A concise retelling comes from testimony before Congress in 1998. Speaking on behalf of the National Retail Federation, Stanton Bluestone, chair of Carson Pirie Scott and Company, explained, "[W]e are in good economic times. Yet nearly one in every 80 households filed for bankruptcy—just in the past year."[60]

Like others who identified bankruptcy "crises" in the 1920s and 1950s to 1960s, Bluestone was sure that declining social stigma was responsible: "In the past, shame kept people away from bankruptcy court. Unfortunately, that has changed." However, as discussed in chapter 4, the assertion that declining stigma causes rising bankruptcy is hard to validate. Stigma is hard to measure. Proxies for stigma, such as measures of promise keeping, religiosity, or social connectivity,[61] can also be correlated with financial precursors of bankruptcy. The most rigorous attempts at untangling the effects of declining stigma from the effects of increasing information indicate that knowing someone who has filed for bankruptcy affects the decision to file mainly by improving knowledge of the process of bankruptcy rather than reducing the guilt of it.[62] And, as the bankruptcy rate rose to new heights, a majority of people came to know someone who had decided to file.[63]

But Bluestone was convinced that people were abusing the law because "several recent studies have revealed that there are a significant number of people who are filing for complete relief under Chapter 7 that could actually afford to pay back a notable portion of their debt." The ultimate result of people using bankruptcy to escape debts that they could pay was that the resulting loss to creditors "ultimately gets paid by the nation's 100 million households."[64]

The most influential of the "several studies" Bluestone cited came from the Credit Research Center, the same university-based center that produced reports for the creditors' earlier coalition.[65] By 1997, the center was at Georgetown University, where it remained until 2006. Its new study, which was partially funded by Visa USA and MasterCard International, used the court records of more than 3,800 people who filed for bankruptcy in 1996.[66] It concluded that "25 percent of Chapter 7 filers had income net of living expenses to repay at least 30 percent of their nonhousing debt over a 5-year repayment period. Five percent of those Chapter 7 filers could have paid all of their nonhousing debts over five years based on the information they provided to courts."[67] Similarly, a 1997 study by Ernst & Young (also funded by Visa USA) concluded that Chapter 7 filers would have been able to pay $4 billion if they had been required to pursue repayment plans under Chapter 13 over a five-year period.[68] Creditors suggested that bankruptcy cheats caused them to pass on $400 in costs each year to consumers who paid. They called it a "bankruptcy tax."[69]

The evidence in support of the creditors' story ranged from weak to nonexistent. Critics of bankruptcy reform, including Elizabeth Warren, challenged the validity of studies paid for by creditors.[70] An academic attempt at replication of the Ernst & Young study found that just 3.6 percent of petitioners seeking discharge could pay only a collective $450 million.[71] At the request of the Senate Committee on the Judiciary, the US General Accounting Office (GAO) analyzed the research suggesting that many filers were capable of paying a substantial portion of their debts. The GAO found that the methodology used by the Credit Research Center and Ernst & Young could not generate an accurate estimate of the share of petitioners for bankruptcy who would be able to pay some portion of their debts. The creditor-funded work contradicted data from the Administrative Office of US Courts on Chapter 13 plans, which did not support the argument that many filers could repay. In fact, the court data showed that even current filers under Chapter 13 were not able to pay. Less than a third of people who chose Chapter 13 successfully completed the repayment plan, and most Chapter 13 cases were dismissed or converted to Chapter 7.[72] The creditor-funded work also contradicted the firsthand experience of legal professionals, who did not believe abuse was widespread.[73] Economist Ian Domowitz testified that the available evidence indicated that petitioners who could pay already sorted themselves into Chapter 13, and therefore forcing people into Chapter 13 would not substantially increase repayment.[74] Peer-reviewed academic research published in the early 1990s showed that the interest rates charged by credit cards did not vary with the costs of funds to card issuers.[75] This suggested that, if creditors got bankruptcy reform, and if reform did decrease their losses, the increase in profits would probably go to shareholders, not to consumers.

The weakness of the evidence did not matter. Newspapers repeated almost every element of the creditors' story.[76] The creditor's story became, in the words of the *Wall Street Journal*, "conventional wisdom."[77] Many Americans came to agree. For example, the National Consumers League found that 71 percent of respondents said that it was too easy to declare bankruptcy. Seventy-six percent said that people should not be able to erase all their debts if they are able to pay. Creditors used survey results in congressional testimony,[78] and public support for reform increased as the issue lingered in Congress.[79]

Campaign contributions to both Democrats and Republicans helped to ensure that lawmakers were listening when the creditors sent prominent lobbyists to tell their story.[80] In 2000 to 2001, targeted contributions from creditors probably kept bankruptcy on the congressional agenda and switched fifteen votes in the House of Representatives from *nay* to *yea*.[81] Campaign contributions from banks of more than $75,000, or more than about 10 percent of total contributions, strongly predicted a *yea* vote on BAPCPA.[82] The National Consumer Bankruptcy Coalition and its member organizations "obtained the services of some of the most prominent lobbyists in Washington, D.C., to make its case in Congress." The list included former White House counsel Lloyd Cutler and former senator Lloyd Bentsen, both Democrats, as well as former Republican National Committee chairs Haley Barbour and Ed Gillespie.[83]

In total, creditors spent a considerable sum of money changing the narrative about bankruptcy and obtaining their desired reforms. It is not possible to say definitively how much. Estimates run as high as $100 million.[84] The Center for Responsive Politics estimated from Federal Election Commission data that contributions by members of the coalition summed to $5.2 million from January 1999 to election day in November 2000.[85] Banks, finance, and credit card companies not in the coalition spent another $9.2 million.[86] Of the $9.2 million, $3.5 million came from MBNA alone.

Creditors probably mounted their campaign for bankruptcy reform with—and to protect—the high profits from growing credit card operations. As noted above, after the *Marquette* decision, the credit card market grew rapidly. Revolving debt outstanding increased from $59.7 billion in 1980 to $238.6 billion in 1990, $675.6 billion in 2000, and $781 billion in 2004.[87]

Credit card operations earned extraordinary profits for issuers. Credit card interest rates were "exceptionally sticky relative to the cost of funds." When the high markup was multiplied by the growing volume, major credit card issuers earned rates of return that were three to five times the ordinary rate of return in banking during the mid-1980s.[88] In the 1990s, credit card interest rates became more responsive to the cost of funds, but credit card lending remained more profitable than banking generally. Legal and technological changes kept profits from cards high. In 1996, the Supreme Court ruled in *Smiley v. Citibank* that the relevant limits on card fees, like usury limits on card interest rates, were the ones in the state where the card issuer was located, not the ones in the state where the card holder was located.[89] Because of the *Smiley* decision, the average monthly late fee in the industry increased from $13 to $29. Revenue from late fees rose from $1.7 billion to $7.3 billion between 1996 and 2002.[90] Information technology made it possible for credit card issuers to keep profits on the marginal card high by tailoring offers to the characteristics of the holder.[91]

In the early twentieth century, legal changes not directly related to bankruptcy law—small loan laws—increased the supply of consumer credit at the extensive margin, which had unanticipated effects of the personal bankruptcy rate, which then had an effect on the bankruptcy law. In the late 1960s, the Consumer Credit Protection Act and the *Sniadach* decision had similar unanticipated effects in the opposite direction. Perhaps it should have been less surprising when the *Marquette* and *Smiley* decisions did the same in the 1980s, 1990s, and early 2000s.

In each episode, consumer creditors and their allies sought tougher bankruptcy law. They argued that rising bankruptcy rates, particularly during periods of economic expansion, indicated that there was a fundamental flaw in the bankruptcy law that enabled abuse. Only a change to the law could stop the increase in bankruptcy.

Consumer creditors got no traction until 1984, when they won minor victories. In the late 1990s, they mounted a more extensive and successful campaign, one that overcame even the opposition of the legal professionals who had played the dominant role in driving legislative change since 1898. In 2005, banks and credit card companies got what consumer creditors wanted since as early as 1932. Rather than simply encouraging debtors to choose a repayment plan or giving judges greater discretion to push debtors into repayment plans, BAPCPA *required* many debtors to pursue a repayment plan.

Appendix to Chapter 6

Chapter 6 discusses the evidence that the expansion of the supply of credit through general-use credit cards, which was spurred by the *Marquette* decision, contributed to an increase in the bankruptcy rate in the 1980s.

Regression Analysis of the Impact of the Marquette *Decision*

The regression analysis in chapter 6 is quite similar to the analysis in chapter 2. In both periods, the key change in credit markets was an increase in usury rates. As described in the text, in *Marquette*, the Supreme Court ruled that the usury rate that applies to credit card lending is the usury rate in the state from which the credit card is issued rather than the state in which the borrower resides. After *Marquette,* several states increased or removed their usury limits on credit cards to attract banks to locate card operations in their state.

State usury rates on credit cards were collected for the study of entrepreneurship.[92] If a state removed its usury limit entirely, we code the limit as equal to the highest usury limit in any state that year. This underestimates the increase in effective interest rates and biases our regression coefficients downwards. Several years of data are missing for Hawaii; it is dropped from the analysis. Because the usury rate affects the share of the population that is in debt, we lag usury rates by one year in the regression analysis.

In states that had usury rates below the median of 18 percent just before *Marquette*, usury rates went up from about 13.6 percent in the 1970s (standard deviation about 2.9) to 19.6 percent (standard deviation about 3.5) in the 1980s. Where the usury rate was 18 percent just before *Marquette*, the maximum interest rate averaged about 18 percent in the 1970s (standard deviation about 1.1) and 21.0 percent in the 1980s (standard deviation about 2.9). In the states with the highest usury rates just before *Marquette*, interest rates rose from 21.0 in the 1970s (standard deviation about 2.9) to 23.4 percent in the 1980s (standard deviation about 2.1).

The 1978 *Marquette* decision not only led to a larger supply of credit by increasing interest rates, but, by 1982, it also created a national credit card market. Statistically speaking, the switch from many state markets to one national market makes it hard to show that *Marquette* mattered by looking at post-*Marquette* data. We instead make use of the fact that, before 1982, few cards were issued out of state, so most debtors and credit card issuers were in the same state. We measure the extent to which a higher state usury rate on credit cards before 1982 is associated with a greater supply of this type of credit, and thereby a higher personal bankruptcy rate.

The dependent variable is the bankruptcy rate in state s and year t. The sources for the calculation of bankruptcy rates are described in the appendix to chapter 1. The regression analysis covers 1971–90. There are 944 total state-years. In states that had usury rates below the median of 18 percent before *Marquette*, the personal bankruptcy rate was about 6.3 (standard deviation 3.4) before 1982 and about 13.8 (standard deviation 8.1) after. In states that had a usury rate of 18 percent before *Marquette*, the bankruptcy rate was about 9.4 (standard deviation 5.3) before 1982 and about 17.5 (standard deviation 11.4) after. In states that set usury above the median before *Marquette*, bankruptcy rates were 13.3 (standard deviation 5.3) before 1982 and 22 (standard deviation 11.3) after.

As in previous regression analyses, we also include vectors of controls for the social and economic determinants of filing (*Files*), of being in default (*InDefault*), as well as other determinants of being in debt (*InDebt*).

ELEMENTS OF *FILES*

State wage garnishment law is categorized as offering the minimum federal protection to consumers under the CCPA (pro-creditor), as offering some additional protection to consumers (mildly pro-debtor), or as offering considerably more protection to consumers (strongly pro-debtor). These data were gathered for a study of cross-state bankruptcy rates, and we cross-checked them against the report of the commission established by the CCPA.[93] About 45 percent of observations fall into the pro-creditor group, 38 percent are mildly pro-debtor, and 17 percent are strongly pro-debtor.

As discussed in the text of chapter 5, the Bankruptcy Reform Act of 1978 introduced federal minimum personal property and homestead exemptions, but it allowed states to opt out and (re)establish their own exemptions. For this period, we measure the value of exemptions separately for homeowners and nonhomeowners and take into account whether a state opted out.[94] Generosity of exemptions is captured using a dummy variable that indicates that the value of state exemptions is among the top one-third of all states in all years. Homestead exemptions were cross-checked against other sources.[95]

ELEMENTS OF *INDEFAULT*

State proxies for the determinants of default are the unemployment rate, the divorce rate, and per capita transfers from public assistance.[96] Assistance rose from $1.13 per person (standard deviation $0.24) to about $2.10 per person (standard deviation about $0.32). At the state level, the household data necessary to calculate the percent of the population that is unemployed and divorced in a consistent way begin in 1977. The percent of the population that was unemployed was about 7 percent during the period and did not differ meaningfully with a state's pre-*Marquette* usury rate or across the 1982 benchmark. The percent of the population that was divorced averaged 7 percent (standard deviation 1.8) and rose from 5.2 percent in 1977 (standard deviation about 1.3) to about 8.5 percent in 1990 (standard deviation about 1.8).

ELEMENTS OF *INDEBT*

In addition to usury rates, other determinants of the demand and supply of credit are income per capita,[97] the share of whites in the population,[98] and the number of locations of FDIC-insured banks.[99] To adjust income for inflation, we use the regional estimate of the CPI for all urban consumers. The base period for price adjustments is 1982–84. Income rose from about $10,700 (standard deviation about $1,800) to about $14,300 (standard deviation about $2,200) and did not differ across states with high and low usury rates before *Marquette*. Bank locations per 10,000 people rose from about 2 (standard deviation about 0.6) to about 2.8 (standard deviation about 0.7). In each year from 1971 to 1990, there were about 0.5 more bank locations per 10,000 people in states that started the period with low usury rates.

RESULTS

Table 6A.1 shows the regression results. For conciseness, table 6A.1 suppresses the coefficients on the other control variables included in the regressions and described above. Specification (1) includes observations for 1971–90. Specification (2) includes observations for 1977–90. The years included are limited by the divorce and unemployment data used here. Specifications (3) and (4) include years up to and including 1982; the start date varies because of the data limitation. Specification (5) includes 1983–90. We estimate specifications (1)–(5) by OLS; specification (6) includes state fixed effects.

As explained in the text of chapter 6 and mentioned above, the credit

	OLS					FE
	1971–1990	1977–1990	1971–1982	1977–1982	1983–1990	1971–1990
	(1)	(2)	(3)	(4)	(5)	(6)
Max. usury rate on credit cards (t-1)	0.954*** (0.254)	0.677*** (0.160)	0.875*** (0.207)	0.694*** (0.126)	0.325 (0.571)	-0.026 (0.239)
After 1982	33.671*** (11.193)	29.040*** (9.555)				25.068*** (5.269)
After 1982* max CC rate	-0.761* (0.513)	-0.542 (0.440)				-0.214 (0.241)
Mildly pro-debtor garnishment	15.739** (7.103)	10.844** (4.985)	11.333* (6.603)	8.695* (5.675)	3.080 (15.365)	-12.919* (6.611)
Strongly pro-debtor garnishment	9.261* (5.915)	10.497* (6.842)	7.469* (4.340)	8.184* (4.743)	6.049 (14.556)	-4.910 (4.768)
Mildly pro-debtor* max CC rate	-1.009** (0.387)	-0.663** (0.296)	-0.801** (0.365)	-0.605* (0.334)	-0.423 (0.687)	0.780** (0.372)
Strongly pro-debtor* max CC rate	-0.982*** (0.323)	-0.994*** (0.365)	-0.867*** (0.233)	-0.877*** (0.244)	-0.941 (0.702)	-0.041 (0.289)
After 1982* mildly pro-debtor	-23.044* (13.547)	-18.555* (11.532)				-4.206 (9.165)
After 1982* strongly pro-debtor	-7.647 (14.217)	-10.103 (13.303)				-3.209 (7.426)
After 1982* mildly* max CC rate	0.991* (0.629)	0.764 (0.533)				-0.177 (0.460)
After 1982* strongly* max CC rate	0.230 (0.686)	0.380 (0.678)				-0.100 (0.349)
Percent unemployed		0.442*** (0.130)		0.332** (0.144)		
Percent divorced		1.508*** (0.396)		1.105*** (0.252)		
Observations	944	694	550	300	394	944
R-squared	0.653	0.715	0.530	0.646	0.645	0.762

Before there was a national credit card market (ca. 1982), higher usury rates on credit cards increased the bankruptcy rate, but only in states that afforded consumers the minimum protection in garnishment under federal law (the omitted group). After 1982, interstate differences in credit card lending do not predict differences in indebtedness in the states. Notes: * p<0.05 ** p<0.01 *** p<0.001. Standard errors are in parentheses and clustered at the state level. Constant, year fixed effects and controls for homestead and personal property exemptions included in all specifications. Controls for enactment of the Bankruptcy Reform Act and controls for additional social and economic conditions are included; see text for details. *Source*: See appendix to chapter 6.

card market was essentially a national market after 1982. We focus on specifications (1)–(3) because we are interested in the impact of the cross-state differences between usury rates before the nationalization of the credit card market. A comparison of specifications (1)–(3) of table 6A.1 shows that coefficients are not much affected by the years included in the regression or the addition of controls for divorce and unemployment. We focus on specification (2), however, because it includes the social and economic controls that have been shown to be important in other work on the determinants of the bankruptcy rate.

The large number of interactions makes the regression coefficients in table 6A.1 difficult to interpret. It is necessary to examine the full marginal effect (including all interactions). In the states that offered only the minimum federal exemptions in garnishment (the omitted garnishment category), a one percentage point increase in the usury rate on credit cards was associated with an increase in personal bankruptcy petitions of about 0.7 per 10,000 people. The full marginal effect is different from zero at the 1 percent level. In states that offered protection in garnishment that went beyond the federal minimum, the point estimate of marginal effects is small and not statistically different from zero. Again, greater supply of credit increases the bankruptcy rate where creditors find it easy to garnish.

Specification (6) includes state fixed effects and is included for completeness. Although some of the coefficients are statistically different from zero, none of the full marginal effects are statistically significant. Changes in the usury rate within a state do not predict the bankruptcy rate because the changes coincide with the increase in out-of-state card offers.

CHAPTER SEVEN

Conclusion and Epilogue

O ur economic history of bankruptcy in America followed the arc of the story from the 1890s to 2005. In 1890, bankruptcy was a seldom-used provision of the US Constitution, but trade creditors wrote and successfully lobbied for a permanent law that would work for them. During the first decades of the twentieth century, bankruptcy was an important tool used mainly by businesses to collect from other businesses. However, as more households used it for relief from consumer debt, bankruptcy law was transformed. By 1950, bankruptcy was an essential part of the American social safety net. In 2000, more households than ever relied on it when things went wrong, but creditors were moving to block access to relief. The creditors were successful in 2005.

Most studies of bankruptcy cover only one episode of the story, and most focus on changes either in the bankruptcy rate or in the bankruptcy law. Our more comprehensive version of the story reveals that, in each historical episode, it was necessary to consider bankruptcy law and the use of the law together because they affected each other. In each historical episode, the specifics of bankruptcy law interacted with the specifics of related state laws governing debtor-creditor relations to determine who used the bankruptcy law and how often it was used in each state. How the bankruptcy law was written and who used it interacted to determine which groups had a stake in reforming the law. The prevailing narrative about who used the bankruptcy law and why they used it influenced the beliefs of Congress and the courts about the primary purpose and social impact of bankruptcy, which led to changes in law. In the previous chapters, we used this framework for understanding how America got the bankruptcy law that is in effect today. Here we briefly retell the story in a way that highlights the main themes.

A Brief Summary

At the end of the nineteenth century, an economic crisis broke a political deadlock; Republicans gained control of both houses of Congress and the White House; and they passed America's first permanent bankruptcy law in 1898. The authors of the law wrote it to solve the problems they encountered when they, as wholesalers and manufacturers, provided inventory to retailers all across the growing American economy and allowed retailers to pay after they sold the inventory. The law became essential to businesses. Most failed businesses used it, or the private out-of-court workouts that bankruptcy enabled, to settle with their creditors. Then they could move on to another venture without the burden of their old debts.

The authors of the bankruptcy law did not bar consumers from using it, and they did not anticipate how well the procedures they wrote for businesses would work for consumers. Innovations in consumer credit in the early twentieth century—including the small loan laws that increased the supply of credit to the working class—put many more people on the path that can lead to bankruptcy. If they happened to default, and if they happened to live in a state where collection law favored creditors, they were much more likely to seek refuge in the federal bankruptcy law, which sheltered them from other collection efforts and provided the benefit of discharge. Bankruptcy quickly became a social safety net for the working class. At the same time, Congress and the courts segued from the belief that the main purpose of the law was the settlement of debts into the belief that bankruptcy was mainly for debtor relief.

The Great Depression highlighted the shift in beliefs. Because Congress believed that the main purpose of bankruptcy was debtor relief, a proposal requiring personal bankrupts to make good on at least some of their debts before receiving a discharge failed in 1932. When Congress wanted to create new ways for businesses and consumers to extend the terms of their debt obligations under the protection of bankruptcy law, proponents cast their amendments as ways to relieve debtors from both the pressure of collections and the stigma of bankruptcy. However, the existence of procedures for court-supervised repayment of consumer debts under Chapter XIII did not erode the belief in the value of the discharge.

In the decades after World War II, consumer credit returned to its path of prewar growth. Retailers began to offer more credit and different forms of credit, including revolving credit accounts that later morphed into modern credit cards. As before, innovations in consumer credit put more people on the path to bankruptcy. As before, when people happened to default, whether they filed for bankruptcy mainly depended on whether they happened to live in a state where collection law favored creditors. Now, whether a particular filer for personal bankruptcy wound up with a quick discharge or with a three-year repayment plan depended almost entirely on whether he or she happened to live in a place and at a time when the bankruptcy referee administering the case favored Chapter XIII. Because relatively few bankruptcy referees promoted Chapter XIII, the discharge of debt in personal bankruptcy remained a central part of the safety net even as Congress created other safety net programs.

Nationally, and in the median state, the bankruptcy rate reached 10 per 10,000 in the mid-1960s. To resolve this "bankruptcy crisis," one interest group wanted to reform the bankruptcy law to make discharge more difficult. A second interest group wanted reforms that would affect people along the first and last steps toward bankruptcy. They wanted tighter regulation of the market for consumer credit and more protection from the state collection laws that favored creditors. The second group motivated Congress to act quickly by tying the cause of consumer credit protection to the civil rights movement. Congress required the states with pro-creditor garnishment to increase consumer protections in collections. The protection from creditors decreased the high personal bankruptcy rates in states such as Tennessee, which caused the national bankruptcy rate to level off. When Congress later turned to bankruptcy reform, it focused on problems of administration and did not make bankruptcy less attractive to debtors in default.

The bankruptcy reforms passed by Congress in 1978 therefore did nothing to keep the lid on the bankruptcy rate after the spread of general-use credit cards put even more people on the path to bankruptcy. The Supreme Court's 1978 *Marquette* decision allowed banks to issue high-rate cards to consumers in any state. The *Marquette* decision delinked a state's own usury laws from the supply of credit to its citizens. It also increased the profit margin on credit cards, so banks offered cards to people who probably could not have otherwise gotten credit. Improvements in information technology kept increasing the supply of consumer credit at the extensive margin. The bankruptcy rate continued to grow. Creditors, led by credit card issuers, resurrected the old narrative: the stigma of bankruptcy was gone, so people ran up debts because they knew they could get a discharge in bankruptcy. Creditors demanded that Congress require personal bankrupts to pay if they could. Republicans agreed, but Democrats kept their bills from becoming law.

By 2000, the personal bankruptcy rate was 50 per 10,000. In the 2002 elections, Republicans gained control of both houses of Congress and the White House for the first time since the 1950s. As in 1898, breaking the political deadlock enabled creditors to pass long-sought-after legislation. Though external events, including the 9/11 attacks, caused delays, America got BAPCPA.

Themes

There are four themes. Each was identified before as central to an individual episode of the story, but our more comprehensive history reveals that all four are present throughout the story arc. Two of the themes became clear through our use of a consistent cliometric approach to describing the determinants of the bankruptcy rate. Two became clear through our consistent use of new institutional methods for understanding the evolution of law.

The first theme is that long-run growth in personal bankruptcy comes from growth in the supply of credit at the extensive margin. Throughout the twentieth century, businesses invented new ways to grow through consumer lending. Throughout the twentieth century, states and courts liberalized usury, which made it profitable for businesses to make riskier loans. In the earliest episode we cover, the key innovation in consumer credit was legal small loans, which states made possible by small loan laws that increased the usury limit for licensed lenders. In the second episode, the key innovation was department store credit. In the third episode, bank-issued credit cards supplanted department store credit. Courts, Congress, and information technology enabled the growth and consolidation of the credit card market. While unfortunate events, from unemployment to illness to accidents, triggered the default of individuals throughout the century, there is not much evidence that a continuous increase in life's uncertainties across the distribution of income or wealth caused the growth of bankruptcy. Similarly, there is not much evidence that people have strategically run up debt to have it discharged in bankruptcy. Personal bankruptcy rates rose because creditors allowed more people onto the path.

The second theme is that the laws governing the collection of debt are key to interpreting geographic and temporal patterns in bankruptcy. When a person defaulted, it was primarily state law that regulated the collection efforts of creditors. Before the 1960s, state collection law varied from extremely pro-debtor to extremely pro-creditor. In the 1960s, federal statutes and case law began to require a minimum level of protection from creditors, but significant variation remained. The costs of collection to debtors—lost wages, lost jobs, lost peace—caused people to seek federal bankruptcy protection. The interaction of collection law and bankruptcy law caused bankruptcy rates to be higher in states with pro-creditor collections. Pro-creditor collection law also magnified the effect of the growth in the credit supply and the effect of recession on the bankruptcy rate in those states. Because of this interaction, states that have pro-creditor garnishment law have an outsize effect on the national bankruptcy rate.

Together the first two themes imply that growth in personal bankruptcy is seldom a "crisis." More personal bankruptcy does not generally indicate bad economic performance. Because recessions increase the bankruptcy rate more in states with pro-creditor collection law, bankruptcy is not a direct measure of the local business cycle. Further, to the extent that a broadening of the market for consumer credit promotes sustained economic growth (by encouraging investment) and reduces cyclical disruption (by smoothing consumption and production), growth in bankruptcy may indicate economic health.

The third theme is that people matter. A small number of individuals had outsized influence on the history of bankruptcy. Jay Torrey, the president of the National Convention of Representatives of Commercial Bodies, pushed for a system of creditor control rather than government administration in his bankruptcy bill, even though creditors had earlier supported a bill that would have relied on government officials. The system of creditor control promoted the rise of personal bankruptcy and the rise of interest groups composed of legal professionals, both of which were key to the evolution of the law in later episodes. Walter Chandler was a second pivotal person. Without Chandler's insistence on keeping the issue of wage earner workouts before Congress, Chapter XIII may not have become part of federal bankruptcy law. The preferences of in-

dividual referees, like Valentine Nesbit, Clarence Allgood, Henry Bundschu, and Charles Pomeroy determined where Chapter XIII would be
employed. Leonor Sullivan chose to expand a truth-in-lending bill to include restrictions on collection methods. The hearings she held also provided the evidence that Justice William O. Douglas used to strike down
prejudgment garnishment. In these matters, none of these individuals
appears to have been responding to the demands of an interest group or
even public opinion; it is likely that they used their positions to shape the
law based on their own beliefs. Toward the end of the story it becomes
difficult to identify the roles of particular individuals, though Robert W.
Johnson and the other academics associated with the Credit Research
Center played a pivotal role. The story that they told was not new. Creditors had long claimed that many debtors who could pay were taking advantage of Chapter 7 and that the costs of these discharged debts were
borne by debtors who did pay. But creditors had to support this story
with anecdotes and occasional small-scale studies. The Credit Research
Center provided specific estimates of the percentage of bankrupts that
could have paid, the amount lost due to their failure to repay, and the
cost borne by other debtors. And although the studies had not been
through the sort of peer review process typically associated with academic research, they bore an academic stamp through the center's associations with Purdue University and Georgetown University. The center
was an innovation that provided creditors with specificity and credibility
that they could not generate on their own.

The final theme is that stories matter.[1] During episodes when interest groups interpreted growth in the personal bankruptcy rate as a "crisis," their proposals to change law to resolve the crisis were crafted to
suit the stories they told about *why* people use the bankruptcy law. Interest groups of creditors told a story about consumers using bankruptcy
to ditch their obligations, so they repeatedly lobbied for changes to restrict access to the discharge. In 1981, for example, a witness reminded
Congress, "The proposal you have before you is not new. Essentially, the
same idea was proposed to the Congress in 1967. . . . [I]n 1932, there was
a similar proposal even before we had Chapter 13."[2] Before the run-up to
BAPCPA, interest groups allied with consumers and legal professionals
and, supported by many legislators, argued that restricting the discharge
was "un-American."[3] The consumer groups told a story about creditors
conning people out of their hard-earned wages and harassing them af-
terward, so they lobbied for changes to regulate lenders. In the debate

over BAPCPA, the interest groups allied with consumers did not have a clear villain. They did not have a loan shark or a dishonest retailer. On the other side, creditors—especially banks that issue credit cards—used their financial resources to create and disseminate a story in which deadbeat borrowers imposed the cost of their consumption on more honest Americans. Creditors won the story and won over Congress.

Epilogue

We end our economic history of bankruptcy with the 2005 passage of BAPCPA, but (of course) the evolution of bankruptcy continues. Personal bankruptcy rates declined by 50 percent in the median state after BAPCPA, as shown in figure 7.1. Even during the Great Recession, rates remained lower than they had been just before BAPCPA in all but the highest-rate states.

There were two elements to the decline. First, it seems likely that from 1999 to 2005, as every Congress passed some version of the creditor's reforms, some people filed in anticipation of eventual enactment. These people would no longer have been "at risk" for filing again immediately after BAPCPA. Second, BAPCPA increased the financial cost of

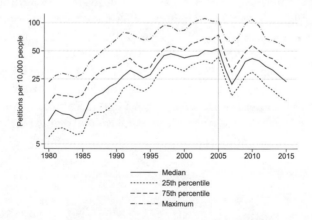

FIG. 7.1. In the median state, the personal bankruptcy rate was steadily high in the years that Congress was considering reforms. After the passage of BAPCPA in 2005, indicated by the vertical line, the rate dropped to less than 50 percent of peak. The rate rose again during the years of the mortgage crisis and Great Recession, but it reached pre-BAPCPA levels only in the states with the very highest rates. *Source*: See appendix to chapter 1.

using the bankruptcy law by 200 to 300 percent.[4] Under BAPCPA, debtors must take a credit counseling course as a prerequisite to filing, and they must take a financial management course as a prerequisite to discharge. They must submit to the court tax returns for the four previous years, plus detailed balance sheet and budget information. Lawyers have to certify the completeness and veracity of all the materials under penalty of fine. Filing fees have also gone up.

With BAPCPA in place, fewer people in default choose to use the federal bankruptcy law. More people simply remain in default. BAPCPA caused the insolvency rate to rise by 25 percent. Remaining in insolvency reduces credit scores and access to credit—not just relative to people who do not default, but also relative to people who can use the bankruptcy law.[5]

In addition to reducing overall use of the bankruptcy law, BAPCPA changed who uses the bankruptcy law and how they use it. Although the reform sought to decrease filings under Chapter 7 by people with higher incomes, the income of Chapter 7 filers did not fall meaningfully right after BAPCPA.[6] But from 2010 to 2016, the *nominal* incomes of filers under both Chapter 7 and Chapter 13 fell.[7] Under BAPCPA, people now postpone seeking bankruptcy protection until they are in extreme financial distress.[8] The debt-to-asset, debt-to-income, and expenses-to-income ratios of filers are higher. Filers are less able to pay now, and the higher fees eat into their estates. Distributions to creditors have fallen.[9]

Because banks that issue credit cards have not much benefited from BAPCPA, they may not be such a keen interest group moving forward. BAPCPA decreased the power of the bankruptcy court and increased the relative power of the US Trustee, part of the Department of Justice.[10] Perhaps trustees will be the interest group that finally moves the US toward officialism. Our framework suggests that the next iteration of the bankruptcy law will likely depend on the narrative that is built around how the law is currently used.

Notes

Preface

1. B. Hansen, "Commercial Associations"; and B. Hansen, "People's Welfare."
2. B. Hansen and M. Hansen, "Role of Path Dependence."
3. B. Hansen and M. Hansen, "Religion."
4. M. Hansen and B. Hansen, "Crisis and Bankruptcy"; and B. Hansen and M. Hansen, "Evolution of Garnishment."
5. M. Hansen, "Sources of Credit."
6. M. Hansen and Ziebarth, "Credit Relationships."

Chapter One

1. United States District Court, Baltimore District of Maryland, "Clutch Case File." To comply with Internal Review Board protocol, we have changed the names and other personally identifying information of filers for personal bankruptcy.
2. United States Courts, "BAPCPA Report—2010."
3. United States, Department of Health and Human Services, "FY 2010 Budget in Brief."
4. Bailey, "Assignment in Insolvency"; Bailey, "Discharge in Insolvency"; Newmyer, *Supreme Court*; and Zainaldin, *Law in Antebellum Society*.
5. Tabb, "Historical Evolution."
6. Ayotte and Yun, "Matching Bankruptcy Laws"; Berkovitch, Israel, and Zender, "Optimal Bankruptcy Law"; Blazy et al., "Severe or Gentle Bankruptcy Law"; Gordon, "Optimal Bankruptcy Code"; Grochulski, "Optimal Personal Bankruptcy Design"; Knot and Vychodil, "What Drives"; and Wang and White, "Optimal Personal Bankruptcy Procedure."

7. The discharge is also defended on ethical grounds. For a discussion, see Tabb, "Historical Evolution."

8. Fan and White, "Personal Bankruptcy."

9. Carlos, Kosack, and Penarrieta, "Bankruptcy, Discharge."

10. The 1800 Bankruptcy Act followed the end of a boom in land speculation. The 1841 law followed the Panics of 1837 and 1839. The 1867 law followed the commercial failures arising from the economic dislocations caused by the Civil War. The 1898 act followed the Panic of 1893.

11. Skeel, *Debt's Dominion*, describes the pattern of passing and repealing bankruptcy laws in the nineteenth century.

12. C. Warren, *Bankruptcy in United States History*, 9. Precedents for Warren's view date back to the 1860s. In a debate on the 1867 Bankruptcy Act, Senator Reverdy Johnson noted, "No bankruptcy law has ever been passed except because of the large amount of existing debts which were depressing the industry of the country and ruining the debtor," United States Congress, *Congressional Record*, 1867, 1004. In an 1890 treatise on mercantile credit, P. R. Earling, a Chicago merchant, described how the past three bankruptcy laws had resulted from periods of crisis: "At each of these periods, the provisions of the Bankrupt Law were invoked for the benefit of the debtor class, who by severe panic had become hopelessly involved," Earling, *Whom to Trust*, 217.

13. Coleman, *Debtors and Creditors*; Jackson, *Logic and Limits*; and Tabb, "History."

14. In addition to the works previously cited, see Balleisen, *Navigating Failure*; Gross, *Failure and Forgiveness*; Jackson, *Logic and Limits*; and Posner, "Political Economy."

15. B. Hansen, "Commercial Associations."

16. Warren was not at all focused on authors of the 1898 act. He made only brief mention of one of the organizations that drafted and lobbied for bankruptcy legislation, the National Convention of Representatives of Commercial Bodies, and mistakenly referred to it as the National Convention of Commercial Organizations. Subsequent authors relied on Warren and continued to misname the organization. See, for example, Coleman, *Debtors and Creditors*; Friedman, *History of American Law*; Frimet, "Birth of Bankruptcy."

17. Skeel, *Debt's Dominion*; Skeel, "Bankruptcy Lawyers"; Skeel, "Evolutionary Theory"; and Skeel, "Genius."

18. Boyes and Faith, "Some Effects"; and Shepard, "Personal Failures"

19. Domowitz and Eovaldi, "Impact of the BRA."

20. Moss and Johnson, "Rise of Consumer Bankruptcy."

21. *Bates v. State Bar of Ariz.*; *Marquette v. Omaha*.

22. Apilado, Dauten, and Smith, "Personal Bankruptcies"; Heck, "Econometric Analysis"; White, "Personal Bankruptcy"; and Lefgren and McIntyre, "Explaining the Puzzle."

23. Agarwal, Liu, and Mielnicki, "Exemption Laws"; and Dawsey and Ausubel, "Informal Bankruptcy." Exemption levels also influence the choice of procedure in bankruptcy; see, e.g., White, "Why Don't More?" and Nelson, "Consumer Bankruptcy."

24. Buckley and Brinig, "Bankruptcy Puzzle"; Fay, Hurst, and White, "Household Bankruptcy Decision"; Gross and Souleles, "Empirical Analysis"; Shiers and Williamson, "Nonbusiness Bankruptcies"; and Weiss, Bhandari, and Robins, "Analysis of State-Wide Variation."

25. Warren and Tyagi, *Two-Income Trap.*

26. Garrett and Wall, "Personal-Bankruptcy Cycles"; Sullivan, Warren, and Westbrook, *As We Forgive*; Sullivan, Warren, and Westbrook, *Fragile Middle Class*; and Weiss, Bhandari, and Robins, "Analysis of State-Wide Variation."

27. Fisher, "Effect of Unemployment Benefits."

28. On the supply of credit, see Livshits, MacGee, and Tertilt, "Accounting for the Rise"; and Livshits, MacGee, and Tertilt, "Democratization of Credit." On the role of state law, see Lefgren and McIntyre, "Explaining the Puzzle."

29. Zywicki, "Economics of Credit Cards," makes this point in an effort to rebut the work of empirical economists, including White, "Bankruptcy Reform and Credit Cards"; and Livshits, MacGee, and Tertilt, "Democratization of Credit," who find that that increases in the supply of credit are the likely cause of increases in personal bankruptcy.

30. Consumer and mortgage credit from Board of Governors of the Federal Reserve System, "Consumer Credit"; Board of Governors of the Federal Reserve System, "Mortgage Debt"; and James and Sylla, "Net Public and Private Debt." Index of real consumption per capita from Jordà, Schularick, and Taylor, "Macrohistory Database."

31. National Bureau of Economic Research, "US Business Cycle."

32. For a summary of the cross-disciplinary debates of the 1960s, see David, "Transport Innovation." On recent differences, see Hilt, "Economic History."

33. Athreya, "Welfare Implications"; White, "Why Don't More?"; and Zhang, Sabarwal, and Gan, "Strategic or Nonstrategic."

34. Recent work in comparative bankruptcy history takes a similar approach; see Ramsay, "US Exceptionalism"; and Ramsay, *Personal Insolvency.*

35. Examples from economics, political science, law, and sociology include Bebchuk and Roe, "Theory of Path Dependence"; David, "Path Dependence"; Greif and Laitin, "Theory"; Hathaway, "Path Dependence"; Mahoney, *Legacies of Liberalism*; North, *Institutions*; North, *Understanding the Process*; and Pierson, "Increasing Returns."

36. Examples include Alexander, "Institutions"; Bridges, "Path Dependence"; and Crouch and Farrell, "Breaking the Path."

37. North, *Understanding the Process*, 77.

38. A good starting point for following the story of corporate bankruptcy is Skeel, "Evolutionary Theory."

39. United States, Administrative Office of the US Courts, *Annual Report of AOUSC*; United States Department of Justice, *Annual Report of the AG*; and United States Courts, "Table F-2."

40. Hansen, Davis, and Fasules, *Bankruptcy Statistics.*

41. Haines and Inter-university Consortium, *Historical.*

42. United States, Department of Commerce, "Personal Income Summary."

43. Roth, *SEER.*

44. Hansen, Chen, and Davis, *USDC Shape Files.*

45. Though sampling every 100th case would have been a desirable strategy, it was not deemed feasible by National Archives staff.

46. M. Hansen and Ziebarth, "Credit Relationships"; and M. Hansen, "Sources of Credit."

47. See particularly the studies summarized in Herrmann, "Families in Bankruptcy"; and Sullivan, Warren, and Westbrook, *As We Forgive.*

48. For example, Zywicki, "Consumer Bankruptcy Crisis."

49. Hyman, "Ending Discrimination, Legitimating Debt"; Ladd, "Equal Credit Opportunity"; and M. Hansen and Miller, "New View of Women."

50. Haines and Inter-university Consortium, *Historical*; and United States, Bureau of the Census, "Households by Household Type."

51. United States, Bureau of the Census, "Household Size."

52. This counting problem has been widely discussed. See especially, Domowitz and Eovaldi, "Impact of the BRA"; and Domowitz and Tamer, "Two Hundred Years."

53. Also see M. Hansen and B. Hansen, "Crisis and Bankruptcy."

54. Hynes, Malani, and Posner, "Political Economy."

55. White, "Bankruptcy and Consumer Behavior."

56. Lefgren and McIntyre, "Explaining the Puzzle."

57. Hausman and Taylor, "Panel Data"; Breusch et al., "FEVD"; and Plümper and Troeger, "Efficient Estimation."

Chapter Two

1. Ellman was born in 1863 and emigrated from Russia in 1881. United States, Bureau of the Census, "1870 Census Manuscript Hornellsville."

2. United States District Court, St. Louis, Eastern District of Missouri, "Ellman Case File."

3. Ancestry.com, *St. Louis, Missouri*, 217.

4. Ancestry.com, 304.

5. United States, Bureau of the Census, "1920 Census Manuscript St. Louis."

6. Eaton, "Lucius Eaton to Merchants Exchange"; and United States Senate, "Memorial of Many Commercial Bodies."

7. United States Senate, "Resolution of Retail Grocers."

8. For a review of state laws as they related to foreign creditors, see Bailey, "Assignment in Insolvency," 281–99; and Dunscomb, *Bankruptcy*, 2:151–67.

9. United States Senate, "Memorial of Many Commercial Bodies," 4.

10. United States Senate, "Memorials, Press Clippings, Etc.," 89.

11. United States Senate, "Memorial of Many Commercial Bodies," 70.

12. Barger, *Distribution's Place*, 33; Nystrom, *Economics of Retailing*, 405. For a description of the role of Chicago wholesalers as creditors, see Cronon, *Nature's Metropolis*, 322–23.

13. Merchants grew from 357,647 to 784,210, and travelers increased from 7,262 to 92,919. Moeckel, *Development of the Wholesaler*, 118.

14. Advocates of the law spoke frequently of the high costs of the last bankruptcy law and the need to ensure that the many fees associated with it were not duplicated. See, e.g., United States Senate, "Memorial of Convention of Commercial Bodies," 11.

15. Dates from United States House of Representatives, "Report of the Internal Commerce"; and National Industrial Conference Board, *Trade Associations*.

16. Quoted in Dunscomb, *Bankruptcy*, 2:147.

17. United States Senate, "Memorials, Press Clippings, Etc."

18. Bensel, *Political Economy*.

19. United States Congress, *Congressional Record*, June 28, 1898, 6435.

20. B. Hansen, "Commercial Associations," 105.

21. B. Hansen, 103.

22. United States Congress, *Congressional Record*, February 16, 1898, 1804.

23. United States Congress, *Congressional Record*, June 28, 1898, 6429.

24. Boshkoff, "Limited, Conditional, Suspended," 108.

25. Lowell, "Bankruptcy."

26. National Convention, *Proceedings*.

27. Compare the 1892 House version to the 1898 Conference Report. United States House of Representatives, "House Report on Bankruptcy, 1892"; and United States Senate, "Senate Report on Bankruptcy, 1898."

28. Skeel, *Debt's Dominion*, 39.

29. B. Hansen, "Commercial Associations."

30. B. Hansen; B. Hansen and M. Hansen, "Role of Path Dependence," 211.

31. There probably was never one referee per county. In 1938, there were about 500. United States, Administrative Office of the US Courts, *Annual Report of AOUSC for 1943*, 15.

32. United States Congress, *Congressional Record*, June 17, 1902, 6945.

33. United States Congress, 6946.

34. B. Hansen and M. Hansen, "Role of Path Dependence," 213.

35. United States, Department of Justice, *Annual Report of the AG 1903*, 125.

36. United States Congress, *Congressional Record*, June 17, 1902, 6940.

37. United States Congress, *Congressional Record*, February 23, 1910, 2265.

38. United States Congress, 2273.

39. The National Convention of Representatives of Commercial Bodies, which was formed for the sole purpose of obtaining bankruptcy legislation, ceased to exist after the law was passed.

40. Skeel, "Genius."

41. Murnane, *Bankruptcy*, 62.

42. Failures and concerns are from United States, Bureau of the Census, *Statistical Abstract*. Net new business formation is the annual change in the number of business concerns. Bankruptcies are from United States, Administrative Office of the US Courts, *Annual Report of AOUSC*.

43. Failures are from United States, Bureau of the Census, *Statistical Abstract*. Bankruptcies are from United States, Administrative Office of the US Courts, *Annual Report of AOUSC*. Though the number of business bankruptcies is strongly correlated with net new business formation, during this period neither the size of the homestead exemption nor the size of the personal property exemption is correlated with new business formation after controlling for income. In contrast, entrepreneurship and exemptions were positively related in the 1980s and 1990s. See Fan and White, "Personal Bankruptcy."

44. Lane and Schary, "Understanding," 93; and Kaplan, *Small Business*.

45. Romer and Romer, "Incentive Effects," suggests that higher and unpredictable marginal tax rates may have contributed to the large fluctuations in new business formation in the 1920s.

46. Remington, "Bankruptcy Law," 591.

47. "Bankruptcy Law Must Stand," 30; and "Failures in 1908," 25.

48. On the history of adjustment bureaus, see Billig, "What Price Bankruptcy?"

49. United States, Department of Justice, *Strengthening of Procedure*, 184; also see Billig, "What Price Bankruptcy?"

50. Brewster, *Legal Aspects of Credit*, 454.

51. Sadd and Williams, *Causes of Bankruptcies*.

52. United States, Department of Justice, *Strengthening of Procedure*, 174.

53. Douglas and Marshall, "Factual Study," 33.

54. Nehemkis, "Boston Poor Debtor Court"; and Sadd and Williams, *Causes of Bankruptcies*. On the use of consumer credit, see Olney, *Buy Now, Pay Later*; and Calder, *Financing the American Dream*.

55. Olney, "Demand"; and Olney, *Buy Now, Pay Later*.

56. Olney, *Buy Now, Pay Later*, 126–28; and Calder, *Financing the American Dream*, 184–91.

57. Snowden, "Evolution."

58. Postel-Vinay, "Debt Dilution."

59. Snowden, "Anatomy"; and Snowden, "Historiography."

60. For detail about the housing bubble and bust, see the essays in White, Snowden, and Fishback, *Housing and Mortgage Markets.*

61. Persons, "Credit Expansion." Long-term mortgage bonds feature prominently in the case that introduces chapter 3.

62. Ryan, "Family Finance," 417.

63. Plummer and Young, *Sales Finance Companies*; and Olney, *Buy Now, Pay Later.*

64. Persons, "Credit Expansion."

65. Olney, "Avoiding Default." United States, Bureau of Foreign and Domestic Commerce, *Causes of Failures and Bankruptcies in New Jersey*, was an early study finding that automobile accident liability judgments were a cause of bankruptcy for many.

66. Calder, *Financing the American Dream*, 147; see also, Hyman, *Debtor Nation*, 13–20; and Olegario, *Engine of Enterprise*, 128–32.

67. Unless otherwise noted, statistics on installment debt are from Ryan, "Family Finance."

68. Despite the efforts of reformers throughout the twentieth century, many Americans continue to depend on financial services that are regarded as less than respectable, if not illegal, such as pawnbroking, payday lending, check cashing, and loan sharks. Caskey, *Fringe Banking*; and Servon, *Unbanking of America.*

69. A 1938 federal suit changed this practice. After the suit, sales finance companies were required to refund equity if the borrower defaulted. Defaults rose, as did options to adjust terms. Olney, "Avoiding Default."

70. Clark, *Financing the Consumer*, 141.

71. Clark, 144.

72. Rockoff, "Prodigals and Projectors."

73. Benmelech and Moskowitz, "Political Economy."

74. There is evidence that wage earners obtained cash loans under these laws to refinance the purchase of assets obtained through installment contracts. Plummer and Young, *Sales Finance Companies.*

75. Carruthers, Guinnane, and Lee, "Bringing 'Honest Capital.'"

76. Calder, *Financing the American Dream*, 147. See also Hyman, *Debtor Nation*, 13–20; and Olegario, *Engine of Enterprise*, 128–32.

77. Benmelech and Moskowitz, "Political Economy." For a literature review, see Hynes and Posner, "Law and Economics."

78. See Fleming, *City of Debtors.*

79. *Massie v. Cessna.*

80. *Massie v. Cessna.*

81. For a list of states and cases, see B. Hansen and M. Hansen, "Evolution of

Garnishment," 32–33. On wage assignment during the early twentieth century generally, see Fleming, "Borrower's Tale"; and Fleming, *City of Debtors.*

82. *Mutual Loan Co. v. Martell.*

83. Nugent and Jones, "Wage Executions Part 1."

84. Hynes, Malani, and Posner, "Political Economy"; and Goodman, "Emergence of Homestead Exemption."

85. M. Hansen and B. Hansen, "Crisis and Bankruptcy."

86. B. Hansen and M. Hansen, "Evolution of Garnishment."

87. Nugent and Jones, "Wage Executions Part 1"; Nugent, Hamm, and Jones, "Wage Executions Part 2"; and M. Hansen and B. Hansen, "Crisis and Bankruptcy." The original study used the term "severe" to indicate pro-creditor law and "ineffective" to indicate pro-debtor law. It covered twenty-three states, and we classified an additional seven states using other sources.

88. M. Hansen and B. Hansen, "Crisis and Bankruptcy"; and Lefgren and McIntyre, "Explaining the Puzzle."

89. United States, Department of Justice, *Annual Report of the AG for 1905,* 95.

90. M. Hansen and B. Hansen, "Crisis and Bankruptcy."

91. In the 1960s and 1970s, a national pro-debtor lobby emerged. It pushed states toward more uniform laws and reduced, but did not eliminate, geographical differences in the personal bankruptcy rate. See chapter 5.

92. National Convention, *Proceedings.*

93. "Judge Landis under Fire," 3.

94. Robertson, "In the Loan Sharks' Grasp."

95. Edwards, "Debt and the 'Loan Sharks.'"

96. "Credit and Loan Sharks," 3.

97. Quoted in Olmstead, "Bankruptcy," 843.

98. *Williams v. United States Fiduciary & Guaranty Co.*

99. *Freshman v. Atkins.*

100. Noel, "Bankruptcy Law," 154.

101. D. Smith, "Elimination of the Unworthy."

102. Prendergast, "Enduring National Bankruptcy System," 382.

103. "Seek Change in Law."

104. "New Association Formed." From 1912 to 1927, it was known as the National Association of Retail Credit Men.

105. American Bar Association, *Report.*

106. American Bar Association, 4.

107. Robinson, "Scope and Effect," 51.

108. Cook, "Analysis," 237; McLaughlin, "Amendment," 341; and Robinson, "Scope and Effect," 49.

109. "Capital Credit Men Leave."

110. "Referees in Bankruptcy."

111. United States Congress, *Congressional Record*, April 17, 1926, 7679.

112. United States Congress, 7680.

113. United States Congress, *Congressional Record*, May 18, 1926, 9610; United States Congress, *Congressional Record*, May 20, 1926, 9749.

114. United States, Bureau of the Census, "1940 Census Manuscript Saverton."

115. United States District Court, St. Louis, Eastern District of Missouri, "Glascock Case File."

116. United States, Bureau of the Census, "1910 Census Manuscript Hannibal."

117. Ancestry.com, *Hannibal, Missouri*.

118. Carruthers, Guinnane, and Lee, "Bringing 'Honest Capital.'"

119. Hubachek, "Development."

120. Hubachek gives 1927 as the date of passage for Missouri. Carruthers, Guinnane, and Lee, "Bringing 'Honest Capital,'" list Missouri as a state without a small loan law as of 1930, but on page 401 discuss "working to pass" the small loan law there in 1927. Missouri is not discussed in their online appendix at http://ssrn.com/abstract=1413905.

121. M. Hansen and B. Hansen, "Crisis and Bankruptcy."

122. M. Hansen and B. Hansen; Nugent and Jones, "Wage Executions Part 1"; Nugent, Hamm, and Jones, "Wage Executions Part 2"; and Nugent, Hamm, and Jones, "Wage Executions Part 3."

123. Goodman, "Emergence of Homestead Exemption"; National Association of Credit Management, *Credit Manual*; and Wickens, "Farmer Bankruptcies."

124. Douglas, *Real Wages*; United States, Bureau of the Census, *Historical Statistics*; and Fishback and Kantor, "Datasets."

125. United States, Bureau of the Census, *Statistical Abstract*.

126. Douglas, *Real Wages*; United States, Bureau of the Census, *Historical Statistics*; and Fishback and Kantor, "Datasets."

127. Fishback and Kantor, *Prelude to the Welfare State*; and Fishback and Kantor, "Datasets."

128. United States, Bureau of Labor Statistics, "CPI."

Chapter Three

1. "Foreclosure Suit."

2. "Reorganization Project."

3. United States District Court, St. Louis, Eastern District of Missouri, "Koplar Case File."

4. The Koplar case was the first in St. Louis and the sixth in the nation under Section 77b. "Suit Discloses Default on Bonds of Park Plaza."

5. Central States Life Insurance Company held a substantial amount of the

bonds secured by the Park Plaza Hotel, but it had not invested in the other properties. It objected to Koplar's plan. After several years of litigation, the Park Plaza case was severed from the proceedings on the other properties. *Central States Life Insurance Co. v. Koplar Co.*

6. Koplar Properties, "Koplarproperties.Com"; and "100 People Who Shaped St. Louis."

7. Bernanke, "Bankruptcy, Liquidity, and Recession," 155; Domowitz and Eovaldi, "Impact of the BRA," 819; Field, "Bankruptcy," 26; and Keller, *Regulating a New Economy*, 98.

8. Richardson and Gou, "Bank Failures."

9. M. Hansen and Ziebarth, "Credit Relationships."

10. M. Hansen, "Sources of Credit."

11. Craig, "Consumption Expenditures." Deflated using the Consumer Price Index for All Urban Consumers (CPI-U).

12. Richardson and Troost, "Monetary Intervention."

13. Statistics on filings by occupation are not available for this period. Cases closed in year *t+1* serves as a proxy for cases filed in year *t*. For a full explanation, see the appendix to chapter 1.

14. Unemployment index taken from Wallis, "Employment in the Great Depression." The ranks of the unemployed grew by 7.2 million in states with pro-debtor or intermediate garnishment, while there were "only" 4.3 million unemployed in states with pro-creditor garnishment. Population data are described in the appendix to chapter 1.

15. United States, Department of Justice, *Annual Report of the AG.* The first mention of debtor fraud is on page 26 of the 1910 *Report.* Referee fraud is first mentioned on page 50 of the 1912 *Report.* The first mention of trustee fraud is on page 63 of the 1915 *Report.*

16. United States, Department of Justice, 1927 *Report*, 49.

17. United States, Department of Justice, 1928 *Report*, 56–57.

18. United States, Department of Justice, 44.

19. Honsberger, "Origins of the NBC."

20. Donovan, *Administration of Bankruptcy Estates.*

21. Cover, *Business and Personal Failure*; Douglas, "Wage Earner Bankruptcies"; Douglas and Marshall, "Factual Study"; Fortas, "Wage Assignments;" and Sadd and Williams, *Causes of Bankruptcies.*

22. United States, Department of Justice, *Strengthening of Procedure*, 3.

23. United States, Department of Justice, 93.

24. "Herbert Hoover: Special Message on Reform."

25. United States Senate, Hearing on S. 3866.

26. See the testimony of W. Randolph Montgomery, general counsel to the National Association of Credit Men, United States Congress, Joint Hearings on S. 3866, 488–51.

27. Joint Hearings on S. 3866, 465.

28. Skeel, *Debt's Dominion*, 90.

29. Douglas, "Wage Earner Bankruptcies," 592.

30. United States Congress, Joint Hearings on S. 3866, 487.

31. Joint Hearings on S. 3866, 487.

32. Joint Hearings on S. 3866, 487.

33. "Herbert Hoover: Special Message on Legislation."

34. "Herbert Hoover: Special Message on Legislation."

35. For more general treatments of mortgage moratoria during the Great Depression, see Alston, "Farm Foreclosure Moratorium Legislation"; Rucker and Alston, "Farm Failures"; and Wheelock, "Changing the Rules."

36. *Louisville Joint Stock Land Bank v. Radford.*

37. *Wright v. Vinton Branch*; also see Hanna, "New Frazier-Lemke Act."

38. *Wright v. Vinton Branch.*

39. B. Hansen, "People's Welfare"; B. Hansen, *Institutions*, 95–128; and Tufano, "Business Failure."

40. See especially Posner, "Political Economy;" Skeel, *Debt's Dominion*; Skeel, "Evolutionary Theory."

41. Kinsley, "Thacher."

42. Dixon, Epstein, and Tweedy, "Where Did Chapter 13 Come From?"

43. Palmer, "Poor Man's Receivership."

44. Palmer, 99.

45. Nehemkis, "Boston Poor Debtor Court."

46. United States Senate, Hearing on S. 3866, 576.

47. "Amortization" in this context meant simply spreading payments over time. The company's commission is mentioned; interest is not.

48. United States, Department of Justice, *Strengthening of Procedure*, 80.

49. United States Senate, Hearing on S. 3866, 288.

50. Hearing on S. 3866, 102.

51. "Wage-Earner Receiverships," 462.

52. United States Congress, Joint Hearings on S. 3866, 934.

53. Joint Hearings on S. 3866, 128–30.

54. Hearing on S. 3866, 508.

55. Joint Hearings on S. 3866, 578.

56. Joint Hearings on S. 3866, 622.

57. Boshkoff, "Limited," 113.

58. Garrison, "Wisconsin's New Personal Receivership."

59. United States House of Representatives, Hearing on H.R. 1981, 2. Recall from chapter 2 that Tennessee had pro-creditor garnishment. It trailed only Alabama in the number and rate of personal bankruptcy cases.

60. Hearing on H.R. 1981, 3.

61. Hearing on H.R. 1981, 6.

62. Hearing on H.R. 1981, 39.

63. United States House of Representatives, Hearing on H.R. 11219, 30.

64. See, for instance, United States House of Representatives, Hearing on H.R. 8046, 62.

65. United States House of Representatives, Hearing on H.R. 1981, 1.

66. Hunt, "National Bankruptcy Conference," 576.

67. Banks, "National Bankruptcy Conference," 116.

68. On the corporate reorganization provisions of the law and how they were used, see Skeel, *Debt's Dominion*.

69. Arrangements include the following from the *Annual Reports of the AG*: cases concluded under Sections 77 and 77b, cases concluded under Sections 80 and 81, compositions under Section 12, compositions under Section 74, and extensions under Section 74.

70. Special to the *New York Times*, "Senate Modifies Bankruptcy Laws."

71. National Association of Credit Management, *Credit Manual*, 467 (1939 edition).

72. United States Congress, *Congressional Record*, August 10, 1937, 8649.

73. Berglof and Rosenthal, "Political Economy."

74. M. Hansen and B. Hansen, "Crisis and Bankruptcy."

75. Flood, *Historical Data*.

76. United States, Bureau of the Census, *Census of Religious Bodies*; and B. Hansen and M. Hansen, "Religion."

77. Nugent, "Small Loan Debt"; Robinson and Nugent, *Regulation*; and Ryan, *Usury*.

78. Flood, *Historical Data*.

79. United States, Bureau of the Census, *Statistical Abstract*.

80. United States, Bureau of the Census.

Chapter Four

1. United States District Court, Kansas City, Western District of Missouri, "Hall Case File."

2. As will be discussed more below, relatively few early users of Chapter XIII were homeowners. The use of Chapter XIII (later renamed to Chapter 13) to save a home became much more prominent after the 1978 Bankruptcy Reform Act, which allowed mortgage payments to be included in the repayment plan. See the last section of chapter 5 and chapter 6. For evidence, see the supplemental results in the appendix to chapter 4.

3. Domowitz and Sartain, "Determinants"; Domowitz and Sartain, "Incentives"; Nelson, "Consumer Bankruptcy"; and Sullivan and Worden, "Rehabilitation or Liquidation."

4. Changes in 1978 that provided a more generous discharge after a completed repayment plan also did not influence chapter choice. Domowitz and Sartain, "Determinants."

5. Lefgren, McIntyre, and Miller, "Chapter 7 or 13."

6. Jagtiani and Li, "Credit Access."

7. Before 2005, all payments were based on the difference between projected monthly income and actual monthly expenses. After 2005, if average actual income over the past six months was greater than median state income, then a debtor was allowed only a standard allowance for exemptions. Lefgren, McIntyre, and Miller, "Chapter 7 or 13."

8. White, "Why Don't More?"

9. Braucher, "Lawyers and Consumer Bankruptcy."

10. Lefgren and McIntyre, "Explaining the Puzzle"; Lefgren, McIntyre, and Miller, "Chapter 7 or 13"; Norberg and Compo, "Report on an Empirical Study;" Sullivan, Warren, and Westbrook, "Laws, Models, and Real People"; and Sullivan, Warren, and Westbrook, "Persistence."

11. United States House of Representatives, Hearing on H.R. 1057 and H.R. 5771.

12. The historical volatility contrasts with modern-day stability. See, e.g., Lefgren, McIntyre, and Miller, "Chapter 7 or 13."

13. Lefgren, McIntyre, and Miller.

14. Heck, "Econometric Analysis."

15. Braucher, Cohen, and Lawless, "Race, Attorney Influence."

16. Braucher, Cohen, and Lawless, 393.

17. Dixon, Epstein, and Tweedy, "Where Did Chapter 13 Come From?"

18. Stanley and Girth, *Bankruptcy*, 46.

19. Norberg and Compo, "Report on an Empirical Study"; Sullivan, Warren, and Westbrook, "Laws, Models, and Real People."

20. Allgood, "Chapter XIII," 20.

21. Woodbridge, "Wage Earners' Plans."

22. Allgood, "Chapter XIII"; Allgood, "Operation"; Benson, "Wage Earners' Plans"; Bobier, "Mecca or Mirage"; Bundschu, "Administration"; Gates, "My Practice"; Hess, "Wage-Earner Plans"; and McDuffee, "Wage Earners' Plan."

23. United States House of Representatives, Hearing on H.R. 1057 and H.R. 5771, 41.

24. United States House of Representatives, 38.

25. United States House of Representatives, 85.

26. Dolphin, *Analysis*, 27.

27. United States House of Representatives, Hearing on H.R. 1057 and H.R. 5771, 41.

28. Efrat, "Evolution of Bankruptcy Stigma," 376.

29. Quoted in Brunner, *Personal Bankruptcies*, 4.

30. "Making Bankruptcy Pay."

31. Stanley and Girth, *Bankruptcy*.

32. Agarwal, Chomsisengphet, and Liu, "Consumer Bankruptcy and Default"; and Buckley and Brinig, "Bankruptcy Puzzle." Alternatively, B. Hansen and M. Hansen, "Religion," argue that social connectivity in the 1920s offered a safety net that helped prevent default.

33. Agarwal, Chomsisengphet, and Liu, "Consumer Bankruptcy and Default," is the strongest of the studies. It proxies social connectivity by migration from place of birth and show that migration about doubles the risk of bankruptcy.

34. Dick, Lehnert, and Topa, "Social Spillovers"; and Miller, "Social Networks."

35. Chen, "Local Spillovers"; Chen and Hansen, "New Evidence of Spillovers"; and Cohen-Cole and Duygan-Bump, "Social Influence and Bankruptcy."

36. Calder, *Financing the American Dream*; Cohen, *Consumers' Republic*; Hyman, *Borrow*; Hyman, *Debtor Nation*; Lauer, *Creditworthy*; and Olegario, *Engine of Enterprise*.

37. Jordà, Schularick, and Taylor, "Macrohistory Database."

38. Projector and Weiss, "1962 Survey." In 1980, when the Federal Reserve series on debt burden begins, payments on consumer debt were about 6 percent of disposable income. Federal Reserve Board, "Household Debt Service."

39. United States House of Representatives, Hearing on H.R. 1057 and H.R. 5771, 102.

40. From 1945–65, for the economy overall, nominal interest rates trended up, but real interest rates did not. Jordà, Schularick, and Taylor, "Macrohistory Database."

41. P. Smith, "Trends."

42. For example, in 1971, almost 100 percent of FHA home improvement loans were made at the highest rate allowed. More than 90 percent of personal loans made by finance companies were made at the highest legal rate. Schober and Shay, *State and Regional Estimates*.

43. Matherly, "Regulation of Consumer Credit."

44. Matherly, 40.

45. James and Sylla, "Net Public and Private Debt."

46. Hyman, *Debtor Nation*; Trumbull, *Consumer Lending*.

47. See, among others, Balleisen, *Navigating Failure*.

48. Calder, *Financing the American Dream*; and Hyman, *Debtor Nation*.

49. This account primarily summarizes the detailed version in Hyman, *Debtor Nation*.

50. They also facilitated information sharing. Lipartito, "Narrative and the Algorithm."

51. Trumbull, *Consumer Lending*; Hyman, *Debtor Nation*.

52. Hyman, *Debtor Nation*, 122.

53. Hyman, 154–69.

54. Early credit card debt is easy to identify because the debt schedules in the bankruptcy case files list creditors such as "Diner's Club." We identified department store account credit by matching the names and locations of unsecured creditors to historical, mostly local, department stores listed in city directories or with Wikipedia entries. In sample cases filed between 1945 and 1965 (the period covered here) there are 6,933 total debts, of which 6,240 are unsecured. Of these, 504 are missing creditor information. Of valid observations, 39.9 percent are utilities/businesses; 10 percent are private persons; 20.6 percent are financial institutions; 12 percent are medical providers; 8.9 percent are department stores; 5.3 percent are credit card companies; and 3.2 percent are other categories of creditors.

55. On the history of credit cards, see Mandell, *Credit Card Industry*; and Nocera, *Piece of the Action*.

56. Other studies have not considered department stores separately from other retail establishments. Herrmann, "Families in Bankruptcy"; and Misbach, "Personal Bankruptcy."

57. Carter, "Index—All Utilities."

58. Craig, "Consumption Expenditures."

59. Hyman, *Debtor Nation*.

60. Data from the Surveys of Consumer Finance, as summarized in Durkin et al., *Consumer Credit*, 69.

61. Nationally, the share of households with mortgages rose from 20 percent in 1950, to 24 percent in 1956, and to 32 percent in 1963. Durkin et al., 68.

62. Misbach, "Personal Bankruptcy."

63. Dolphin, *Analysis of Personal Factors*.

64. Specifically, $31 per capita in pro-debtor states versus $27 in pro-creditor states (in 1984 dollars).

65. National Association of Credit Management, *Credit Manual*.

66. Stanley and Girth, *Bankruptcy*.

67. Schober and Shay, *State and Regional Estimates*; and Shuchman and Jantscher, "Effects."

68. United States, Department of Commerce, "Personal Income Summary."

69. National Bureau of Economic Research, "US Business Cycle."

70. Flood, *Historical Data*.

71. Federal Deposit Insurance Corp., "Historical Statistics on Banking."

72. Federal Deposit Insurance Corp.; and Flood, *Historical Data*.

73. Roth, *SEER*.

74. Haines and Inter-university Consortium, *Historical*.

75. Dawsey, Hynes, and Ausubel, "Non-Judicial Debt Collection"; Domowitz and Sartain, "Determinants"; and White and Zhu, "Saving Your Home."

76. Ghent, "How Do Case Law and Statute Differ?"

77. National Association of Credit Management, *Credit Manual*.

78. Haines and Inter-university Consortium, *Historical*.

79. Federal Deposit Insurance Corp., "Historical Statistics on Banking"; and Flood, *Historical Data*.

80. Haines and Inter-university Consortium, *Historical*.

Chapter Five

1. United States District Court, Portland District of Southern Maine, "Nayers Case File."

2. Mintz, "47,877 Garnished."

3. Mintz, "Easy Credit."

4. Patterson, "Wage Garnishment." For a similar analysis of garnishment in California, see Brunn, "Wage Garnishment in California."

5. Grosse and Lean, "Wage Garnishment in Washington."

6. "Days Jewelry Store."

7. United States House of Representatives, Hearing on H.R. 11601, 70.

8. United States House of Representatives, 424.

9. Herrmann, "Families in Bankruptcy"; and Stanley and Girth, *Bankruptcy*.

10. Brunn, "Wage Garnishment in California."

11. Jablonski, "Wage Garnishment."

12. Mintz, "Easy Credit."

13. Caplovitz, *Poor Pay More*.

14. Jacob, "Winners and Losers."

15. The districts were Northern Alabama, Northern Illinois, Northern Ohio, Southern California, and Oregon. Stanley and Girth, *Bankruptcy*, 46.

16. National Advisory Commission on Civil Disorders, *Report*, 139–40.

17. "Kerner Urges Credit Reform."

18. Brunn, "Wage Garnishment in California," 1223.

19. For a detailed legislative history of the Consumer Credit Protection Act, see Rubin, "Legislative Methodology."

20. United States House of Representatives, Hearing on H.R. 11601, 88.

21. Hearing on H.R. 11601, 69.

22. Hearing on H.R. 11601, 424.

23. Hearing on H.R. 11601, 419.

24. United States Congress, *Congressional Record*, 1968, 1832.

25. United States House of Representatives, Hearing on H.R. 11601, 242.

26. National Association of Credit Management, *Credit Manual* (various years).

27. *Hodgson v. Housing Authority of Kansas City*; *Brennan v. General Telephone Co. of Florida*; *Brennan v. Pitts Pontiac*; and *Brennan v. Kroger Co.*

28. See *Hodgson v. Cleveland Municipal Court*; and *Hodgson v. Sheriff of Grand Forks*.

29. *Hodgson v. Hamilton Municipal Court.*

30. *Dunlop v. First National Bank of Arizona*; *John O. Melby & Co. Bank v. Anderson.*

31. *Western v. Hodgson.*

32. Cole, "Personal Finance." The states are Alaska, Arizona, Arkansas, California, Idaho, Iowa, Kansas, Minnesota, Montana, New Hampshire, New Mexico, North Dakota, Oklahoma, Oregon, Utah, Washington, and Wisconsin.

33. *Sniadach v. Family Finance Corp.*

34. B. Hansen and M. Hansen, "Evolution of Garnishment."

35. Angell, "Some Effects"; Day and Brandt, "Consumer Research"; and Mandell, "Consumer Perception."

36. Rubin, "Legislative Methodology," 252.

37. Danziger and Bailey, *Legacies of the War on Poverty.*

38. United States House of Representatives, Hearing on H.R. 11601, 158.

39. Bailey and Duquette, "How Johnson Fought."

40. These paragraphs summarize pertinent findings in Fasules, "Impact of Medicare."

41. More recently, bankruptcy and financial distress among the elderly has been growing; see Lusardi, Mitchell, and Oggero, "Debt and Financial Vulnerability"; and Pottow, "Rise in Elder Bankruptcy."

42. See also Himmelstein et al., "Illness and Injury"; Jacoby, Sullivan, and Warren, "Rethinking the Debates."

43. Finkelstein et al., "Oregon Health Insurance Experiment."

44. Zelenko, "Role of the Referee," 103.

45. Stanley and Girth, *Bankruptcy*, 4.

46. Posner, "Political Economy."

47. United States, Department of Justice, *Annual Report of the AG for 1916*, 63–66.

48. United States, Administrative Office of the US Courts, *Annual Report of AOUSC for 1940*, 12–13.

49. United States Congress, Referee Salary Act.

50. United States, Department of Justice, *Annual Report of the AG for 1948*, 62.

51. Judicial Conference is the modern name of the policymaking body of the federal courts. United States Courts, "Governance and the Judicial Conference."

52. United States, Administrative Office of the US Courts, *Annual Report of AOUSC for 1954*, 68.

53. Calculated from Hansen, Davis, and Fasules, *Bankruptcy Statistics.*

54. United States, Administrative Office of the US Courts, *Annual Report of AOUSC for 1964*, 193.

55. *Annual Report of AOUSC for 1964*, 193.

56. *Annual Report of AOUSC for 1964*, 18.

57. Klee, "Legislative History"; and Posner, "Political Economy."

58. Berglof and Rosenthal, "Political Economy," 57.

59. Article III of the Constitution establishes the judicial branch of the government and specifies, among other things, that judges "shall hold their offices during good behavior," in other words, lifetime appointment.

60. Posner, "Political Economy," makes the case that the core of the dispute was over patronage opportunities.

61. Commission on the Bankruptcy Laws of the United States, *Report*, 8.

62. Posner, "Political Economy," 70.

63. For an extended discussion of the political economy of exemptions under the Code, see Hynes, Malani, and Posner, "Political Economy."

64. For example, the commission wanted to eliminate the right of creditors to petition against discharge because of mistakes that debtors made on credit applications. The law merely added ways for debtors to be reimbursed for the expenses of defending themselves against false claims that they had tried to defraud creditors.

65. The implication of this change for computing the bankruptcy rate is discussed in the appendix to chapter 1.

66. United States Congress, Bankruptcy Reform Act of 1978 § 524(a)(1).

67. Domowitz and Eovaldi, "Impact of the BRA."

68. United States Congress, Bankruptcy Reform Act of 1978 § 524(c)–(d).

69. Bankruptcy Reform Act § 525.

70. Businesses could also liquidate or reorganize. On the changes to corporate reorganization, see Skeel, *Debt's Dominion*, 160–83.

71. Commission on the Bankruptcy Laws of the United States, *Report*, pt. 1, 9.

72. Posner, "Political Economy," argues that the debate over exemptions caused creditors to fight among themselves.

73. Stanley and Girth, *Bankruptcy.*

74. Shuchman and Jantscher, "Effects."

75. Schober and Shay, *State and Regional Estimates.*

76. National Association of Credit Management, *Credit Manual.*

77. Stanley and Girth, *Bankruptcy.*

78. National Bureau of Economic Research, "US Business Cycle."

79. Fasules, "Impact of Medicare."

80. Haines and Inter-university Consortium, *Historical.*

81. Schober and Shay, *State and Regional Estimates.*

82. United States, Department of Commerce, "Personal Income Summary."

83. Roth, *SEER.*

84. Haines and Inter-university Consortium, *Historical.*

85. Federal Deposit Insurance Corp., "Historical Statistics on Banking."

86. Federal Deposit Insurance Corp., "Historical Statistics on Banking."

87. Cole, "Personal Finance."

Chapter Six

1. Warren, "Bankruptcy Crisis"; and Zywicki, "Consumer Bankruptcy Crisis." In the late 1970s and mid-1980s, there was a surge in business bankruptcy, which rose briefly to about 18 percent of petitions. More recently, some business bankruptcies have been counted as personal bankruptcies, likely because filers used personal credit cards to finance small businesses. Lawless and Warren, "Myth"; see also, Chatterji and Seamans, "Entrepreneurial Finance."

2. Boyes and Faith, "Some Effects"; Peterson and Aoki, "Bankruptcy Filings"; Shepard, "Personal Failures"; and Weiss, Bhandari, and Robins, "Analysis of State-Wide Variation."

3. Domowitz and Eovaldi, "Impact of the BRA."

4. Fay, Hurst, and White, "Household Bankruptcy Decision"; Gross and Souleles, "Empirical Analysis"; Zywicki, "Consumer Bankruptcy Crisis."

5. Warren and Tyagi, *Two-Income Trap.*

6. For example, Congress curtailed the activities of third-party collection agencies, and the Federal Trade Commission extended the CCPA's restrictions on garnishment to wage assignments. It is not possible to identify the effects of these changes because they were coincident with changes to the bankruptcy law. Herbert, "Straining the Gnat"; Rogalski, "Examination of the FDCPA"; Schulman, "Effectiveness of the FDCPA."

7. Moss and Johnson, "Rise of Consumer Bankruptcy"; and White, "Bankruptcy Reform and Credit Cards."

8. Dick and Lehnert, "Personal Bankruptcy"; Livshits, MacGee, and Tertilt, "Democratization of Credit." Livshits, MacGee, and Tertilt, "Accounting for the Rise," point out that advances in information technology reinforced the effect of legal changes.

9. Benmelech and Moskowitz, "Political Economy."

10. Usury data collected by Chatterji and Seamans, "Entrepreneurial Finance."

11. Lefgren and McIntyre, "Explaining the Puzzle."

12. Vanatta, "Citibank"; and Wright, "Wall Street."

13. Furletti, "Debate."

14. It is generally presumed that states acted strategically. However, we cannot rule out that banking and business interest groups lobbied for removing usury limits as a response to the profit squeeze that resulted from the combination of high inflation and usury laws. Wright, "Wall Street."

15. Vanatta, "Citibank," also notes that, without deposits, Citibank's operations in South Dakota had to raise funds through financialization.

16. Wright, "Wall Street."

17. Livshits, MacGee, and Tertilt, "Democratization of Credit."

18. Again, data on credit card usury rates before and after *Marquette* are from Chatterji and Seamans, "Entrepreneurial Finance."

19. The local market is Maryland, the District of Columbia, Virginia, or West Virginia.

20. One widely cited statistic, published in the *American Banker*, is that in 1984 less than 10 percent of "customers with incomes above $15,000 held a card from an out-of-state bank." Knittel and Stango, "Price Ceilings," report this statistic without citation.

21. Of course, some of the new credit card lending stayed within the states that had eliminated usury. In 1982–83, households in states with no usury limit on cards had 30 percent more card debt than residents in states with limits. Chatterji and Seamans, "Entrepreneurial Finance."

22. Kroszner and Strahan, "What Drives Deregulation?"

23. DeMuth, "Case."

24. The demand for consumer credit was probably growing especially quickly around the time of *Marquette*. Consumers wanted to buy on credit in anticipation of continuing inflation. The president of Citibank wrote that "consumers show unimpeachable logic and common sense by saving less and borrowing more" because they recognize "that if they borrow at 9 or 12 percent when inflation is 18, they're beating the system." Quoted in Wriston, "Outsmarting Inflation."

25. Chatterji and Seamans, "Entrepreneurial Finance"; and M. Hansen and Miller, "New View of Women." The Equal Credit Opportunity Acts gave an assist; see Hyman, "Ending Discrimination, Legitimating Debt."

26. Livshits, MacGee, and Tertilt, "Accounting for the Rise"; and Livshits, MacGee, and Tertilt, "Democratization of Credit."

27. Chatterji and Seamans, "Entrepreneurial Finance"; and DeMuth, "Case." In the Maryland sample of case files, there is no association between the total (real) value of a filer's assets and the probability that they have a card from a no-limit state; however, assets are also not a strong predictor of credit card holding before *Marquette*.

28. Livshits, MacGee, and Tertilt, "Democratization of Credit."

29. White, "Bankruptcy Reform and Credit Cards," further argues that the

substitution of credit card debt for installment debt has increased the sensitivity of households to adverse events.

30. Between 1980 and 2000 (the period shown in the figure), there are 17,860 debts in the sample, of which 3,276 were owed to a bank and 1,283 were owed on credit cards. Financial institutions are identified by name. Credit card debt can be identified if the network name (e.g., "Visa") is given as part of the creditor's name or if the promotional brand of the card is listed (e.g., "Capital One Venture Card"). However, if the creditor listed is a bank ("Capital One") and the debt is described vaguely ("miscellaneous," "household items"), then it is classified as being unsecured bank debt.

31. Domowitz and Eovaldi, "Impact of the BRA," give a clear listing.

32. United States Senate, Hearings on the Bankruptcy Reform Act of 1978, 11.

33. The Credit Research Center was headed by Professor Robert W. Johnson who had previously served on the National Commission on Consumer Finance. Durkin and Staten, "Introduction."

34. Credit Research Center, *Consumer Bankruptcy Study*, 1:49.

35. Credit Research Center, 67.

36. United States Senate, Hearings on the Bankruptcy Reform Act of 1978, 20.

37. Hearings on the Bankruptcy Reform Act of 1978, 1334; Warren, "Market for Data," 8.

38. United States Senate, Hearings on the Bankruptcy Reform Act of 1978, 6.

39. Hearings on the Bankruptcy Reform Act of 1978, 121.

40. There were only four roll call votes on the 1984 amendments. The House passed the Conference Report by a vote of 394 to 0, and the Senate agreed to the report by a voice vote. Congress.gov, "Actions—H.R. 5174—98th Congress (1983–1984)."

41. Article III makes exceptions for territories, courts-martial, and matters involving the legislature or public agencies.

42. Hinds, "Are Changes Needed?"

43. For a description of the changes relevant to consumer bankruptcy, see Morris, "Substantive Consumer Bankruptcy Reform."

44. Case law eventually determined that ability to pay was "a primary factor" courts should consider in dismissal for substantial abuse under Section 707(b) of the Code as amended in 1984. See, among many sources, footnotes 3 and 7 of Culhane and White, "Test Drive."

45. Hynes, Malani, and Posner, "Political Economy."

46. Quoted in Jensen, "Legislative History," 486.

47. Klein, "Consumer Bankruptcy in the Balance," 293.

48. Jensen, "Legislative History," 499.

49. Jensen.

50. Jensen, 493–94.

51. Jensen, 526.

52. Jensen, 501.

53. For a brief summary of key changes made by BAPCPA, see White, "Bankruptcy Reform and Credit Cards," 192.

54. The final version of the bill did shield some groups from the changes in the law: Child support, social security and veteran benefits were excluded from income used in the means test. Dickerson, "Regulating Bankruptcy," 1882–83.

55. Veto-proof margins were not guaranteed. Hayes, "Bankruptcy Reform"; and Nunez and Rosenthal, "Bankruptcy 'Reform' in Congress." There were more than eighteen roll call votes on the House version of the 2000 bill that President Clinton vetoed. Congress.gov, "Actions—H.R. 2415—106th Congress (1999–2000)."

56. Zingales, *Capitalism for the People*, 53.

57. Grodzicki, "Evolution of Competition," 10.

58. American Bankruptcy Institute, "Statements." The list of members is from Nunez and Rosenthal, "Bankruptcy Reform" 534.

59. Landry, "Policy and Forces."

60. United States Senate, Hearing on S. 1301, 12–13.

61. Agarwal, Chomsisengphet, and Liu, "Consumer Bankruptcy and Default"; Buckley and Brinig, "Bankruptcy Puzzle"; B. Hansen and M. Hansen, "Religion."

62. Agarwal, Chomsisengphet, and Liu, "Consumer Bankruptcy and Default"; Cohen-Cole and Duygan-Bump, "Household Bankruptcy Decision."

63. Dugas, "Going Broke."

64. United States Senate, Hearing on S. 1301, 12–13.

65. For a list of studies through 1999, see Culhane and White, "Test Drive."

66. Barron and Staten, "Personal Bankruptcy."

67. United States Senate, Hearing on S. 1301, 89.

68. Hearing on S. 1301, 89.

69. Jensen, "Legislative History," 502; and United States Senate, Hearing on S. 1301, 12–13. Visa spread the "tax" idea around; see, e.g., Layman, "Current Bankruptcy Legislation."

70. Warren, "Market for Data."

71. Culhane and White, "Test Drive."

72. United States Senate, Hearing on S. 1301, 12–13.

73. Douglas Boshkof, Professor Emeritus of Indiana University, and Randall Picker, Professor at University of Chicago Law School, spoke on behalf of the National Bankruptcy Conference. United States Senate, Hearing on S. 1301, 157–83.

74. United States Senate, Hearing on Consumer Credit.

75. Ausubel, "Failure of Competition"; and more recently, Grodzicki, "Evolution of Competition."

76. For examples of articles, editorials, and advertisements, see Landry, "Policy and Forces," 520; Warren, "Bankruptcy Crisis," 1089–1090; and Warren, "Market for Data," 5.

77. Schlesinger, "Card Games."

78. United States Congress, *Congressional Record*, September 10, 1998, 19877.

79. "Almost Three Quarters."

80. Campaign finance watchdogs reported a 75 percent increase (from about $21 to about $38 million) in donations to Congress between 1998 and 2000. About 60 percent went to Republicans. Shapiro, "Let the Hogfest Begin!"

81. Nunez and Rosenthal, "Bankruptcy 'Reform' in Congress"; Zywicki, "Past, Present, and Future Bankruptcy Law in America," argues that special interests were less important than ideology. However, interest groups, constituent interests, and ideology were all in alignment. It is not possible to separate them through an analysis of voting.

82. Hayes, "Bankruptcy Reform."

83. Jensen, "Legislative History," 499.

84. Studies cite Opensecrets.com, but details are scarce. Several studies use the $100 million estimate without citation; see, e.g., Hayes, "Bankruptcy Reform," 68; Mann, "Sweat Box," 382; and White, "Bankruptcy Reform and Credit Cards," 175. Cappiello, "Price of Inequality," 432, cites the earlier studies.

85. Center for Responsive Politics, "Bankruptcy."

86. Nunez and Rosenthal, "Bankruptcy 'Reform' in Congress," 535.

87. United States, President and CEA, *Economic Report of the President 2006*, table B-77.

88. Ausubel, "Failure of Competition," 50.

89. *Smiley v. Citibank*.

90. Westrich and Bush, "Blindfolded into Debt," 6.

91. Grodzicki, "Evolution of Competition," 13.

92. Chatterji and Seamans, "Entrepreneurial Finance."

93. Lefgren and McIntyre, "Explaining the Puzzle"; and Schober and Shay, *State and Regional Estimates*.

94. We follow the method in Hynes, Malani, and Posner, "Political Economy."

95. M. Hansen and B. Hansen, "Crisis and Bankruptcy"; National Association of Credit Management, *Credit Manual*; Stanley and Girth, *Bankruptcy*; and Wickens, "Farmer Bankruptcies."

96. United States, Bureau of the Census, *CPS*. Garrett and Wall, "Bankruptcy Cycles," show that the differences in state unemployment rates explain differences in bankruptcy rates in modern data, but state-level unemployment rates are not generally available historically.

97. United States, Department of Commerce, "Personal Income Summary."

98. Roth, *SEER*.

99. Federal Deposit Insurance Corp., "Historical Statistics on Banking."

Chapter Seven

1. In recent years, some economists and legal scholars have rigorously examined the influence of narratives. See Ramsay, "Personal Insolvency"; Shiller, "Narrative Economics"; and Skeel, "Competing Narratives."

2. United States Senate, Hearings on the Bankruptcy Reform Act of 1978, 74.

3. Hearings on the Bankruptcy Reform Act of 1978, 74.

4. Lawless et al., "Did Bankruptcy Reform Fail?"; Lupica, "Costs of BAPCPA"; and White, "Bankruptcy Reform and Credit Cards."

5. Albanesi and Nosal, "Insolvency."

6. Lawless et al., "Did Bankruptcy Reform Fail?"

7. United States Courts, "Table F-2."

8. Albanesi and Nosal, "Insolvency"; and Lawless et al., "Did Bankruptcy Reform Fail?"

9. Lupica, "Consumer Bankruptcy Creditor Distribution Study."

10. Tabb, "Top Twenty."

Sources

US Statutes

1898 An Act to establish a uniform system of bankruptcy throughout the United States, Pub. L. No. 55-541, 30 Stat. 544.

1926 An Act to amend an Act entitled "An Act to establish a uniform system of bankruptcy throughout the United States," approved July 1, 1898, and Acts amendatory thereof and supplementary thereto, Pub. L. No. 69-301, 44 Stat. 662.

1933 An Act to amend an Act entitled "An Act to establish a uniform system of bankruptcy throughout the United States," approved July 1, 1898, and Acts amendatory thereof and supplementary thereto, Pub. L. No. 72-420, 47 Stat. 1467.

1934 An Act to amend an Act entitled "An Act to establish a uniform system of bankruptcy throughout the United States," approved July 1, 1898, and Acts amendatory thereof and supplementary thereto, Pub. L. No. 73-296, 48 Stat. 911.

1934 An Act to amend an Act entitled "An Act to establish a uniform system of bankruptcy throughout the United States," approved July 1, 1898, and Acts amendatory thereof and supplementary thereto, Pub. L. No. 73-486, 48 Stat. 1289 (Frazier-Lemke Act).

1938 An Act to amend an Act entitled "An Act to establish a uniform system of bankruptcy throughout the United States," approved July 1, 1898, and Acts amendatory thereof and supplementary thereto; and to repeal section 76 thereof and all Acts and parts of Acts inconsistent therewith, Pub. L. No. 75-696, 52 Stat. 840 (Chandler Act).

1946 An Act to amend an Act entitled "An Act to establish a uniform system of bankruptcy throughout the United States," approved July 1, 1898, and Acts amendatory thereof and supplementary thereto, Pub. L. No. 79-464, 60 Stat. 323 (Referees' Salary Act).

1968 An Act to safeguard the consumer in connection with the utilization of credit by requiring full disclosure of the terms and conditions of finance charges in credit transactions or in offers to extend credit; by restricting the garnishment of wages; and by creating the National Commission on Consumer Finance to study and make recommendations on the need for further regulation of the consumer finance industry; and for other purposes, Pub. L. No. 90-321, 82 Stat. 146 (Consumer Credit Protection Act).

1978 An Act to establish a uniform Law on the Subject of Bankruptcies, Pub. L. No. 95-598, 92 Stat. 2549 (Bankruptcy Reform Act).

1984 An Act to amend title 28 of the United States Code regarding jurisdiction of bankruptcy proceedings, to establish new Federal judicial positions, to amend title 11 of the United States Code, and for other purposes, Pub. L. No. 98-353, 98 Stat. 333 (Bankruptcy Amendments and Federal Judgeship Act).

2005 An Act to amend title 11 of the United States Code, and for other purposes, Pub. L. No. 109-8, 119 Stat. 23 (Bankruptcy Abuse Prevention and Consumer Protection Act).

Court Cases

Bates v. State Bar of Arizona, 433 U.S. 350 (1977).

Brennan v. General Telephone Co. of Florida, 488 F.2d 157 (5th Cir. 1973).

Brennan v. Kroger Co., 74 Lab. Cas. (CCH) P33,085 (N.D. Ind. 1974).

Brennan v. Pitts Pontiac, 73 Lab. Cas. (CCH) P33,046 (W.D.N.Y. 1974).

Central States Life Ins. Co. v. Koplar Co., 80 F.2d 754 (8th Cir. 1936).

Dunlop v. First National Bank of Arizona, 399 F. Supp. 855 (D. Ariz. 1975).

Freshman v. Atkins, 269 U.S. 121 (1925).

Hodgson v. Christopher, 365 F. Supp. 583 (D.N.D. 1973).

Hodgson v. Cleveland Municipal Court, 326 F. Supp. 419 (N.D. Ohio 1971).

Hodgson v. Hamilton Municipal Court, 349 F. Supp. 1125 (S.D. Ohio 1972).

Hodgson v. Housing Authority of Kansas City, 71 Lab. Cas. (CCH) P32,887 (W.D. Mo. 1973).

John O. Melby & Co. Bank v. Anderson, 88 Wis. 2d 252 (1979).

Louisville Joint Stock Land Bank v. Radford, 295 U.S. 555 (1935).

Marquette National Bank of Minneapolis v. First of Omaha Service Corp., 439 U.S. 299 (1978).

Massie v. Cessna, 239 Ill. 352 (1909).

Mutual Loan Co. v. Martell, 222 U.S. 225 (1911).

Smiley v. Citibank (South Dakota), N. A., 517 U.S. 735 (1996).

Sniadach v. Family Finance Corp., 395 U.S. 337 (1969).

State Street Furniture Co. v. Armour & Co., 345 Ill. 160 (1931).

Western v. Hodgson, 494 F.2d 379 (4th Cir. 1974).

Williams v. United States Fidelity & Guaranty Co., 236 U.S. 549 (1915).
Wright v. Vinton Branch of Mountain Trust Bank of Roanoke, Virginia, 300 U.S. 440 (1937).

Government Reports and Websites

Barron, John M., and Michael E. Staten. "Personal Bankruptcy: A Report on Petitioners' Ability-to-Pay," October 6, 1997. http://govinfo.library.unt.edu/nbrc/report/g2b.pdf.

Commission on the Bankruptcy Laws of the United States. *Report of the Commission on Bankruptcy Laws of the United States*. Washington, DC: GPO, 1973.

Congress.gov. "Actions—H.R. 2415—106th Congress (1999–2000): Bankruptcy Reform Act of 2000." Last modified December 19, 2000. https://www.congress.gov/bill/106th-congress/house-bill/2415/all-actions.

———. "Actions—H.R. 5174—98th Congress (1983–1984): Bankruptcy Amendments and Federal Judgeship Act of 1983." Last modified July 10, 1984. https://www.congress.gov/bill/98th-congress/house-bill/5174/all-actions.

Donovan, William J. *Administration of Bankruptcy Estates (also known as the Donovan Report)*. Washington, DC: GPO, 1931.

"Herbert Hoover: Special Message to the Congress on Bankruptcy Legislation," April 11, 1933. http://www.presidency.ucsb.edu/ws/index.php?pid=23408.

"Herbert Hoover: Special Message to the Congress on Reform of Judicial Procedure," February 29, 1932. http://www.presidency.ucsb.edu/ws/index.php?pid=23469.

National Advisory Commission on Civil Disorders. *Report of the National Advisory Committee on Civil Disorders*. Washington, DC: GPO, 1968.

Projector, Dorothy S., and Gertrude S. Weiss. "1962 Survey of Financial Characteristics of Consumers and 1963 Survey of Changes in Family Finances." Board of Governors of the Federal Reserve System, 1966. https://www.federalreserve.gov/econres/scf_6263.htm.

Sadd, Victor, and Robert T. Williams. *Causes of Bankruptcies among Consumers*. Washington, DC: GPO, 1933.

Schober, Milton W., and Robert P. Shay. *State and Regional Estimates of the Price and Volume of the Major Types of Consumer Instalment Credit in Mid-1971*. National Commission on Consumer Finance Technical Studies vol. 3. Washington, DC: GPO, 1974.

United States, Administrative Office of the US Courts. *Annual Report of the Director of the Administrative Office of the US Courts*. Washington, DC: GPO, various years.

United States, Bureau of Foreign and Domestic Commerce. *Domestic Com-*

merce Series No. 54: Causes of Business Failures and Bankruptcies of Individuals in New Jersey. Washington, DC: GPO, 1931.

United States Congress. *Congressional Record*, various dates.

———. Joint Hearings on S. 3866, Subcommittees of the Committees on the Judiciary on S. 3866 (1932).

United States Courts. "BAPCPA Report—2010." Statistics and Reports. Last updated December 31, 2010. http://www.uscourts.gov/statistics-reports/bapcpa-report-2010.

———. "Governance and the Judicial Conference." United States Courts. Accessed January 30, 2019. http://www.uscourts.gov/about-federal-courts/governance -judicial-conference.

United States, Department of Health and Human Services, Assistant Secretary for Financial Resources (ASFR). "FY 2010 Budget in Brief." HHS Budgets in Brief and Performance Reports. Last modified on February 28, 2016. https://www.hhs.gov/about/agencies/asfr/budget/budgets-in-brief-performance -reports/index.html.

United States, Department of Justice. *Annual Report of the Attorney General of the United States*. Washington, DC: GPO, various years.

———. *Strengthening of Procedure in the Judicial System: Message from the President of the United States Recommending the Strengthening of Procedure in the Judicial System, Together with the Report of the Attorney General on Bankruptcy Law and Practice (also known as the Thacher Report)*. United States 72nd Congress, 1st Session, Senate Document No. 65. Washington: GPO, 1932.

United States House of Representatives. "A Uniform System of Bankruptcy," House Report No. 1674, 52nd Congress, 1st Session, 1892.

———. Hearing on H.R. 1057 and H.R. 5771: Wage Earner Plans under the Bankruptcy Act, Subcommittee No. 4 of the Committee on the Judiciary (1967).

———. Hearing on H.R. 1981, Subcommittee on Bankruptcy and Reorganization of the Committee on the Judiciary (1937).

———. Hearing on H.R. 8046, Committee on the Judiciary (1937).

———. Hearing on H.R. 11219, Committee on the Judiciary (1936).

———. Hearing on H.R. 11601, Subcommittee on Consumer Affairs of the Committee on Banking and Currency (1967).

———. "Report on the Internal Commerce of the U.S.," 51st Cong. 1st Sess., H. Doc. 6, Serial 2738, 1890.

United States, President and Council of Economic Advisers. *Economic Report of the President Transmitted to the Congress, February 2006 Together with the Annual Report of the Council of Economic Advisers*. Washington, DC: GPO, 2006. https://www.govinfo.gov/content/pkg/ERP-2006/pdf/ERP-2006 .pdf.

United States Senate. Hearing on Examining the Increase of Personal Bankruptcies and the Crisis in Consumer Credit, Subcommittee on Administrative Oversight and the Courts of the Committee on the Judiciary (1997).

———. Hearing on S. 1301, Subcommittee on Administrative Oversight and the Courts of the Committee on the Judiciary (1998).

———. Hearing on S. 3866, Subcommittees of the Committees on the Judiciary (1932).

———. Hearings on the Bankruptcy Reform of 1978, Subcommittees on Courts of the Committee on the Judiciary (1981).

———. "Memorial of Many Commercial Bodies for Passage of Torrey Bankrupt Bill," 54th Congress, 2nd Session, S. Misc. Doc. 182, Serial 2907, 1892.

———. "Memorials, Press Clippings, Resolutions and Documents on Torrey Bankruptcy Bill," 54th Cong., 1st Sess., S. Doc. 237, Serial 3354, 1896.

———. "Proceedings of the National Association of Credit Men," 55th Congress, 2nd Session, S. Doc. 156, Serial 3600, 1898.

———. "Resolution of Retail Grocers Association of Illinois Etc. on Bankruptcy," 55th Congress 2nd Session, S. Doc. 155, Serial 3600, 1898.

———. "Uniform System of Bankruptcy," Senate Document No. 294, 55th Congress, 2nd Session, 1898.

Physical and Digital Archives

American Bankruptcy Institute. "Statements on Bankruptcy Reform Legislation," October 15, 1998. http://lobby.la.psu.edu/046_Bankruptcy_Reform/Organizational_Statements/American_Bankruptcy_Institute/ABI_Bankruptcy_Statements.htm.

Ancestry.com. Hannibal, Missouri, City Directory, 1929. Provo, UT: US City Directories, 1822–1995 [database online], 2011.

———. St. Louis, Missouri, City Directory, 1904. Provo, UT: US City Directories, 1822–1995 [database online], 2011.

Center for Responsive Politics. "Bankruptcy." Archived Profile: Bankruptcy. Accessed January 30, 2019. http://www.opensecrets.org/news/issues/bankruptcy/.

Eaton, Lucius. "Lucius Eaton to Merchants Exchange of St. Louis, Miscellaneous Correspondence, Merchants Exchange Collection," October 18, 1881. Missouri Historical Society.

Koplar Properties. "St. Louis' Most Memorable Commercial and Residential Landmarks: Koplar Properties." Accessed January 30, 2019. http://koplarproperties.com/about/.

United States, Bureau of the Census. "1870 United States Federal Census, Hornellsville, Steuben, New York; Roll M593_1095 Page 264A; Family History Library Film 552594," 2004. Ancestry.com.

———. "1910 United States Federal Census, Hannibal Ward 4, Marion, Missouri; Roll T624_798 Page 4B," 2004. Ancestry.com.

———. "1920 United States Federal Census, St. Louis Ward 25, Tract Y6, Precincts 11–12; Page 3A; Enumeration District 506; Image 358," 2004. Ancestry.com.

———. "1940 United States Federal Census, Saverton, Ralls, Missouri; Roll T627–2142; Page 8A," 2004. Ancestry.com.

United States District Court, Baltimore District of Maryland. "Bankruptcy Case File of Glenda Clutch (Case No. 0269489)," 2002. Bankruptcy Act of 1898 Case Files Box 212.

United States District Court, Portland, District of Southern Maine. "Bankruptcy Case File of W.H. Nayers (Case No. BK-63–489)," 1963. Bankruptcy Act of 1898 Case Files Box 31.

United States District Court, Kansas City, Western District of Missouri. "Bankruptcy Case File of Wendell T. Hall, Jr. (Case No. 18490)," 1949. Bankruptcy Act of 1898 Case Files Box 30.

United States District Court, St. Louis, Eastern District of Missouri. "Bankruptcy Case File of Jasper C. Glascock (Case No. 5282)," 1928. Bankruptcy Act of 1898 Case Files Box 802.

———. "Bankruptcy Case File of John Ellman (Case No. 3)," 1898. Bankruptcy Act of 1898 Case Files Box 280.

———. "Bankruptcy Case File of the Koplar Company (Case No. 7636)," 1932. Bankruptcy Act of 1898 Case Files Box 274.

Data Sets

Board of Governors of the Federal Reserve System. "G.19 Release: Consumer Credit." Accessed January 30, 2019. https://www.federalreserve.gov/releases/ g19/hist/cc_hist_mt_levels.html and https://www.federalreserve.gov/releases/ g19/hist/cc_hist_mh_levels.html.

———. "Mortgage Debt Outstanding." Accessed January 20, 2017. https://www .federalreserve.gov/econresdata/releases/mortoutstand/current.htm.

Carter, Susan B. "Index of Industrial Production—All Utilities: 1939–2001 (Table Dh227)." In *Historical Statistics of the United States: Millennial Edition Online*, edited by Susan B. Carter, Scott Sigmund Gartner, Michael R. Haines, Alan L. Olmstead, Richard Sutch, and Gavin Wright. Cambridge: Cambridge University Press, 2017.

Craig, Lee A. "Consumption Expenditures, by Type: 1929–1999 (Table Cd153–263)." In *Historical Statistics of the United States: Millennial Edition Online*, edited by Susan B. Carter, Scott Sigmund Gartner, Michael R. Haines, Alan L. Olmstead, Richard Sutch, and Gavin Wright. Cambridge: Cambridge University Press, 2017.

Federal Deposit Insurance Corp.. "Historical Statistics on Banking: Commercial Banks." Accessed January 30, 2019. https://www5.fdic.gov/hsob/SelectRpt.asp?EntryTyp=10&Header=1.

Federal Reserve Board. "Household Debt Service and Financial Obligations Ratios." Accessed January 30, 2019. https://www.federalreserve.gov/releases/housedebt/.

Fishback, Price V., and Shawn Everett Kantor. "Datasets from Published Research Projects: Workers' Compensation Project Data." Accessed January 30, 2019. http://www.u.arizona.edu/~fishback/Published_Research_Data sets.html.

Flood, Mark D. *United States Historical Data on Bank Market Structure, 1896–1955.* Inter-university Consortium of Political and Social Research [distributor], 1998. http://doi.org/10.3886/ICPSR02393.v1.

Haines, Michael R., and Inter-university Consortium for Political and Social Research. *Historical, Demographic, Economic, and Social Data: The United States, 1790–2002.* Ann Arbor, MI: ICPSR [distributor], 2010. http://doi.org/10.3886/ICPSR02896.v3.

Hansen, Mary Eschelbach, Jess Chen, and Matthew Davis. *United States District Court Boundary Shapefiles (1900–2000).* Ann Arbor, MI: Inter-university Consortium of Political and Social Research [distributor], 2016. http://doi .org/10.3886/E100069V1.

Hansen, Mary Eschelbach, Matthew Davis, and Megan Fasules. *United States Bankruptcy Statistics by District, 1899–2007.* Ann Arbor, MI: Inter-university Consortium of Political and Social Research [distributor], 2016. http://doi.org/10.3886/E100062V4.

James, John A., and Richard Sylla. "Net Public and Private Debt, by Major Sector: 1916–1976 (Table Cj889)." In *Historical Statistics of the United States: Millennial Edition Online*, edited by Susan B. Carter, Scott Sigmund Gartner, Michael R. Haines, Alan L. Olmstead, Richard Sutch, and Gavin Wright. Cambridge: Cambridge University Press, 2017.

Jordà, Òscar, Moritz Schularick, and Alan M. Taylor. "Jordà-Schularick-Taylor Macrohistory Database," Accessed January 30, 2019. http://www .macrohistory.net/data/#DownloadData.

National Bureau of Economic Research. "US Business Cycle Expansions and Contractions." Accessed January 30, 2019. http://www.nber.org/cycles.html.

Roth, Jean. *Survey of Epidemiology and End Results (SEER) County Population Data.* National Bureau of Economic Research, 2012. http://www.nber .org/data/seer_u.s._county_population_data.html.

United States, Bureau of the Census. *Census of Religious Bodies 1926, Part I: Summary and Detailed Tables.* Washington, DC: GPO, 1930. http://www .thearda.com/Archive/Files/Descriptions/1926CENSCT.asp.

———. "Changes in Household Size (Figure HH-6)." Families and Living

Arrangements. Accessed January 30, 2019. https://www.census.gov/data/
tables/time-series/demo/families/households.html.

———. *Current Population Surveys, March 1971–1990.* Santa Monica, CA: Uni-
con Research Corp. [distributor], 2014.

———. *Historical Statistics of the United States, Colonial Times to 1970.* Washington, DC: US Department of Commerce, Bureau of the Census, 1975.

———. "Households by Household Type." Social Explorer. Accessed October 3,
2016. https://www.socialexplorer.com/explore/tables.

———. *Statistical Abstract of the United States*, various years. Accessed January
30, 2019. http://www.census.gov/library/publications/time-series/statistical
_abstracts.html.

United States, Bureau of Labor Statistics. "Consumer Price Index (CPI)." Accessed January 30, 2019. https://www.bls.gov/cpi/.

United States Courts. "Table F-2 12-Month, US Bankruptcy Courts: Business
and Nonbusiness Bankruptcy Cases Commenced, by Chapter of the Bankruptcy Code during the Twelve Month Period Ended Sep. 30." Caseload Statistics Data Tables. Accessed January 30, 2019. http://www.uscourts.gov/
statistics-reports/caseload-statistics-data-tables.

United States, Department of Commerce, Bureau of Economic Affairs. "Table
SA1 Personal Income Summary." Accessed March 15, 2017. https://www.bea
.gov/itable/iTable.cfm?ReqID=70&step=1#reqid=70&step=1&isuri=1.

Popular and Trade Periodicals

"100 People Who Shaped St. Louis." *St. Louis Magazine*, December 27, 2007.
https://www.stlmag.com/St-Louis-Magazine/December-2007/100-People
-Who-Shaped-St-Louis/.

Allgood, Clarence W. "Chapter XIII: Wage Earners' Plans." *Journal of the National Association of Referees in Bankruptcy* 15, no. 1 (October 1940): 20–21,
HeinOnline.

"Almost Three Quarters of Americans (73%) Support Tougher Bankruptcy
Laws and If Enacted, 79% Would Be Less Likely to File for Bankruptcy, According to the Cambridge Consumer Credit Index." *PR Newswire*, June 6,
2003.

"Bankruptcy Law Must Stand." *Bulletin of the National Association of Credit
Men*, January 1917.

Banks, Charles S. J. "The National Bankruptcy Conference and the Bankruptcy
Act." *Journal of the National Association of Referees in Bankruptcy* 22, no. 4
(July 1948): 115–17, HeinOnline.

Benson, Edward H. "Wage Earner Plans in Bankruptcy Court." *Michigan State
Bar Journal* 41, no. 8 (August 1962): 10–22, HeinOnline.

Bobier, Harold H. "Chapter XIII: Mecca or Mirage." *Detroit Lawyer* 32 (1964): 23–42.

"Capital Credit Men Leave for Session: Retail Association to Open Convention in Memphis Next Tuesday." *Washington Post*, June 16, 1934.

Cappiello, Brendan A. "The Price of Inequality and the 2005 Bankruptcy Abuse Prevention and Consumer Protection Act." *North Carolina Banking Institute* 17, no. 1 (2013): 401–34.

Cole, Robert J. "Personal Finance: Wage Garnishment." *New York Times*, April 28, 1969.

Cook, Robert A. B. "An Analysis of the Amendatory Bankruptcy Law of 1926." *Commercial Law League Journal* 31 (June 1926): 237–39, HeinOnline.

"Credit and Loan Sharks." *Industrial Lenders News*, March 1924.

"Days Jewelry Store." *Portland Press Herald*, June 3, 1949.

Dugas, Christine. "Going Broke: Bankruptcy Stigma Lessens:" *USA Today*, June 10, 1997, sec. News.

Edwards, Edna. "Debt and the 'Loan Sharks.'" *Washington Post*, April 30, 1905.

"Failures in 1908." *Bradstreet's*, January 9, 1909.

"Foreclosure Suit Is Filed against Four Apartments." *St. Louis Post-Dispatch*, March 28, 1932, sec. A.

Gates, Louis R. "My Practice in Chapter XIII Proceedings." *Journal of the National Association of Referees in Bankruptcy* 17, no. 3 (April 1943): 95–97, HeinOnline.

Hess, Henry L., Jr. "Wage-Earner Plans in Oregon." *Journal of the National Conference of Referees in Bankruptcy* 42, no. 3 (July 1968): 72–79, HeinOnline.

Hinds, Michael deCourcy. "Are Changes Needed in Bankruptcy Laws?" *New York Times*, May 31, 1982. http://www.nytimes.com/1982/05/31/business/issue-and-debate-are-changes-needed-in-bankruptcy-laws.html.

Hunt, Reuben G. "The National Bankruptcy Conference." *Commercial Law Journal* 39, no. 11 (November 1934): 576–78, HeinOnline.

"Judge Landis under Fire." *Literary Digest*, March 1924, 3.

"Kerner Urges Credit Reform Legislation." *Chicago Daily Tribune*, August 1, 1960, sec. A.

Kinsley, Philip. "Thacher Calls U.S. Bankruptcy Law Corrupting: Solicitor General Speaks before Bar Assn." *Chicago Daily Tribune*, August 22, 1930.

Layman, Thomas. "The Current Bankruptcy Legislation Will Bring about Real Reform." *Pittsburgh Post–Gazette*, July 2, 1998.

"Making Bankruptcy Pay." *Time*, February 22, 1963.

Mintz, Morton. "Easy Credit Writ Large on Seventh St." *Washington Post*, February 1, 1959, sec. E.

———. "47,877 Garnished under Antique Law." *Washington Post*, February 2, 1959, sec. A.

"New Association Formed." *Cairo Bulletin*, August 20, 1913.

Patterson, Mark T. "Wage Garnishment: An Extraordinary Remedy Run Amuck." *Washington Law Review* 43, no. 4 (1968): 735–42.

Prendergast, William A. "An Enduring National Bankruptcy System the Inherent Ally of Commerce." *Bankers Magazine*, September 1905, 380–87.

"Referees in Bankruptcy Form National Organization." *American Bar Association Journal* 12, no. 9 (September 1926): 622–23.

"Reorganization Project for Four Apartments Here." *St. Louis Star and Times*, August 18, 1932, evening ed.

Robertson, Thomas. "In the Loan Sharks' Grasp, Many Victims Squirm and Pay Their 'Pound of Flesh.'" *Chicago Daily Tribune*, September 20, 1908.

Schlesinger, Jacob M. "Card Games: As Bankruptcies Surge, Creditors Lobby Hard to Get Tougher Laws—But Whether Many People Shirk Bills They Can Pay Remains Open to Debate—Changing the Lenders' Image." *Wall Street Journal*, eastern ed., June 17, 1998.

"Seek Change in Law on Debtor Discharge: Credit Men to Urge Bankruptcy Act Amendment—Stores Seen as Hit by Current Practices." *New York Times*, December 6, 1931, sec. N.

Shapiro, Bruce. "Let the Hogfest Begin!" *Salon*, March 12, 2001. https://www.salon.com/2001/03/12/bankruptcy_2/.

Special to the *New York Times*. "Senate Modifies Bankruptcy Laws." *New York Times*, June 11, 1938.

"Suit Discloses Default on Bonds of Park Plaza." *St. Louis Post-Dispatch*, June 9, 1934, sec. A.

"Wage-Earner Receiverships." *University of Chicago Law Review* 6, no. 3 (1939): 459–67.

Wriston, Walter B. "Outsmarting Inflation." *Washington Post*, March 13, 1980.

Books, Journal Articles, and Other Secondary Sources

Agarwal, Sumit, Souphala Chomsisengphet, and Chunlin Liu. "Consumer Bankruptcy and Default: The Role of Individual Social Capital." *Journal of Economic Psychology* 32, no. 4 (August 2011): 632–50. https://doi.org/10.1016/j.joep.2010.11.007.

Agarwal, Sumit, Chunlin Liu, and Lawrence Mielnicki. "Exemption Laws and Consumer Delinquency and Bankruptcy Behavior: An Empirical Analysis of Credit Card Data." *Quarterly Review of Economics and Finance* 43, no. 2 (Summer 2003): 273–89. https://doi.org/10.1016/S1062-9769(02)00156-4.

Albanesi, Stefania, and Jaromir Nosal. "Insolvency after the 2005 Bankruptcy Reform." Working paper, National Bureau of Economic Research, August 2018. https://doi.org/10.3386/w24934.

Alexander, Gerard. "Institutions, Path Dependence, and Democratic Consolidation." *Journal of Theoretical Politics* 13, no. 3 (July 2001): 249–69. https:// doi.org/10.1177/095169280101300302.

Allgood, Clarence W. "Operation of the Wage Earner's Plan in the Northern District of Alabama." *Rutgers Law Review* 14, no. 3 (Spring 1960): 578–86, HeinOnline.

Alston, Lee J. "Farm Foreclosure Moratorium Legislation: A Lesson from the Past." *American Economic Review* 74, no. 3 (June 1984): 445–57. https://www .jstor.org/stable/1804019.

American Bar Association. *Report of the Committee on Commercial Law: Bankrupt Law*. Chicago: American Bar Association, 1905.

Angell, Frank J. "Some Effects of the Truth-in-Lending Legislation." *Journal of Business* 44, no. 1 (January 1971): 78–85. https://www.jstor.org/stable/ 2351838.

Apilado, Vincent P., Joel J. Dauten, and Douglas E. Smith. "Personal Bankruptcies." *Journal of Legal Studies* 7, no. 2 (June 1978): 371–92. https://www.jstor .org/stable/724221.

Athreya, Kartik B., "Welfare Implications of the Bankruptcy Reform Act of 1999." *Journal of Monetary Economics* 49, no. 8 (November 2002): 1567–95. https://doi.org/10.1016/S0304-3932(02)00176-9.

Ausubel, Lawrence M. "The Failure of Competition in the Credit Card Market." *American Economic Review* 81, no. 1 (March 1991): 50–81. https://www.jstor .org/stable/2006788.

Ayotte, Kenneth, and Hayong Yun. "Matching Bankruptcy Laws to Legal Environments." *Journal of Law, Economics, and Organization* 25, no. 1 (May 2009): 2–30. https://doi.org/10.1093/jleo/ewm048.

Bailey, Hollis R. "An Assignment in Insolvency, and Its Effect upon Property and Persons out of the State." *Harvard Law Review* 7, no. 5 (December 1893): 281–99. https://doi.org/10.2307/1321416.

——."A Discharge in Insolvency, and Its Effect on Non-Residents." *Harvard Law Review* 6, no. 7 (February 1893): 349–68. https://doi.org/10.2307/ 1321620.

Bailey, Martha J., and Nicolas J. Duquette. "How Johnson Fought the War on Poverty: The Economics and Politics of Funding at the Office of Economic Opportunity." *Journal of Economic History* 74, no. 2 (June 2014): 351–88. http://dx.doi.org/10.1017/S0022050714000291.

Balleisen, Edward J. *Navigating Failure: Bankruptcy and Commercial Society in Antebellum America*. Chapel Hill: University of North Carolina Press, 2001.

Barger, Harold. *Distribution's Place in the American Economy since 1869*. Princeton, NJ: Princeton University Press, 1955.

Bebchuk, Lucien, and Mark Roe. "Theory of Path Dependence in Corporate Ownership and Governance." *Stanford Law Review* 52, no. 1 (November 1999): 127–70, HeinOnline.

Benmelech, Efraim, and Tobias J. Moskowitz. "The Political Economy of Financial Regulation: Evidence from US State Usury Laws in the 19th Century." *Journal of Finance* 65, no. 3 (June 2010): 1029–73. https://doi.org/10.1111/j .1540-6261.2010.01560.x.

Bensel, Richard Franklin. *The Political Economy of American Industrialization, 1877–1900.* Cambridge: Cambridge University Press, 2000.

Berglof, Eric, and Howard Rosenthal. "The Political Economy of American Bankruptcy: The Evidence from Roll Call Voting, 1800–1978." Paper presented at the UFA meeting in Frankfurt, November 2000. https://legacy .voteview.com/pdf/Berglof_Rosenthal_Bankruptcy.pdf.

Berkovitch, Elazar, Ronen Israel, and Jaime F. Zender. "Optimal Bankruptcy Law and Firm-Specific Investments." *European Economic Review* 41, no. 3–5 (April 1997): 487–97. https://doi.org/10.1016/S0014-2921(97)00016-0.

Bernanke, Ben S. "Bankruptcy, Liquidity, and Recession." *American Economic Review* 71, no. 2 (May 1981): 155–59. https://www.jstor.org/stable/pdf/1815710 .pdf.

Billig, Thomas Clifford. "What Price Bankruptcy? A Plea for Friendly Adjustment." *Cornell Law Quarterly* 14, no. 4 (June 1929): 413–4, HeinOnline.

Blazy, Regis, Bruno Deffains, Gisele Umbhauer, and Laurent Weill. "Severe or Gentle Bankruptcy Law: Which Impact on Investing and Financing Decisions?" *Economic Modelling* 34 (August 2013): 129–44. http://dx.doi.org/10 .1016/j.econmod.2013.02.001.

Boshkoff, Douglass G. "Limited, Conditional, and Suspended Discharges in Anglo-American Bankruptcy Proceedings." *University of Pennsylvania Law Review* 131, no. 1 (November 1982): 69–126. https://www.jstor.org/stable/ 3311830.

Boyes, William J., and Roger L. Faith. "Some Effects of the Bankruptcy Reform Act of 1978." *Journal of Law & Economics* 29, no. 1 (April 1986): 139–49. https://www.jstor.org/stable/725405.

Braucher, Jean. "Lawyers and Consumer Bankruptcy: One Code, Many Cultures." *American Bankruptcy Law Journal* 67, no. 4 (Fall 1993): 501–84, HeinOnline.

Braucher, Jean, Dov Cohen, and Robert M. Lawless. "Race, Attorney Influence, and Bankruptcy Chapter Choice." *Journal of Empirical Legal Studies* 9, no. 3 (September 2012): 393–429. https://doi.org/10.1111/j.1740-1461.2012.01264.x.

Breusch, Trevor, Michael B. Ward, Hoa Thi Minh Nguyen, and Tom Kompas. "FEVD: Just IV or Just Mistaken?" *Political Analysis* 19, no. 2 (Spring 2011): 165–69. https://www.jstor.org/stable/pdf/23011260.pdf.

Brewster, Stanley Farrar. *Legal Aspects of Credit.* New York: Ronald Press, 1923.

Bridges, Amy. "Path Dependence, Sequence, History, Theory." *Studies in American Political Development* 14, no. 1 (April 2000): 109–12.

Brunn, George. "Wage Garnishment in California: A Study and Recommendations." *California Law Review* 53, no. 5 (December 1965): 1214–53, HeinOnline.

Brunner, George Allen. *Personal Bankruptcies: Trends and Characteristics.* Ohio State University. Bureau of Business Research, Monograph No. 124. Columbus: Bureau of Business Research, Division of Research, College of Commerce and Administration, Ohio State University, 1965.

Buckley, F. H., and Margaret F. Brinig. "The Bankruptcy Puzzle." *Journal of Legal Studies* 27, no. 1 (January 1998): 187–207. https://doi.org/10.1086/468018.

Bundschu, Henry A. "Administration of Wage Earners' Plans in the Bankruptcy Court." *Journal of the National Association of Referees in Bankruptcy* 18, no. 2 (January 1944): 55–57, HeinOnline.

Calder, Lendol. *Financing the American Dream: A Cultural History of Consumer Credit.* Princeton, NJ: Princeton University Press, 2009.

Caplovitz, David. *The Poor Pay More: Consumer Practices of Low-Income Families.* Report of the Bureau of Applied Social Research, Columbia University. New York: Free Press of Glencoe, 1963.

Carlos, Ann M., Edward Kosack, and Luis Castro Penarrieta. "Bankruptcy, Discharge, and the Emergence of Debtor Rights in Eighteenth-Century England." *Enterprise & Society* 20, no. 2 (June 2019): 475–506. https://doi.org/10.1017/eso.2018.69.

Carruthers, Bruce G., Timothy W. Guinnane, and Yoonseok Lee. "Bringing 'Honest Capital' to Poor Borrowers: The Passage of the US Uniform Small Loan Law, 1907–1930." *Journal of Interdisciplinary History* 42, no. 3 (Winter 2012): 393–418. https://www.jstor.org/stable/41291234.

Caskey, John P. *Fringe Banking: Check-Cashing Outlets, Pawnshops, and the Poor.* New York: Russell Sage Foundation, 1994.

Chatterji, Aaron K., and Robert C. Seamans. "Entrepreneurial Finance, Credit Cards, and Race." *Journal of Financial Economics* 106, no. 1 (October 2012): 182–95. https://doi.org/10.1016/j.jfineco.2012.04.007.

Chen, Jess, and Mary Eschelbach Hansen. "New Evidence of Spillovers in Personal Bankruptcy Using Point-Coded Data." *Spatial Economic Analysis* (forthcoming). http://doi.org/10.1080/17421772.2019.1636128.

Chen, X. Jess. "Local Spillovers in Bankruptcy: Analysis Using the Local Modified Moran's I and Other Methods." PhD diss., American University, 2016.

Clark, Evans. *Financing the Consumer.* New York: Harper & Brothers, 1930.

Cohen, Lizabeth. *A Consumers' Republic: The Politics of Mass Consumption in Postwar America.* New York: Knopf, 2003.

Cohen-Cole, Ethan, and Burcu Duygan-Bump. "Household Bankruptcy Decision: The Role of Social Stigma vs. Information Sharing." Federal Reserve Bank of Boston, Quantitative Analysis Unit Working Paper: QAU08–6, 2008, November 12, 2008. http://www.bos.frb.org/bankinfo/qau/wp/2008/qau0806.pdf.

———. "Social Influence and Bankruptcy: Why Do So Many Leave So Much on the Table?" Unpublished manuscript, 2009. http://papers.ssrn.com/abstract=1423964.

Coleman, Peter J. *Debtors and Creditors in America: Insolvency, Imprisonment for Debt, and Bankruptcy, 1607–1900.* Madison: State Historical Society of Wisconsin, 1974.

Cover, John H. *Business and Personal Failure and Readjustment in Chicago.* Vol. 3. University of Chicago; Graduate School of Business; Studies in Business Administration. Chicago: University of Chicago Press, 1933.

Credit Research Center, Arthur D. Little Inc., and Opinion Research Corp.. *Consumer Bankruptcy Study.* Vol. 1, *Consumers' Right to Bankruptcy Origins and Effects.* Monograph No. 23. West Lafayette, IN: Credit Research Center, Krannert Graduate School of Management, Purdue University, 1982.

Cronon, William. *Nature's Metropolis: Chicago and the Great West.* New York: W. W. Norton, 1991.

Crouch, Colin, and Henry Farrell. "Breaking the Path of Institutional Development? Alternatives to the New Determinism." *Rationality and Society* 16, no. 1 (February 2004): 5–43. https://doi.org/10.1177%2F1043463104039874.

Culhane, Marianne B., and Michaela M. White. "Taking the New Consumer Bankruptcy Model for a Test Drive: Means-Testing Real Chapter 7 Debtors." *American Bankruptcy Institute Law Review* 7, no. 1 (Spring 1999): 27–78, HeinOnline.

Danziger, Sheldon, and Martha J. Bailey. *Legacies of the War on Poverty.* National Poverty Center Series on Poverty and Public Policy. New York: Russell Sage Foundation, 2013. https://doi.org/10.1177%2F1043463104039874.

David, Paul A. "Path Dependence, Its Critics, and the Quest for 'Historical Economics.'" In *Evolution and Path Dependence in Economic Ideas: Past and Present,* edited by Pierre Garrouste, and Stavros Ioannides, 15–40. Cheltenham: Edward Elgar, 1994.

———. "Transport Innovation and Economic Growth: Professor Fogel on and off the Rails." *Economic History Review* 22, no. 3 (December 1969): 506–25. https://doi.org/10.2307/2594124.

Dawsey, Amanda E., and Lawrence M. Ausubel. "Informal Bankruptcy," Unpublished manuscript, University of North Carolina Greensboro and University of Maryland, April 12, 2004. http://www.ausubel.com/creditcard-papers/informal-bankruptcy.pdf.

Dawsey, Amanda E., Richard M. Hynes, and Lawrence M. Ausubel. "Non-Judicial Debt Collection and the Consumer's Choice among Repayment, Bankruptcy and Informal Bankruptcy." *American Bankruptcy Law Journal* 87, no. 1 (Winter 2013): 1–26, HeinOnline.

Day, George S., and William K. Brandt. "Consumer Research and the Evaluation of Information Disclosure Requirements: The Case of Truth in Lend-

ing." *Journal of Consumer Research* 1, no. 1 (June 1974): 21–32. http://www
.jstor.org/action/showPublication?journalCode=jconsrese.

DeMuth, Christopher C. "The Case against Credit Card Interest Rate Regulation." *Yale Journal on Regulation* 3, no. 2 (Spring 1986): 201–42, HeinOnline.

Dick, Astrid A., and Andreas Lehnert. "Personal Bankruptcy and Credit Market Competition." *Journal of Finance* 65, no. 2 (April 2010): 655–86. https://
doi.org/10.1111/j.1540-6261.2009.01547.x.

Dick, Astrid, Andreas Lehnert, and Giorgio Topa. "Social Spillovers in Personal
Bankruptcies." Federal Reserve Bank of New York Working Paper, June
2008. https://www.newyorkfed.org/medialibrary/media/research/economists/
topa/DLT_062808.pdf.

Dickerson, A. Mechele. "Regulating Bankruptcy: Public Choice, Ideology &
Beyond." *Washington University Law Review* 84, no. 7 (2006): 1861–1906,
HeinOnline.

Dixon, Timothy W., and David G. Epstein. "Where Did Chapter 13 Come from
and Where Should It Go?" *American Bankruptcy Institute Law Review* 10,
no. 2 (Winter 2002): 741–64, HeinOnline.

Dolphin, Robert. *An Analysis of Economic and Personal Factors Leading to
Consumer Bankruptcy.* Bureau of Business and Economic Research, Michigan State University, Occasional Paper No. 15. East Lansing: Bureau of Business and Economic Research, Graduate School of Business Administration,
Michigan State University, 1965.

Domowitz, Ian, and Thomas L. Eovaldi. "The Impact of the Bankruptcy Reform Act of 1978 on Consumer Bankruptcy." *Journal of Law & Economics*
36, no. 2 (October 1993): 803–35. https://www.jstor.org/stable/725808.

Domowitz, Ian, and Robert L. Sartain. "Determinants of the Consumer Bankruptcy Decision." *Journal of Finance* 54, no. 1 (February 1999): 403–20.
https://doi.org/10.1111/0022-1082.00110.

———. "Incentives and Bankruptcy Chapter Choice: Evidence from the Reform
Act of 1978." *Journal of Legal Studies* 28, no. 2 (June 1999): 461–87. https://
www.jstor.org/stable/10.1086/468058.

Domowitz, Ian, and Elie Tamer. "Two Hundred Years of Bankruptcy: A Tale
of Legislation and Economic Fluctuations." IPR working paper, Institute for
Policy Research at Northwestern University, 1997. https://ideas.repec.org/p/
wop/nwuipr/97-25.html.

Douglas, Paul. *Real Wages in the United States, 1890–1926.* New York: Houghton Mifflin, 1930.

Douglas, William O. "Wage Earner Bankruptcies: State vs. Federal Control."
Yale Law Journal 42, no. 4 (February 1933): 591–642, HeinOnline.

Douglas, William O., and J. Howard Marshall. "A Factual Study of Bankruptcy
Administration and Some Suggestions." *Columbia Law Review* 32, no. 1
(January 1932): 25–59. https://www.jstor.org/stable/1115117.

Dunscomb, S. Whitney. *Bankruptcy: A Study in Comparative Legislation.* Vol. 2. Studies in History, Economics and Public Law. New York: Columbia College, 1893.

Durkin, Thomas A., Gregory Elliehausen, Michael E. Staten, and Todd J. Zywicki. *Consumer Credit and the American Economy.* New York: Oxford University Press, 2014.

Durkin, Thomas A., and Michael E. Staten. "Introduction." In *The Impact of Public Policy on Consumer Credit,* edited by Thomas A. Durkin and Michael E. Staten, 1–22. New York: Springer Science & Business Media, 2002.

Earling, Peter R. *Whom to Trust: A Practical Treatise on Mercantile Credits.* Chicago: Rand, McNally, 1889.

Efrat, Rafael. "The Evolution of Bankruptcy Stigma." *Theoretical Inquiries in Law* 7, no. 2 (July 2006): 365–93. https://doi.org/10.2202/1565-3404.1130.

Fan, Wei, and Michelle J. White. "Personal Bankruptcy and the Level of Entrepreneurial Activity." *Journal of Law and Economics* 46, no. 2 (October 2003): 543–67. https://doi.org/10.1086/382602.

Fasules, Megan Lynn. "The Impact of Medicare on Personal Bankruptcy." PhD diss., American University, 2015.

Fay, Scott, Erik Hurst, and Michelle J. White. "The Household Bankruptcy Decision." *American Economic Review* 92, no. 3 (June 2002): 706–18. https://www.jstor.org/stable/pdf/3083362.pdf.

Field, Alexander J. "Bankruptcy, Debt, and the Macroeconomy: 1919–1946." *Research in Economic History* 20 (2001): 99–133. https://doi.org/10.1016/S0363 -3268(01)20004-4.

Finkelstein, Amy, Sarah Taubman, Bill Wright, Mira Bernstein, Jonathan Gruber, Joseph P. Newhouse, Heidi Allen, and Katherine Baecker. "The Oregon Health Insurance Experiment: Evidence from the First Year." *Quarterly Journal of Economics* 127, no. 3 (August 2012): 1057–1106. https://doi.org/10 .1093/qje/qjs020.

Fishback, Price V., and Shawn Everett Kantor. *A Prelude to the Welfare State: The Origins of Workers' Compensation.* Chicago: University of Chicago Press, 2007.

Fisher, Jonathan D. "The Effect of Unemployment Benefits, Welfare Benefits, and Other Income on Personal Bankruptcy." *Contemporary Economic Policy* 23, no. 4 (October 2005): 483–92. https://doi.org/10.1093/cep/byi036.

Fleming, Anne. "The Borrower's Tale: A History of Poor Debtors in Lochner Era New York City." *Law and History Review* 30, no. 4 (November 2012): 1053–98. https://doi.org/10.1017/S0738248012000533.

———. *City of Debtors: A Century of Fringe Finance.* Cambridge, MA: Harvard University Press, 2018.

Fortas, A. "Wage Assignments in Chicago: *State Street Furniture Co. v. Armour*

& Co." *Yale Law Journal* 42, no. 4 (February 1933): 526–60. https://www.jstor
.org/stable/pdf/791157.pdf.

Friedman, Lawrence M. *A History of American Law.* New York: Simon and
Schuster, 1973.

Frimet, Rhett. "The Birth of Bankruptcy in the United States." *Commercial
Law Journal* 96 (1991): 160–89, HeinOnline.

Furletti, Mark. "The Debate over the National Bank Act and the Preemption of
State Efforts to Regulate Credit Cards." *Temple Law Review* 77, no. 2 (Summer 2004): 425–56, HeinOnline.

Garrett, Thomas A., and Howard J. Wall. "Personal-Bankruptcy Cycles."
Macroeconomic Dynamics 18, no. 7 (October 2014): 1488–1507. http://dx.doi
.org/10.1017/S1365100512001058.

Garrison, Lloyd K. "Wisconsin's New Personal Receivership Law." *Wisconsin
Law Review* 1938 (March 1938): 201–28, HeinOnline.

Ghent, Andra. "How Do Case Law and Statute Differ? Lessons from the Evolution of Mortgage Law." *Journal of Law and Economics* 57, no. 4 (November
2014): 1085–1122. https://doi.org/10.1086/680931.

Goodman, Paul. "The Emergence of Homestead Exemption in the United
States: Accommodation and Resistance to the Market Revolution, 1840–
1880." *Journal of American History* 80, no. 2 (September 1993): 470–98.
https://doi.org/10.2307/2079867.

Gordon, Grey. "Optimal Bankruptcy Code: A Fresh Start for Some." *Journal
of Economic Dynamics and Control* 85 (December 2017): 123–49. https://doi
.org/10.1016/j.jedc.2017.10.005.

Greif, Avner, and David D. Laitin. "A Theory of Endogenous Institutional
Change." *American Political Science Review* 98, no. 4 (November 2004):
633–52. https://doi.org/10.1017/S0003055404041395.

Grochulski, Borys. "Optimal Personal Bankruptcy Design under Moral Haz-
ard." *Review of Economic Dynamics* 13, no. 2 (April 2010): 350–78. http://dx
.doi.org/10.1016/j.red.2009.06.004.

Grodzicki, Daniel. "The Evolution of Competition in the Credit Card Market."
Unpublished manuscript, Pennsylvania State University, 2017. https://sites
.google.com/site/danieljosegrodzicki/research.

Gross, David B., and Nicholas S. Souleles. "An Empirical Analysis of Personal
Bankruptcy and Delinquency." *Review of Financial Studies* 15, no. 1 (January 2002): 319–47. https://doi.org/10.1093/rfs/15.1.319.

Gross, Karen. *Failure and Forgiveness: Rebalancing the Bankruptcy System.*
Contemporary Law Series. New Haven: Yale University Press, 1997.

Grosse, C. Kenneth, and Charles W. Lean. "Wage Garnishment in Washington:
An Empirical Study Project." *Washington Law Review* 43, no. 4 (April 1968):
743–98, HeinOnline.

Hanna, John. "New Frazier-Lemke Act." *Missouri Law Review* 1, no. 1 (January 1936): 1–19, HeinOnline.

Hansen, Bradley A. "Commercial Associations and the Creation of a National Economy: The Demand for Federal Bankruptcy Law." *Business History Review* 72, no. 1 (Spring 1998): 86–113. https://doi.org/10.2307/3116596.

——. *Institutions, Entrepreneurs, and American Economic History: How the Farmers' Loan and Trust Company Shaped the Laws of Business from 1822 to 1929.* New York: Palgrave Macmillan, 2009.

——. "The People's Welfare and the Origins of Corporate Reorganization: The Wabash Receivership Reconsidered." *Business History Review* 74, no. 3 (Autumn 2000): 377–405. https://doi.org/10.2307/3116432.

Hansen, Bradley A., and Mary Eschelbach Hansen. "The Evolution of Garnishment and Wage Assignment Law in Illinois." *Essays in Economic & Business History* 32 (March 2014): 19–46. http://www.ebhsoc.org/journal/index.php/journal/article/view/268.

——. "Religion, Social Capital and Business Bankruptcy in the United States, 1921–1932." *Business History* 50, no. 6 (November 2008): 714–27. https://doi.org/10.1080/00076790802420252.

——. "The Role of Path Dependence in the Development of US Bankruptcy Law, 1880–1938." *Journal of Institutional Economics* 3, no. 2 (August 2007): 203–25. https://doi.org/10.1017/S174413740700063X.

Hansen, Mary Eschelbach. "Sources of Credit and the Extent of the Credit Market: A View from Bankruptcy Records in Mississippi, 1929–1936." In *Enterprising America: Businesses, Banks, and Credit Markets in Historical Perspective*, edited by William J. Collins and Robert A. Margo, 179–212. Chicago: University of Chicago Press, 2015.

Hansen, Mary Eschelbach, and Bradley A. Hansen. "Crisis and Bankruptcy: The Mediating Role of State Law, 1920–1932." *Journal of Economic History* 72, no. 2 (June 2012): 448–68. https://doi.org/10.1017/S0022050712000095.

Hansen, Mary Eschelbach, and Michelle McKinnon Miller. "A New View of Women in Bankruptcy." *American Bankruptcy Institute Journal* 35, no. 11 (November 2016): 82–83.

Hansen, Mary Eschelbach, and Nicolas L. Ziebarth. "Credit Relationships and Business Bankruptcy during the Great Depression." *American Economic Journal: Macroeconomics* 9, no. 2 (April 2017): 228–55. https://doi.org/10.1257/mac.20150218.

Hathaway, Oona A. "Path Dependence in the Law: The Course and Pattern of Legal Change in a Common Law System." *Iowa Law Review* 86, no. 2 (January 2001): 601–66, HeinOnline.

Hausman, Jerry A., and William E. Taylor. "Panel Data and Unobservable Individual Effects." *Econometrica* 49, no. 6 (November 1981): 1377–98. https://doi.org/10.2307/1911406.

Hayes, Thomas J. "Bankruptcy Reform and Congressional Action: The Role of Organized Interests in Shaping Policy." *Social Science Research* 64 (May 2017): 67–78. https://doi.org/10.1016/j.ssresearch.2016.09.026.

Heck, Ramona. "An Econometric Analysis of Interstate Differences in Nonbusiness Bankruptcy and Chapter Thirteen Rates." *Journal of Consumer Affairs* 15, no. 1 (Summer 1981): 13–32. https://doi.org/10.1111/j.1745-6606.1981.tb00687.x.

Herbert, Michael J. "Straining the Gnat: A Critique of the 1984 Federal Trade Commission Consumer Credit Regulations." *South Carolina Law Review* 38, no. 2 (Winter 1987): 329–62, HeinOnline.

Herrmann, Robert O. "Families in Bankruptcy: A Survey of Recent Studies." *Journal of Marriage and Family* 28, no. 3 (August 1966): 324–30. https://doi.org/10.2307/349882.

Hilt, Eric. "Economic History, Historical Analysis, and the 'New History of Capitalism.'" *Journal of Economic History* 77, no. 2 (June 2017): 511–36. https://doi.org/10.1017/S002205071700016X.

Himmelstein, David U., Elizabeth Warren, Deborah Thorne, and Steffie Woolhandler. "Illness and Injury as Contributors to Bankruptcy." *Health Affairs* 24 (June 2005): W5-63–W5-73. https://doi.org/10.1377/hlthaff.W5.63.

Honsberger, John D. "The Origins of the National Bankruptcy Conference: A Hinge-Point of Change 1932–1933." National Bankruptcy Conference, 1985. http://nbconf.org/wp-content/uploads/2015/10/NBC-History-1.pdf.

Hubachek, Frank Brookes. "The Development of Regulatory Small Loan Laws." *Law and Contemporary Problems* 8, no. 1 (Winter 1941): 108–45. https://doi.org/10.2307/1189378.

Hyman, Louis. *Borrow: The American Way of Debt.* New York: Vintage Books, 2012.

———. *Debtor Nation: The History of America in Red Ink.* Princeton, NJ: Princeton University Press, 2011.

———. "Ending Discrimination, Legitimating Debt: The Political Economy of Race, Gender, and Credit Access in the 1960s and 1970s." *Enterprise & Society* 12, no. 1 (June 2011): 200–232. https://doi.org/10.1017/S1467222700009770.

Hynes, Richard M., Anup Malani, and Eric A. Posner. "The Political Economy of Property Exemption Laws." *Journal of Law and Economics* 47, no. 1 (April 2004): 19–43. https://doi.org/10.1086/386276.

Hynes, Richard M., and Eric A. Posner. "The Law and Economics of Consumer Finance." *American Law and Economics Review* 4, no. 1 (January 2002): 168–207. https://doi.org/10.1093/aler/4.1.168.

Jablonski, James A. "Wage Garnishment as a Collection Device." *Wisconsin Law Review* 1967, no. 3 (1967): 759–73, HeinOnline.

Jackson, Thomas H. *The Logic and Limits of Bankruptcy.* Cambridge, MA: Harvard University Press, 1986.

Jacob, Herbert. "Winners and Losers: Garnishment and Bankruptcy in Wisconsin." *Society* 6, no. 7 (May 1969): 24–32. https://doi.org/10.1007/BF03180877.

Jacoby, Melissa B., Teresa A. Sullivan, and Elizabeth Warren. "Rethinking the Debates over Health Care Financing: Evidence from the Bankruptcy Courts." *New York University Law Review* 76, no. 2 (May 2001): 375–418, HeinOnline.

Jagtiani, Julapa, and Wenli Li. "Credit Access and Credit Performance after Consumer Bankruptcy Filing: New Evidence." Federal Reserve Bank of Philadelphia Working Paper No. 13–24, 2013. https://dx.doi.org/10.2139/ssrn.2269621.

Jensen, Susan. "A Legislative History of the Bankruptcy Abuse Prevention and Consumer Protection Act of 2005." *American Bankruptcy Law Journal* 79, no. 3 (Summer 2005): 485–570, HeinOnline.

Kaplan, A. D. H. *Small Business: Its Place and Problems.* Committee for Economic Development, Research Study. New York: McGraw-Hill, 1948.

Keller, Morton. *Regulating a New Economy: Public Policy Change in America, 1900–1933.* Cambridge, MA: Harvard University Press, 1990.

Klee, Kenneth N. "Legislative History of the New Bankruptcy Code." *American Bankruptcy Law Journal* 54, no. 3 (Summer 1980): 275–98, HeinOnline.

Klein, Gary. "Consumer Bankruptcy in the Balance: The National Bankruptcy Review Commission's Recommendations Tilt toward Creditors." *American Bankruptcy Institute Law Review* 5, no. 2 (Winter 1997): 293–340, HeinOnline.

Knittel, Christopher R., and Victor Stango. "Price Ceilings as Focal Points for Tacit Collusion: Evidence from Credit Cards." *American Economic Review* 93, no. 5 (December 2003): 1703–29. https://doi.org/10.1257/000282803322655509.

Knot, Ondrej, and Ondrej Vychodil. "What Drives the Optimal Bankruptcy Law Design?" *Czech Journal of Economics and Finance* 55, no. 3–4 (2005): 110–23. http://journal.fsv.cuni.cz/storage/1011_s_110_123.pdf.

Kroszner, Randall S., and Philip E. Strahan. "What Drives Deregulation? Economics and Politics of the Relaxation of Bank Branching Restrictions." *Quarterly Journal of Economics* 114, no. 4 (November 1999): 1437–67. https://doi.org/10.1162/003355399556223.

Ladd, Helen F. "Equal Credit Opportunity: Women and Mortgage Credit." *American Economic Review* 72, no. 2 (May 1982): 166–70. http://www.jstor.org/stable/1802323.

Landry, Robert J., III. "The Policy and Forces behind Consumer Bankruptcy Reform: A Classic Battle over Problem Definition." *University of Memphis Law Review* 33, no. 3 (2003): 509–28, HeinOnline.

Lane, Sarah J., and Martha Schary. "Understanding the Business Failure Rate." *Contemporary Economic Policy* 9, no. 4 (October 1991): 93–105. https://doi.org/10.1111/j.1465-7287.1991.tb00353.x.

Lauer, Josh. *Creditworthy: A History of Consumer Surveillance and Financial Identity in America.* Columbia Studies in the History of US Capitalism; New York: Columbia University Press, 2017.

Lawless, Robert M., Angela K. Littwin, Katherine M. Porter, John A. E. Pottow, Deborah K. Thorne, and Elizabeth Warren. "Did Bankruptcy Reform Fail—An Empirical Study of Consumer Debtors." *American Bankruptcy Law Journal* 82, no. 3 (Summer 2008): 349–406, HeinOnline.

Lawless, Robert M., and Elizabeth Warren. "The Myth of the Disappearing Business Bankruptcy." *California Law Review* 93, no. 3 (May 2005): 743–96, HeinOnline.

Lefgren, Lars, and Frank McIntyre. "Explaining the Puzzle of Cross-State Differences in Bankruptcy Rates." *Journal of Law and Economics* 52, no. 2 (May 2009): 367–93. https://doi.org/10.1086/596561.

Lefgren, Lars, Frank L. McIntyre, and Michelle Miller. "Chapter 7 or 13: Are Client or Lawyer Interests Paramount?" *BE Journal of Economic Analysis & Policy* 10, no. 1 (2010): art. 82. https://doi.org/10.2202/1935-1682.2512.

Lipartito, Kenneth. "The Narrative and the Algorithm: Genres of Credit Reporting from the Nineteenth Century to Today." Unpublished manuscript, Florida International University, January 6, 2011. https://ssrn.com/abstract=1736283.

Livshits, Igor, James MacGee, and Michèle Tertilt. "Accounting for the Rise in Consumer Bankruptcies." *American Economic Journal: Macroeconomics* 2, no. 2 (April 2010): 165–93. https://doi.org/10.1257/mac.2.2.165.

——. "The Democratization of Credit and the Rise in Consumer Bankruptcies." *Review of Economic Studies* 83, no. 4 (October 2016): 1673–1710. https://doi.org/10.1093/restud/rdw011.

Lowell, John. "Bankruptcy." In *Cyclopedia of Political Science, Political Economy and the Political History of the United States.* New York: Maynard, Merill, 1899.

Lupica, Lois R. "The Consumer Bankruptcy Creditor Distribution Study: Final Report." American Bankruptcy Institute and National Conference of Bankruptcy Judges, 2013. http://abi-org.s3.amazonaws.com/Endowment/Research_Grants/Creditor_Distributions_ABI_Final.pdf.

——. "The Costs of BAPCPA: Report of the Pilot Study of Consumer Bankruptcy Cases." *American Bankruptcy Institute Law Review* 18, no. 1 (Spring 2010): 43–88, HeinOnline.

Lusardi, Annamaria, Olivia S. Mitchell, and Noemi Oggero. "Debt and Financial Vulnerability on the Verge of Retirement." NBER Working Paper 23664, 2017. http://www.nber.org/papers/w23664.pdf.

Mahoney, James. *The Legacies of Liberalism: Path Dependence and Political Regimes in Central America.* Baltimore: John Hopkins University Press, 2001.

Mandell, Lewis. "Consumer Perception of Incurred Interest Rates: An Empirical Test of the Efficacy of the Truth-in-Lending Law." *Journal of Finance* 26, no. 5 (December 1971): 1143–54. https://doi.org/10.1111/j.1540-6261.1971.tb01754.x.

———. *The Credit Card Industry: A History.* Twayne's Evolution of American Business Series, no. 4. Boston: Twayne, 1990.

Mann, Ronald J. "Bankruptcy Reform and the Sweat Box of Credit Card Debt." *University of Illinois Law Review* no. 1 (2007): 375–404, HeinOnline.

Matherly, Walter J. "The Regulation of Consumer Credit." *Southern Economic Journal* 11, no. 1 (July 1944): 34–44. https://doi.org/10.2307/1053165.

McDuffee, Reginald W. "The Wage Earners' Plan in Practice." *Vanderbilt Law Review* 15, no. 1 (1961): 173–94, HeinOnline.

McLaughlin, James Angell. "Amendment of the Bankruptcy Act." *Harvard Law Review* 40, no. 3 (January 1927): 341–91, HeinOnline.

Miller, Michelle M. "Social Networks and Personal Bankruptcy." *Journal of Empirical Legal Studies* 12, no. 2 (June 2015): 289–310. https://doi.org/10.1111/jels.12073.

Misbach, Grant L. "Personal Bankruptcy in the United States and Utah." PhD diss., College of Business, University of Utah, 1964.

Moeckel, Bill. *The Development of the Wholesaler in the United States, 1860–1900.* New York: Garland, 1986.

Morris, Jeffrey W. "Substantive Consumer Bankruptcy Reform in the Bankruptcy Amendments Act of 1984." *William and Mary Law Review* 27, no. 1 (Fall 1985): 91–164, HeinOnline.

Moss, David A., and Gibbs A. Johnson. "The Rise of Consumer Bankruptcy: Evolution, Revolution, or Both?" *American Bankruptcy Law Journal* 73, no. 2 (Spring 1999): 311–52, HeinOnline.

Murnane, M. Susan. *Bankruptcy in an Industrial Society: A History of the Bankruptcy Court for the Northern District of Ohio.* Akron: University of Akron Press, 2015.

National Association of Credit Management. *Credit Manual of Commercial Laws.* New York: National Association of Credit Management, various years.

National Convention of the Representatives of Commercial Bodies of the United States. *Proceedings of the First Session of the National Convention of the Representatives of Commercial Bodies.* St. Louis: Nixon-Jones, 1889.

National Industrial Conference Board. *Trade Associations: Their Economic Significance and Legal Status.* New York: National Industrial Conference Board, 1925.

Nehemkis, Peter R., Jr. "The Boston Poor Debtor Court—A Study in Collection Procedure." *Yale Law Journal* 42, no. 4 (February 1933): 561–90, HeinOnline.

Nelson, Jon P. "Consumer Bankruptcy and Chapter Choice: State Panel Evidence." *Contemporary Economic Policy* 17, no. 4 (October 1999): 552–66. https://doi.org/10.1111/j.1465-7287.1999.tb00704.x.

Newmyer, R. Kent. *The Supreme Court under Marshall and Taney.* Crowell American History Series. New York: Crowell, 1968.

Nocera, Joseph. *A Piece of the Action: How the Middle Class Joined the Money Class.* New York: Simon and Schuster, 1994.

Noel, F. Regis. "Bankruptcy Law as It Affects Credit." *Georgetown Law Journal* 13, no. 2 (1924): 131–55, HeinOnline.

Norberg, Scott F., and Nadja Schreiber Compo. "Report on an Empirical Study of District Variations, and the Roles of Judges, Trustees and Debtors' Attorneys in Chapter 13 Bankruptcy Cases." *American Bankruptcy Law Journal* 81 (Fall 2007): 431–70, HeinOnline.

North, Douglass C. *Institutions, Institutional Change and Economic Performance.* Cambridge: Cambridge University Press, 1990.

——. *Understanding the Process of Economic Change.* Princeton, NJ: Princeton University Press, 2005.

Nugent, Rolf. "Small Loan Debt in the United States." *Journal of Business of the University of Chicago* 7, no. 1 (January 1934): 1–21. http://www.jstor.org/stable/2349472.

Nugent, Rolf, John E. Hamm, and Frances Jones. "Wage Executions for Debt: Part 2. Characteristics of Debts and Debtors." *Monthly Labor Review* 42, no. 3 (March 1936): 578–92. https://www.jstor.org/stable/41814782.

——. "Wage Executions for Debt: Part 3. Most Frequent Creditors, Costs of Executions, and Employers' Policies." *Monthly Labor Review* 43, no. 4 (July 1936): 51–60. https://www.jstor.org/stable/41814867.

Nugent, Rolf, and Frances Jones. "Wage Executions for Debt: Part 1: Frequency of Wage Executions." *Monthly Labor Review* 42, no. 2 (February 1936): 285–300. https://www.jstor.org/stable/41814753.

Nunez, Stephen, and Howard Rosenthal. "Bankruptcy 'Reform' in Congress: Creditors, Committees, Ideology, and Floor Voting in the Legislative Process." *Journal of Law, Economics, and Organization* 20, no. 2 (October 2004): 527–57. https://doi.org/10.1093/jleo/ewh044.

Nystrom, Paul H. *Economics of Retailing.* New York: Ronald Press, 1930.

Olegario, Rowena. *The Engine of Enterprise: Credit in America.* Cambridge, MA: Harvard University Press, 2016.

Olmstead, James M. "Bankruptcy: A Commercial Regulation." *Harvard Law Review* 15, no. 10 (1902): 829–43, HeinOnline.

Olney, Martha L. "Avoiding Default: The Role of Credit in the Consumption Collapse of 1930." *Quarterly Journal of Economics* 114, no. 1 (February 1999): 319–35. https://doi.org/10.1162/003355399555927.

———. *Buy Now, Pay Later: Advertising, Credit, and Consumer Durables in the 1920s.* Chapel Hill: University of North Carolina Press, 1991.

———. "Demand for Consumer Durable Goods in 20th Century America." *Explorations in Economic History* 27, no. 3 (July 1990): 322–49. https://doi.org/10.1016/0014-4983(90)90017-S.

Palmer, J. P. "A Poor Man's Receivership—Discussing a New Nebraska Statute." *Central Law Journal* 85 (August 1917): 99 100, HeinOnline.

Persons, Charles E. "Credit Expansion, 1920 to 1929, and Its Lessons." *Quarterly Journal of Economics* 45, no. 1 (November 1930): 94–130. https://doi.org/10.2307/1882528.

Peterson, Richard L., and Kiyomi Aoki. "Bankruptcy Filings before and after Implementation of the Bankruptcy Reform Law." *Journal of Economics and Business* 36, no. 1 (February 1984): 95–105. https://doi.org/10.1016/0148-6195(84)90015-8.

Pierson, Paul. "Increasing Returns, Path Dependence, and the Study of Politics." *American Political Science Review* 94, no. 2 (June 2000): 251–67. https://doi.org/10.2307/2586011.

Plummer, Wilbur C., and Ralph A. Young. *Sales Finance Companies and Their Credit Practices.* Boston: National Bureau of Economic Research, 1940. https://www.nber.org/books/plum40-1.

Plümper, Thomas, and Vera E. Troeger. "Efficient Estimation of Time-Invariant and Rarely Changing Variables in Finite Sample Panel Analyses with Unit Fixed Effects." *Political Analysis* 15, no. 2 (Spring 2007): 124–39. https://doi.org/10.1093/pan/mpm002.

Posner, Eric A. "The Political Economy of the Bankruptcy Reform Act of 1978." *Michigan Law Review* 96, no. 1 (October 1997): 47. https://doi.org/10.2307/1290141.

Postel-Vinay, Natacha. "Debt Dilution in 1920s America: Lighting the Fuse of a Mortgage Crisis." *Economic History Review* 70, no. 2 (May 2017): 559–85. https://doi.org/10.1111/ehr.12342.

Pottow, John A. E. "The Rise in Elder Bankruptcy Filings and Failure of US Bankruptcy Law." *Elder Law Journal* 19, no. 1 (Spring 2011): 119–57, HeinOnline.

Ramsay, Iain. *Personal Insolvency in the 21st Century: A Comparative Analysis of the US and Europe.* Oxford: Hart, 2017.

———. "US Exceptionalism, Historical Institutionalism, and the Comparative Study of Consumer Bankruptcy Law." *Temple Law Review* 87, no. 4 (Summer 2015): 947–74, HeinOnline.

Remington, Harold. "Bankruptcy Law and Peaceable Settlements of Business Failures." *Yale Law Journal* 18, no. 8 (June 1909): 590–95, HeinOnline.

Richardson, Gary, and Michael Gou. "Bank Failures Trigger Firm Bankruptcies: Causal Evidence from the Federal Reserve's Formative Years." Unpublished manuscript, University of California at Irvine. Accessed January 30, 2019. http://eml.berkeley.edu/~webfac/cromer/e211_f12/Richardson.pdf.

Richardson, Gary, and William Troost. "Monetary Intervention Mitigated Banking Panics during the Great Depression: Quasi-Experimental Evidence from a Federal Reserve District Border, 1929–1933." *Journal of Political Economy* 117, no. 6 (December 2009): 1031–73. https://doi.org/10.1086/649603.

Robinson, James J. "Scope and Effect of the 1926 Amendments to the Bankruptcy Act." *Cornell Law Quarterly* 12, no. 1 (1926): 49–56, HeinOnline.

Robinson, Louis N., and Rolf Nugent. *Regulation of the Small Loan Business.* Small Loan Series. New York: Russell Sage Foundation, 1935.

Rockoff, Hugh. "Prodigals and Projectors: An Economic History of Usury Laws in the United States from Colonial Times to 1900." In *Human Capital and Institutions: A Long-Run View*, edited by David Eltis, Frank D. Lewis, and Kenneth L. Sokoloff, 285–324. New York: Cambridge University Press, 2009.

Rogalski, Martin L. "An Examination of the Fair Debt Collection Practices Act: The Pendulum Swings toward the Debtor." *Detroit College of Law Review*, Winter 1978, 663–88, HeinOnline.

Romer, Christina D., and David H. Romer. "The Incentive Effects of Marginal Tax Rates: Evidence from the Interwar Era." *American Economic Journal: Economic Policy* 6, no. 3 (August 2014): 242–81. https://doi.org/10.1257/pol.6.3.242.

Rubin, Edward L. "Legislative Methodology: Some Lessons From the Truth in Lending Act." *Georgetown Law Journal* 80, no. 2 (December 1991): 233–308, HeinOnline.

Rucker, Randall R., and Lee J. Alston. "Farm Failures and Government Intervention: A Case Study of the 1930s." *American Economic Review* 77, no. 4 (September 1987): 724–30. http://www.jstor.org/stable/1814543.

Ryan, Franklin W. "Family Finance in the United States." *Journal of Business of the University of Chicago* 3, no. 4 (October 1930): 402–23. http://www.jstor.org/stable/2349306.

———. *Usury and Usury Laws.* Boston: Houghton Mifflin, 1924.

Schulman, David A. "The Effectiveness of the Federal Fair Debt Collection Practices Act (FDCPA)." *Bankruptcy Developments Journal* 2 (1985): 171–200, HeinOnline.

Servon, Lisa J. *The Unbanking of America: How the New Middle Class Survives.* Boston: Houghton Mifflin Harcourt, 2017.

Shepard, Lawrence. "Personal Failures and the Bankruptcy Reform Act of 1978." *Journal of Law and Economics* 27, no. 2 (October 1984): 419–37. http://www.jstor.org/stable/725583.

Shiers, Alden F., and Daniel P. Williamson. "Nonbusiness Bankruptcies and the

Law: Some Empirical Results." *Journal of Consumer Affairs* 21, no. 2 (Winter 1987): 277–92. https://doi.org/10.1111/j.1745-6606.1987.tb00203.x.

Shiller, Robert J. "Narrative Economics." *American Economic Review* 107, no. 4 (April 2017): 967–1004. https://doi.org/10.1257/aer.107.4.967.

Shuchman, Philip, and Gerald R. Jantscher. "Effects of the Federal Minimum Exemption from Wage Garnishment on Nonbusiness Bankruptcy Rates." *Commercial Law Journal* 77, no. 11 (December 1972): 360–63, HeinOnline.

Skeel, David A., Jr. "Bankruptcy Lawyers and the Shape of American Bankruptcy Law." *Fordham Law Review* 67, no. 2 (November 1998): 497–522, HeinOnline.

———. "Competing Narratives in Corporate Bankruptcy: Debtor in Control vs. No Time to Spare." *Michigan State Law Review* no. 4 (Winter 2009): 1187–206, HeinOnline.

———. *Debt's Dominion: A History of Bankruptcy Law in America*. Princeton, NJ: Princeton University Press, 2001.

———. "Evolutionary Theory of Corporate Law and Corporate Bankruptcy." *Vanderbilt Law Review* 51, no. 5 (October 1998): 1323–98, HeinOnline.

———. "The Genius of the 1898 Bankruptcy Act." *Bankruptcy Developments Journal* 15, no. 2 (1999): 321–42, HeinOnline.

Smith, David Sellers. "The Elimination of the Unworthy: Credit Men and Small Retailers in Progressive Era Capitalism." *Journal of the Gilded Age and Progressive Era* 9, no. 2 (April 2010): 197–220. https://doi.org/10.1017/S1537781400003935.

Smith, Paul F. "Trends in Cost of Providing Consumer Credit." In *Consumer Credit Costs, 1949–59*, edited by Paul F. Smith, 98–116. Princeton, NJ: Princeton University Press, 1964. http://www.nber.org/books/smit64-1.

Snowden, Kenneth. "The Anatomy of a Residential Mortgage Crisis: A Look Back to the 1930s." In *The Panic of 2008: Causes, Consequences and Implications for Reform*, edited by Lawrence E. Mitchell and Arthur E. Wilmarth, Jr., 51–75. Cheltenham: Edward Elgar, 2010.

———. "The Evolution of Interregional Mortgage Lending Channels, 1870–1940: The Life Insurance-Mortgage Company Connection." In *Coordination and Information: Historical Perspectives on the Organization of Enterprise*, edited by Naomi R. Lamoreaux and Daniel M. G. Raff, 209–56. Chicago: University of Chicago Press and NBER, 1995. http://www.nber.org/chapters/c8755.pdf.

———. "A Historiography of Early NBER Housing and Mortgage Research." In *Housing and Mortgage Markets in Historical Perspective*, edited by Eugene N. White, Kenneth Snowden, and Price Fishback, 15–34. Chicago: University of Chicago Press, 2014.

Stanley, David T., and Marjorie L. Girth. *Bankruptcy: Problem, Process, Reform*. Washington, DC: Brookings Institution, 1971.

Sullivan, A. Charlene, and Debra Drecnik Worden. "Rehabilitation or Liquidation: Consumers' Choices in Bankruptcy." *Journal of Consumer Affairs* 24, no. 1 (Summer 1990): 69–88. https://doi.org/10.1111/j.1745-6606.1990.tb00259.x.

Sullivan, Teresa A., Elizabeth Warren, and Jay Lawrence Westbrook. *As We Forgive Our Debtors: Bankruptcy and Consumer Credit in America*. New York: Oxford University Press, 1989.

——. *The Fragile Middle Class: Americans in Debt*. New Haven, CT: Yale University Press, 2000.

——. "Laws, Models, and Real People: Choice of Chapter in Personal Bankruptcy." *Law and Social Inquiry* 13, no. 4 (Fall 1988): 661–706. https://doi.org/10.1111/j.1747-4469.1988.tb01132.x.

——. "Persistence of Local Legal Culture: Twenty Years of Evidence from the Federal Bankruptcy Courts." *Harvard Journal of Law & Public Policy* 17, no. 3 (Summer 1994): 801–66, HeinOnline.

Tabb, Charles Jordan. "The Historical Evolution of the Bankruptcy Discharge." *American Bankruptcy Law Journal* 65, no. 3 (Spring 1991): 325–72, HeinOnline.

——. "The History of the Bankruptcy Laws in the United States." *American Bankruptcy Institute Law Review* 3, no. 1 (Spring 1995): 5–52, HeinOnline.

——. "The Top Twenty Issues in the History of Consumer Bankruptcy." *University of Illinois Law Review* 2007, no. 1 (2007): 9–30, HeinOnline.

Trumbull, Gunnar. *Consumer Lending in France and America: Credit and Welfare*. New York: Cambridge University Press, 2014.

Tufano, Peter. "Business Failure, Judicial Intervention, and Financial Innovation: Restructuring US Railroads in the Nineteenth Century." *Business History Review* 71, no. 1 (Spring 1997): 1–40. https://doi.org/10.2307/3116328.

Vanatta, Sean H. "Citibank, Credit Cards, and the Local Politics of National Consumer Finance, 1968–1991." *Business History Review* 90, no. 1 (Spring 2016): 57–80. https://doi.org/10.1017/S0007680515001038.

Wallis, John Joseph. "Employment in the Great Depression: New Data and Hypotheses." *Explorations in Economic History* 26, no. 1 (January 1989): 45–72.

Wang, Hung-Jen, and Michelle J. White. "An Optimal Personal Bankruptcy Procedure and Proposed Reforms." *Journal of Legal Studies* 29, no. 1 (January 2000): 255–86. https://doi.org/10.1086/468070.

Warren, Charles. *Bankruptcy in United States History*. Cambridge, MA: Harvard University Press, 1935.

Warren, Elizabeth. "The Bankruptcy Crisis." *Indiana Law Journal* 73, no. 4 (Fall 1998): 1079–1110, HeinOnline.

———. "The Market for Data: The Changing Role of Social Sciences in Shaping the Law." *Wisconsin Law Review* 2002, no. 1 (2002): 1–44, HeinOnline.

Warren, Elizabeth, and Amelia Warren Tyagi. *The Two-Income Trap: Why Middle-Class Mothers and Fathers Are Going Broke*. New York: Basic Books, 2003.

Weiss, Lawrence A., Jagdeep S. Bhandari, and Russell Robins. "An Analysis of State-Wide Variation in Bankruptcy Rates in the United States." *Bankruptcy Developments Journal* 17, no. 2 (2001): 407–24, HeinOnline.

Westrich, Tim, and Malcolm Bush. "Blindfolded into Debt: A Comparison of Credit Card Costs and Conditions at Banks and Credit Unions." Chicago: Woodstock Institute, 2005. https://www.fdic.gov/news/conferences/affordable/woodstock2.pdf.

Wheelock, David C. "Changing the Rules: State Mortgage Foreclosure Moratoria during the Great Depression." *Federal Reserve Bank of St. Louis Review* 90, no. 6 (November/December 2008): 569–83.

White, Eugene N., Kenneth Snowden, and Price Fishback. *Housing and Mortgage Markets in Historical Perspective*. Chicago: University of Chicago Press, 2014.

White, Michelle J. "Bankruptcy and Consumer Behavior: Theory and Evidence from the United States." In *The Economics of Consumer Credit*, edited by Giuseppe Bertola, Richard Disney, and Charles Grant, 239–74. Cambridge, MA: MIT Press, 2006.

———. "Bankruptcy Reform and Credit Cards." *Journal of Economic Perspectives* 21, no. 4 (Fall 2007): 175–200. https://doi.org/10.1257/jep.21.4.175.

———. "Personal Bankruptcy under the 1978 Bankruptcy Code: An Economic Analysis." *Indiana Law Journal* 63, no. 1 (1987): 1–54, HeinOnline.

———. "Why Don't More Households File for Bankruptcy?" *Journal of Law, Economics, & Organization* 14, no. 2 (October 1998): 205–31. http://www.jstor.org/stable/765103.

White, Michelle J., and Ning Zhu. "Saving Your Home in Chapter 13 Bankruptcy." *Journal of Legal Studies* 39, no. 1 (January 2010): 33–61. https://doi.org/10.1086/605096.

Wickens, David L. "Farmer Bankruptcies, 1898–1935." United States Department of Agriculture Circular No. 414, 1936.

Woodbridge, Frederick. "Wage Earners' Plans in the Federal Courts." *Minnesota Law Review* 26, no. 7 (June 1942): 775–823, HeinOnline.

Wright, Robert E. "Wall Street on the Prairie." *Financial History*, no. 106 (Spring 2013): 24–26.

Zainaldin, Jamil S. *Law in Antebellum Society: Legal Change and Economic Expansion*. New York: Alfred A. Knopf, 1983.

Zelenko, Benjamin L. "The Role of the Referee in Legislative Reform of the

Bankruptcy Act." *Journal of the National Conference of Referees in Bankruptcy* 43, no. 4 (October 1969): 101–3, HeinOnline.

Zhang, Shuoxun, Tarun Sabarwal, and Li Gan. "Strategic or Nonstrategic: The Role of Financial Benefit in Bankruptcy." *Economic Inquiry* 53, no. 2 (2015): 1004–18. https://doi.org/10.1111/ecin.12163.

Zingales, Luigi. *A Capitalism for the People: Recapturing the Lost Genius of American Prosperity.* New York: Basic Books, 2014.

Zywicki, Todd J. "An Economic Analysis of the Consumer Bankruptcy Crisis." *Northwestern Law Review* 99, no. 4 (2005): 1463–1541, HeinOnline.

———. "The Economics of Credit Cards." *Chapman Law Review* 79, no. 3 (2000): 80–150, HeinOnline.

———. "The Past, Present, and Future of Bankruptcy Law in America." *Michigan Law Review* 101, no. 6 (May 2003): 2016–36. https://www.jstor.org/stable/3595342.

Index

Pages in italics refer to illustrations.